The American Revolution and the Birth of the USA

1740–1801

ALAN FARMER

SECOND EDITION

HODDER
EDUCATION
AN HACHETTE UK COMPANY

The Publishers would like to thank Nicholas Fellows and David Ferriby for their contribution to the Study Guide.

The Publishers would like to thank the following for permission to reproduce copyright material:

Photo credits: p6 Library of Congress, LC-D4-11342; **p13** Library of Congress, LC-DIG-det-4a26115; **p22** Library of Congress, LC-USZ62-7819; **p43** Library of Congress, LC-USZ62-102271; **p46** Library of Congress, LC-DIG-ppmsca-01657.; **p50** Library of Congress, LC-USZ62-9487; **p64** Library of Congress, LC-DIG-pga-00085; **p70** Library of Congress, LC-DIG-det-4a2629; **p71** Library of Congress, LC-DIG-pga-05288; **p86** Library of Congress, LC-DIG-det-4a26226; **p87** Library of Congress, LC-DIG-det-4a26164; **p120** The Granger Collection/TopFoto; **p141** Library of Congress, LC-DIG-ppmsca-19166; **p147** Mary Evans Picture Library; **p156** Library of Congress, LC-USZ62-45589; **p169** Library of Congress, LC-DIG-det-4a26166; **p185** Library of Congress, LC-USZ62-13002.

The Publishers thank OCR for permission to use specimen exam questions on page 200, from OCR's A Level History A specification H505 © OCR 2014. OCR have neither seen nor commented upon any model answers or exam guidance related to these questions.

Acknowledgements: Faber & Faber, *His Excellency George Washington* by Joseph Ellis, 2004. Grafton Books, *Redcoats and Rebels: The War for America 1770–1781* by Christopher Hibbert, 1990. D.C. Heath, *Major Problems in the Era of the American Revolution 1760–1791* by R.D. Brown (editor), 1992. D.C. Heath, *The Causes of the American Revolution* by J.C. Wahlke (editor), 1962. D.C. Heath, *The Declaration of Independence and the Constitution* by E. Latham (editor), 1962. Longman, *Longman History of the United States of America* by Hugh Brogan, 1985. Oxford University Press, *Sources and Documents Illustrating the American Revolution 1764–1788 and the Formation of the Federal Constitution* by S.E. Morison (editor), 1972. Oxford University Press, *The Age of Federalism: The Early American Republic 1788–1800* by S. Elkins and E. McKitrick, 1993. Oxford University Press, *The Glorious Cause: The American Revolution 1763–1789* by Robert Middlekauff, 1982. Oxford University Press, *The Limits of Liberty: American History 1607–1992* by Maldwyn A. Jones, 1995. Penguin, *The American Revolution* by Edward Countryman, 1991. US Census Bureau, 1978. Larzer Ziff, 1987.

Every effort has been made to trace all copyright holders, but if any have been inadvertently overlooked the Publishers will be pleased to make the necessary arrangements at the first opportunity.

Although every effort has been made to ensure that website addresses are correct at time of going to press, Hodder Education cannot be held responsible for the content of any website mentioned in this book. It is sometimes possible to find a relocated web page by typing in the address of the home page for a website in the URL window of your browser.

Hachette UK's policy is to use papers that are natural, renewable and recyclable products and made from wood grown in sustainable forests. The logging and manufacturing processes are expected to conform to the environmental regulations of the country of origin.

Orders: please contact Bookpoint Ltd, 130 Milton Park, Abingdon, Oxon OX14 4SB. Telephone: +44 (0)1235 827720. Fax: +44 (0)1235 400454. Lines are open 9.00a.m.–5.00p.m., Monday to Saturday, with a 24-hour message answering service. Visit our website at www.hoddereducation.co.uk

© Alan Farmer 2015

First published in 2015 by
Hodder Education
An Hachette UK Company
Carmelite House,
50 Victoria Embankment
London EC4Y 0DZ

Impression number	10	9	8	7	6
Year	2019	2018			

Cover photo: Washington Crossing the Delaware River, 25th December 1776, 1851 (oil on canvas) (copy of an original painted in 1848), Leutze, Emanuel Gottlieb (1816–68)/© Metropolitan Museum of Art, New York, USA/Bridgeman Images
Produced, illustrated and typeset in Palatino LT Std by Gray Publishing, Tunbridge Wells
Printed and bound by CPI Group (UK) Ltd, Croydon CR0 4YY

A catalogue record for this title is available from the British Library

ISBN 978 1471838767

Contents

Dedication

Keith Randell (1943–2002)

The *Access to History* series was conceived and developed by Keith, who created a series to 'cater for students as they are, not as we might wish them to be'. He leaves a living legacy of a series that for over 20 years has provided a trusted, stimulating and well-loved accompaniment to post-16 study. Our aim with these new editions is to continue to offer students the best possible support for their studies.

The American colonies by 1763

The establishment of the British colonies in North America seemed, by the mid-eighteenth century, to have been a huge success. In 1763 British North America ran from Hudson Bay in the north to Florida in the south. Few Americans or Britons expected that within twelve years they would be at war – a war that the Americans would win. This chapter will examine the relationship between Britain and its American colonies pre-1763 by focusing on the following themes:

★ The development of the thirteen colonies

★ Colonial government

★ Colonial economy, society and culture

★ The struggle with France

★ Britain by 1763

The key debate on *page 23* of this chapter asks the question: To what extent were there signs in 1763 that the colonies were likely to break their ties with Britain?

Key dates

1607	Virginia established	**1759**	Britain captured Quebec
1754	Albany conference	**1760**	Accession of George III
1756–63	The French–Indian (or Seven Years') War	**1763**	Peace of Paris

1 The development of the thirteen colonies

▶ *Why did the American population grow so quickly in the eighteenth century?*

The first successful English **colony** was established in Virginia in 1607. The second major colony followed the sailing of the ***Mayflower*** to Massachusetts in 1620. By 1650, four further colonies – Connecticut, New Hampshire, Rhode Island and Maryland – had been added. New York was captured from the Dutch in 1664, New Jersey and North and South Carolina were founded during the

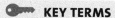

🔑 **KEY TERMS**

Colony Territory, usually overseas, occupied by settlers from a 'mother country' that continues to have political power over the settlers.

Mayflower The name of the ship on which the Pilgrim Fathers, a small group of English Puritans, sailed to America in 1620.

1660s and Pennsylvania and Delaware during the 1680s. The establishment of Georgia in 1732 completed the thirteen British colonies on the American mainland. They stretched about 2400 km (1500 miles) along the Atlantic seaboard from Canada to Florida. Pre-1763, most colonists lived to the east of the Appalachian mountains (see Figure 1.1).

Colonial division

There were three colonial groups:

- the New England colonies – New Hampshire, Massachusetts, Rhode Island and Connecticut
- the middle colonies – New York, New Jersey, Pennsylvania and Delaware
- the southern colonies – Maryland, Virginia, North Carolina, South Carolina and Georgia.

Population growth

Between 1700 and 1763 the population of the thirteen colonies increased eightfold from 250,000 to reach 2 million. Between 1750 and 1770 England and Wales's population rose from 6.5 million to 7.5 million – a fifteen per cent increase. In the same period, the thirteen colonies' population expanded from

Abbreviations for US states used in this book:	
CT	Connecticut
DE	Delaware
GA	Georgia
IL	Illinois
IN	Indiana
KY	Kentucky
MA	Massachusetts
MD	Maryland
ME	Maine
MI	Michigan
NC	North Carolina
NH	New Hampshire
NJ	New Jersey
NY	New York
OH	Ohio
PA	Pennsylvania
RI	Rhode Island
SC	South Carolina
TN	Tennessee
VA	Virginia
VT	Vermont
WI	Wisconsin

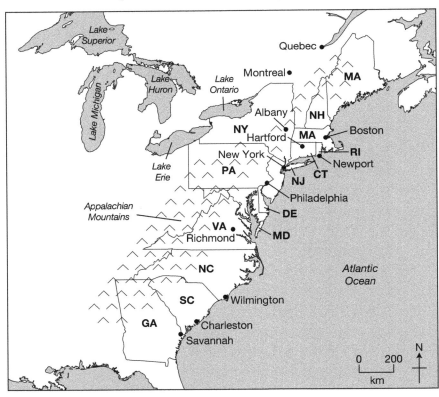

Figure 1.1 The thirteen colonies in 1763.

1.25 million to over 2.3 million – an almost 100 per cent increase. There were three reasons for the population growth:

- a high birth rate: the average American woman had a family of seven children
- a low death rate: Americans, well fed and generally prosperous, lived longer than most Europeans
- immigration (see below).

Nevertheless, America was far from densely populated. The vast majority of colonists lived on farms. Almost half lived in the South, a quarter in the middle colonies and a quarter in New England. By 1770:

- Virginia was the largest colony in population and land area, with some 500,000 inhabitants.
- Pennsylvania and Massachusetts each had about 275,000 inhabitants.
- Maryland and North Carolina each had 200,000.
- New York, South Carolina and New Jersey each had more than 100,000.
- New Hampshire and Rhode Island each had just over 50,000.
- Delaware had 40,000.
- Georgia had only 30,000.

American towns

There were only five towns of any size, all of which were seaports: Philadelphia (with 23,750 inhabitants), New York (18,000), Boston (15,600), Newport (10,000) and Charleston (10,000). By 1760 their combined population was 73,000 – only 3.5 per cent of the total population.

The colonial melting pot

Some 400,000 people from Europe and Africa migrated to the thirteen colonies between 1700 and 1763. While most of the seventeenth-century settlers were of English stock, less than a fifth of the eighteenth-century migrants were English.

European settlement

The largest group of immigrants (some 150,000) were Scots-Irish Protestants from Ulster. Discontented with the land system, recurrent bad harvests and the decline of the linen trade, most Scots-Irish left their homeland for economic reasons.

About 65,000 Germans, mainly peasants from the Rhineland, hoping to improve their economic lot and attracted by the religious tolerance in the colonies, crossed the Atlantic. Many settled in Pennsylvania, making up almost a third of the colony's population by the 1760s. Smaller immigrant groups included Dutch and Swedes.

Indentured servitude

European immigrants crossing the Atlantic tended to travel in groups, either as part of colonisation schemes or, more frequently, under a system of temporary servitude designed to meet the colonies' severe labour shortage. The system enabled people to obtain free passage by entering into a contract (or indenture) pledging their labour for a specified number of years – usually four. Between a half and two-thirds of all white immigrants during the colonial period were indentured servants.

African settlement

The first black slaves landed in Virginia in 1619. Their numbers at first grew slowly. In the eighteenth century, however, the importation of slaves soared. By 1763 there were 350,000 slaves – one in six of the overall population. Most came from west Africa. The demand for slaves was so high that the black population in America grew more rapidly than the white population. While there were African-Americans in all the colonies, 90 per cent lived in the South (see page 12). They made up less than five per cent of the total population in New England but 40 per cent in Virginia, Maryland and Georgia, and 67 per cent in South Carolina.

Native Americans

The British and European settlers did not assimilate with the **Native Americans**. Divided, less advanced technologically and hit hard by European diseases, the Indians had been unable to resist the newcomers establishing themselves down the Atlantic seaboard. Nevertheless, Native American tribes remained a powerful force to the west of the Appalachians (see Figure 1.1).

The results of immigration

By 1760 only about half the American population was of English stock. Another fifteen per cent was Welsh, Scottish or Scots-Irish. Africans comprised over twenty per cent and Germans eight per cent of the population. While most European newcomers quickly blended into colonial culture and society, Germans retained an important degree of religious and cultural **autonomy**.

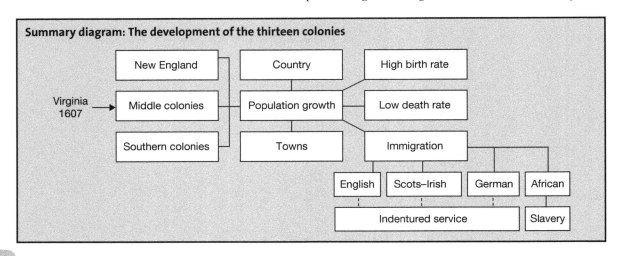

Summary diagram: The development of the thirteen colonies

Colonial government

 ▶ *To what extent did the colonists govern themselves?*

All the colonies had, by 1760, a similar governmental structure, consisting of a governor and a legislative assembly.

Governors

In most colonies, the governor was appointed and could be removed only by the British king, to whom he was responsible. The exceptions were the following:

- the **proprietary colonies** of Maryland, Pennsylvania and Delaware, where the proprietor who ran the colony appointed the governor
- the **corporate colonies** of Connecticut and Rhode Island, where governors were popularly elected and responsible to the legislatures.

Responsible for internal administration, the governors (in theory) had enormous powers. In reality, however, their authority was limited:

- They could be dismissed at will by the British government.
- They were dependent for revenue (including their own salaries) on the colonial assemblies.

Colonial assemblies

Most colonial legislatures (usually called assemblies) consisted of two houses:

- Upper houses (or councils) were normally appointed by the governor. Chosen from the colonial elite, their members served as an advisory board to the governor.
- Lower houses were elected. Although they could be summoned and dismissed and their legislation vetoed by the governor, the power of the assemblies was considerable.
- They were responsible for initiating money bills and controlling expenditures.
- They represented their communities in a way that neither the governors nor the councils did.

Assemblies usually met in the spring or autumn for four to six weeks. As well as dealing with money matters, they made local laws, At least 50 (and in some colonies as much as 80) per cent of American white adult males could vote, compared with only fifteen per cent in Britain.

Nevertheless, the colonies were far from democratic:

- Not all white men owned sufficient property to entitle them to vote.
- Women and slaves could not vote.
- Higher property qualifications for office as well as custom and deference towards men of high social standing ensured that great landowners, rich merchants or lawyers were usually elected.

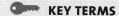

KEY TERMS

Proprietary colonies
Colonies in which the Crown had vested political authority in the hands of certain families: the Calverts (in Maryland) and the Penns (in Pennsylvania and Delaware).

Corporate colonies
Connecticut and Rhode Island possessed charters granted by the king, which gave them extensive autonomy.

SOURCE A

? The Massachusetts assembly met in the State House in Boston. What does the nature of the building shown in Source A suggest about the power of the colony's legislature?

The State House in Boston.

Local government

In New England, where settlements were relatively compact, authority over local affairs was vested in town meetings in which all **freeholders** had voting rights. Elected annually, the town meetings fixed local taxes and chose men to administer the town's business. In the middle and southern colonies, a wider variety of practices prevailed. Some communities had New England-style town governments; in others local government was organised by county or parish.

🔑 **KEY TERM**

Freeholders People who own, rather than rent, their land.

British rule in the colonies

Charters were the umbilical cords attaching the colonies to Britain – the mother country. Granted in the seventeenth century, the charters tied the colonies to the Crown rather than to Parliament. The governors continued to be appointed by – and represented – the Crown. The Crown's authority was somewhat ambiguous in the proprietary colonies and even more tenuous in the corporate colonies.

After 1696 the British sovereign and the **Privy Council** had joint authority, conferred by Parliament, to review colonial laws. (Only five per cent of the 8500 colonial measures submitted between 1691 and 1775 were disallowed by Britain.)

For most of the eighteenth century, responsibility for colonial supervision rested with the Board of Trade, which advised on colonial appointments, drew up government instructions and reviewed colonial legislation.

The secretary of state for the Southern Department also had responsibility for colonial affairs. Both the Board of Trade and the secretary communicated with governors on policy and routine administration. Governors submitted regular reports to the secretary on colonial affairs generally and to the Board of Trade on commercial matters.

Other agencies – the Treasury, the War Office and the Admiralty – also had some role in imperial administration. Given that British administration affecting the colonies lacked central control, confusion and duplication often characterised the bureaucracy.

In order to follow developments concerning colonial matters, as well as to lobby Parliament and the Board of Trade on behalf of their interests, most colonies employed agents in Britain. These agents warned the colonies of pending measures by the Crown or Parliament and informed British officials of colonial thinking.

Salutary neglect

In the early eighteenth century, British governments realised it was best not to stir up trouble in the colonies. Given that they were 4800 km (3000 miles) away from Britain, the colonies were left largely to their own devices. This detached policy is often referred to as 'salutary neglect'.

Despite salutary neglect, the common presumption in Britain was that the colonies were subject to parliamentary legislation. The colonists did not necessarily accept this view. However, this was not a major issue pre-1763 because Parliament gave so little attention to colonial affairs. Trade regulation apart, there was hardly a single parliamentary act that touched on the internal affairs of the colonies. Few colonists, therefore, gave much thought to their relationship with Britain.

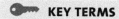

KEY TERMS

Charters Formal documents, granting or confirming titles, rights or privileges.

Privy Council The private council of the British king, advising on the administration of government.

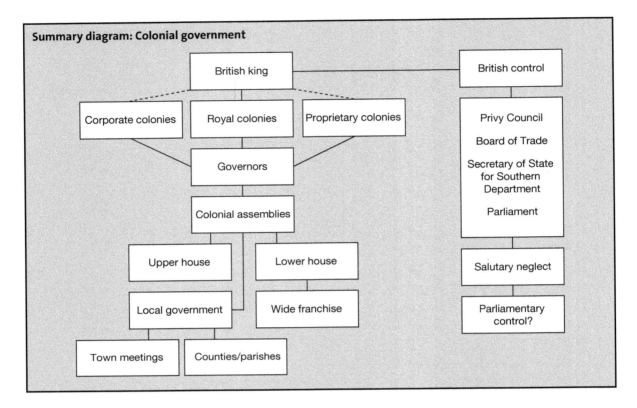

Summary diagram: Colonial government

The importance of agriculture and fishing

 Colonial economy, society and culture

> ▶ *To what extent were the colonies linked to Britain – economically, socially and culturally?*

Between 1650 and 1770 the colonial economy grew by an annual average of 3.2 per cent. This was the result of several factors:

- expanding inter-colonial trade
- increased trade with Britain and its Empire
- availability of credit and capital from Britain
- the rapid increase in population
- availability of new land
- increasing diversification; for example, the development of iron production, textiles and shipbuilding.

The importance of agriculture and fishing

Farming remained the dominant economic activity, employing nine-tenths of the working population. There was great diversity from region to region:

- Lacking extensive rich soils, New England remained a land of small subsistence farms. The sea, however, provided it with a profitable alternative. From the Newfoundland Banks and the shores of Nova Scotia, New England fishermen brought back great quantities of cod, to be dried and exported. More than half of New England's thriving export trade was with the West Indies, which supplied the colonies in return with sugar, molasses and other tropical products. New England distillers turned molasses into rum.
- The middle colonies were a major source of wheat and flour products for export to other colonies, the West Indies and Europe.
- Tobacco was the mainstay of the southern economy, tobacco exports rising from £14 million in the 1670s to £100 million by the 1770s. Rice, indigo and grain were also produced for export. Development was most advanced in the **Tidewater**, where the population was densest. Population pressure and the search for higher profits ensured that the **backcountry** was filling rapidly.

🔑 **KEY TERMS**

Tidewater The eastern areas nearest the coast.

Backcountry The western areas furthest from the coast.

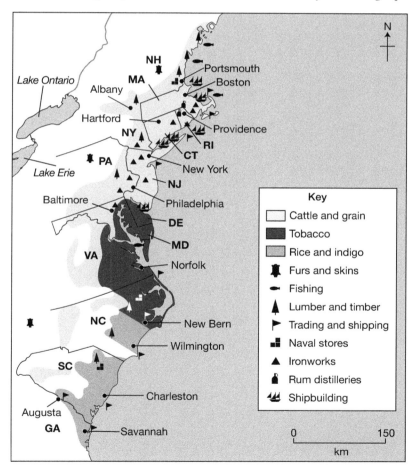

Figure 1.2 The colonial economy.

Mercantilism

In the seventeenth and eighteenth centuries, most European governments believed in **mercantilism** and **economic self-sufficiency**. Mercantilists assumed that colonies existed to supply the mother country with raw materials, buy its manufactures and provide employment for its shipping.

Between 1651 and 1673 the Trade and Navigation Acts were designed to establish an English monopoly of the colonial carrying trade, the colonial market and certain colonial products:

- All cargoes to or from the colonies were to be carried in ships built and owned in England or the colonies and manned by predominantly English crews.
- Certain **enumerated commodities** – sugar, cotton, indigo, dyewoods, ginger and tobacco – could be exported only from the colonies to England even if their ultimate destination lay elsewhere.
- European goods bound for America had, with few exceptions, to be landed first in England and then reshipped.

English/British colonial policy remained strictly mercantilist through the early eighteenth century. The list of enumerated commodities was steadily extended until by 1763 it included practically everything the colonies produced except fish, grain and lumber. Laws were also passed to restrict colonial manufacturing:

- The Woollen Act (1699) forbade the export of woollen yarn and cloth outside the colony in which it was produced.
- The Hat Act (1732) prohibited the export of colonial beaver hats.
- The Iron Act (1750) banned the export of colonial iron outside the Empire.

The effects of the mercantilist system

Few Americans complained about mercantilist regulations. This was partly because the system was not well enforced. While the Navigation Acts levied high duties, they were rarely collected. The chief posts in the colonial customs service were **sinecures**, filled by men who remained in Britain. The ill-paid deputies who were sent to perform their duties could easily be bribed by the colonists, ensuring that they often turned a blind eye to infractions of the trade laws. The laxity of control particularly prevailed during Prime Minister Robert Walpole's long rule (1721–42). Although Lord Halifax, president of the Board of Trade from 1748 to 1761, tried to tighten imperial control, the colonies were able to avoid most of the trade laws and smuggling was a fact of colonial economic life.

The few laws restricting colonial production had little effect. The Woollen Act had a limited impact because sheep and wool rarely exceeded local demand. The Hat Act affected an industry of minor importance. The prohibitions of the Iron Act were disregarded. Moreover, the act was not wholly restrictive.

Designed to check the expansion of the iron-finishing industry, it aimed to encourage crude-iron production and allowed colonial bar and pig iron to enter Britain free of duty. By the 1770s the colonies had outstripped Britain as producers of crude iron.

On balance, mercantilism probably benefited the colonies:

- American products enjoyed a protected market in Britain and its Empire.
- American shipping profited by the exclusion of foreign ships from colonial trade.

As the eighteenth century progressed, colonial trade played an increasingly important role in the British economy. By the 1760s a third of British imports and exports crossed the Atlantic. The colonies imported British manufactured goods, exporting tobacco, flour, fish, rice and wheat in return. Both Britain and the colonies benefited from increasing trade.

SOURCE B

Peter Kalm, a Swedish biologist travelling in North America 1748–51, http://nationalhumanitiescenter.org/pds/becomingamer/economies/text1/ europeanperspectives.pdf

For the English colonies … have increased so much in their number of inhabitants and in their riches that they almost vie with Old England. Now in order to keep up the authority and trade of their mother country and to answer several other purposes, they are forbidden to establish new manufactures, which would turn to the disadvantage of the British commerce … They have not the liberty of trading with any parts that do not belong to the British dominion, except a few places; nor are foreigners allowed to trade with the English colonies of North America. These and some other restrictions occasion the inhabitants of the English colonies to grow less tender for their mother country. This coldness is kept up by the many foreigners such as Germans, Dutch and French, who live among the English and have no particular attachment to Old England.

> Why, according to Source B, were the ties between Britain and the colonies starting to strain? **?**

Colonial society

In every colony a wealthy elite – great landowners, **planters** and wealthy merchants – had emerged whose pre-eminence was evident in its possessions, lifestyles and in their control of politics. Several landowners received returns from their lands rivalling the incomes of the great British landed families. Yet the colonial elites lacked the titles, privileges and often the possessions that gave automatic social prestige and political authority to the British aristocracy. The American elite were hard-working capitalists, intensely and of necessity absorbed in land speculation and in the business of marketing commercial crops. Since their capital was largely tied up in land (and slaves in the South), their **liquid assets** were not impressive by European standards.

> **🔑 KEY TERMS**
>
> **Planters** Southern landowners who owned more than twenty slaves.
>
> **Liquid assets** Wealth that may be easily converted into cash.

Below the elite were the professionals – ministers, lawyers, doctors, schoolmasters. Respected in their communities, they often held positions of public responsibility. Eighty per cent of free males were farmers. Most owned and (with the help of their families) worked their own land – usually between 50 and 500 acres (20 and 200 hectares). In the towns, two-thirds of the population were shopkeepers and self-employed craftsmen.

Below the property holders were those who laboured for others. This was a diverse group, ranging from tenant farmers to slaves. Approximately a third of land was farmed by tenants who rented rather than owned the land. Only about a fifth of adult white males, many of whom were recent immigrants, were landless labourers. The availability of cheap frontier lands limited the numbers of tenants and landless agricultural workers. In the towns, the property-less included apprentices, sailors, servants and labourers.

Black slaves were at the bottom of the social structure. Slaves were subject to the will of their owners and could be bought and sold. While some slaves were used as domestic servants, most worked on plantations producing tobacco and rice.

A middle-class world?

According to historian Richard Hofstadter (1948), colonial America was 'a middle-class world'. The groups at the top and bottom of the British social pyramid – the nobility and the poor – were under-represented in America. Availability of land meant that, unlike in Britain, where farm tenancy was the norm, most colonial farmers tilled their own soil. In the cities, **artisans** capitalised on their scarcity value by demanding and getting higher wages.

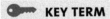

KEY TERM

Artisans Skilled manual workers.

Nevertheless, American society was hierarchical and there were huge differences between rich and poor. While society may have been more mobile than that in Britain, the notion of widespread social mobility should not be exaggerated. Only a few individuals rose from humble beginnings to wealth and power.

Families

The basic unit of American life was the family. At its head was a white male. Households were hierarchical. Children were subordinate to elders, females to males, servants to family, blacks to whites. While it has been claimed that the preponderance of males among early American settlers helped to raise the status of women, this seems doubtful. Irrespective of wealth or condition they were assigned a subordinate role and were denied the political and civil rights enjoyed by men. Wives, for example, had no legal right to property.

American culture

By the 1760s Americans could boast their own cultural and intellectual achievements.

Benjamin Franklin

1706	Born in Boston
1729	Purchased the *Pennsylvania Gazette*
1751–64	Sat in the Pennsylvania Assembly
1757–75	Pennsylvania's colonial agent in London
1775	Sat as a delegate in the Second Continental Congress
1776	Helped to draw up the Declaration of Independence
1776–85	Head of a diplomatic mission in France, he helped to bring France into the War of Independence
1787	Helped to draft the Constitution
1790	Died

A self-made man, Franklin was a many-sided genius who succeeded in everything he tried: journalism, business, invention, politics and diplomacy. Largely self-educated, he prospered as owner of a printing business in Philadelphia and as editor of the *Pennsylvania Gazette*. He was a prolific pamphleteer on politics, economics, religion and other topics. His passion for learning and civic improvement led him to play a leading role in founding, among other things, a subscription library, a city hospital and the American Philosophical Society.

Franklin became famous in America and Europe as a result of his inventions, including the lightning rod and bifocal spectacles, and still more for his research into the nature of electricity. In all his endeavours Franklin displayed a faith in reason and a humanitarianism that were characteristic of the Enlightenment.

Education

Education was strongly encouraged. By 1763, 75 per cent of white male American adults were literate, compared with 60 per cent in England, and there were nine colleges and universities. Printing presses and booksellers were common. More than thirty newspapers were in circulation by 1763.

The colonial intellectual elite were influenced by the **Enlightenment**, the ideas of which permeated every branch of thought from science to politics. By the mid-eighteenth century Americans could boast their own intellectual achievements. Learned organisations were founded, most notably the American Philosophical Society (1743). Some Americans, for example Benjamin Franklin, gained international notice for their work.

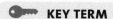 **KEY TERM**

Enlightenment The name given to a school of European thought of the eighteenth century. Those influenced by the Enlightenment believed in reason and human progress.

Religion

Church membership was high, especially in New England. Most Americans were Protestants, a fact that shaped their cultural, social and political attitudes as well as defining their theological principles. However, in contrast to most European states, there was no dominant religious denomination in the colonies as a whole or even within most individual colonies. The tendency towards religious division, together with the immigration of sectarians from different countries, produced a multiplicity of denominations – Congregationalists, Presbyterians, Quakers, Baptists, Anglicans, Lutherans, German and Dutch Reformed and Methodists. There was an established church in nine colonies; Rhode Island, Pennsylvania, Delaware and New Jersey were the exceptions. The Congregational Church was the established church in the New England colonies. The Anglican Church was established in Virginia and other southern colonies. Established churches enjoyed certain privileges, including support from taxation.

Table 1.1 Estimated religious census for 1775

	Number	Chief locale
Congregationalists	575,000	New England
Anglicans	500,000	NY, South
Presbyterians	410,000	Frontier
German churches (incl. Lutherans)	200,000	PA
Dutch reformed	75,000	NY, NJ
Quakers	40,000	PA, NJ, DE
Baptists	25,000	RI, PA, NJ, DE
Roman Catholics	25,000	MD, PA
Methodists	5,000	Scattered
Jews	2,000	NY, RI
Total membership	1,857,000	
Total population	2,493,000	
Percentage church members	74%	

The plethora of diverse religious groups forced Americans to acknowledge a degree of religious tolerance. Tolerance, however, was largely confined to other Protestant groups. Most Americans were strongly anti-Catholic.

The Great Awakening

A wave of religious revivals known as the Great Awakening swept through the colonies in the early eighteenth century. Popular preachers, emphasising the individual's personal relationship with God, drew enormous crowds. Although some scholars have claimed that the Great Awakening aroused an egalitarian and democratic spirit as all souls were now considered eligible for salvation, its levelling tendencies may have been overstated. While it tended to undermine the position of the established clergy, it did not develop into a general challenge to traditional forms of authority.

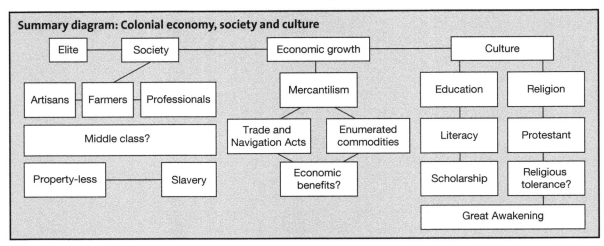

Summary diagram: Colonial economy, society and culture

4 The struggle with France

> ▶ *What were the main results of the British–French struggle for control of North America?*

Warfare was a fact of colonial life in the seventeenth century. To secure their foothold on the American continent early colonists had to overcome Native American resistance. Towards the end of the seventeenth century warfare between colonists and Native Americans merged with a larger struggle between Britain and France (which ruled Canada and Louisiana) for control of North America.

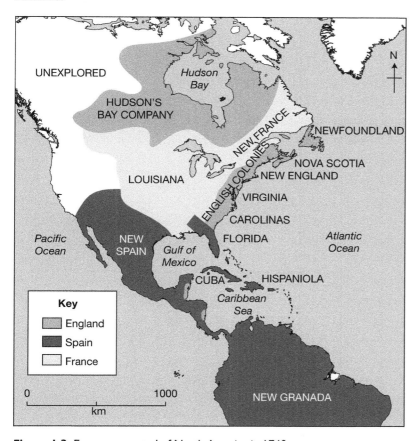

Figure 1.3 European control of North America in 1740.

Spain, which ruled most of Central and South America, had some interest in developments in North America. It controlled Florida and its Mexican boundaries extended north into territory that is now part of the USA. However, there were very few Spaniards in North America, and Spain was declining as a great power. It tended to ally with France against Britain but usually offered little assistance to its partner.

The wars

Between 1689 and 1763 Britain and France fought four wars:

- the War of the League of Augsburg (1689–97)
- the War of Spanish Succession (1702–13)
- the War of Austrian Succession (1740–48)
- the Seven Years' War (1756–63).

The first three wars began in Europe, and were essentially about the balance of power within that continent. Conflict then spread across the Atlantic. That the colonists viewed them essentially as foreign wars in which they became embroiled only as subjects of the British Crown was evident from the labels they attached to the first three of them: King William's War, Queen Anne's War and King George's War. Nonetheless, they were eager to defeat French and Spanish neighbours whose Catholicism they loathed and whom they regarded with fear and suspicion.

The War of Austrian Succession

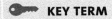

KEY TERM

Militia A force, made up of all military-aged civilians, called out in times of emergency.

In the War of Austrian Succession, Britain was too absorbed in Europe to send much help to the colonists. But France and Spain had similar problems. The fact that the Royal Navy was stronger than the French and Spanish navies also made it difficult for Britain's enemies to send assistance to their colonists. Britain left most of the fighting to the colonial **militia**. The English-speaking colonists outnumbered the French fifteen to one but inter-colonial disputes and French alliances with Native American tribes largely offset the British advantage. The colonists' greatest military achievement was the capture of Louisbourg in 1745. Proud of their victory, the colonists were appalled when the Treaty of Aix-la-Chapelle (1748) handed Louisbourg back to France.

The Albany Congress

As far as America was concerned, the 1748 peace was simply a truce. No sooner had it been signed than British and French colonists redoubled their efforts to control the Ohio Valley. In the spirit of salutary neglect, there were only about 500 British troops in America. The Board of Trade recognised that Native American support could be vital in the coming struggle against the French. It thus called on the colonies from Virginia northward to send delegates to a meeting at Albany to discuss joint Native American policy. The Albany Congress (June 1754) failed to secure an alliance with the Iroquois, the tribe best disposed towards the British. However, the Congress did adopt a scheme, drawn up by Benjamin Franklin, for a permanent inter-colonial confederation. Franklin's Plan of Union envisaged an elected colonial Parliament with authority over Native American affairs and defence and with power to levy taxes to support an army. The British government might well have vetoed the proposal since it went much further than it had intended. But the colonial assemblies saved it the trouble by either rejecting or ignoring the Plan of Union.

Fort Duquesne

In 1753–54 a group of Virginia planters organised the Ohio Company and secured from the British government a grant of some 200,000 acres (about 80,000 hectares) in the trans-Allegheny region. When the French began to build a chain of forts between Lake Erie and the Allegheny River, a Virginian force, led by George Washington (see page 87), was sent to forestall them. But Washington found that the French were already in possession of the key site, the forks of the Ohio River (present-day Pittsburgh), where they were busy constructing Fort Duquesne. In the fighting that followed, Washington was forced to surrender (July 1754). Although war was as yet undeclared, Britain sent General Braddock and 2000 troops to America. On his way to Fort Duquesne, Braddock blundered into a French–Indian ambush. He was killed and his army routed (July 1755). Over the next two years Native American war parties devastated scores of frontier settlements.

The Seven Years' War

In 1756 Britain declared war on France. The Seven Years' War – or the French–Indian War as it was known in America – developed into a worldwide conflict. There was fighting in Europe, the West Indies, Africa and India as well as in North America. At first things went badly for Britain. French General Montcalm captured Fort Oswego on Lake Ontario in 1756 and Fort William Henry at the southern end of Lake George in 1757. These reverses reflected the inability of the Earl of Loudon, the British commander, to induce the colonists to unite in their own defence. Miserly assemblies, dominated by men from the secure seaboard, were unperturbed by the threat to remote frontiers.

Once **William Pitt** was recalled to power in Britain in 1757, the tide began to turn. Determined to expand Britain's imperial power, Pitt judged that defeat of the French in North America was the key to ultimate victory. He thus sent 25,000 troops to America under the command of Jeffrey Amherst and James Wolfe, and paid for raising a further 25,000 colonists. As never before, the British government was preoccupied with America. The war proved an economic bonanza for the colonies. They were paid good money to support the British forces.

Meanwhile Pitt provided subsidies to Frederick the Great of Prussia to preoccupy the French in Europe. The strategy worked brilliantly. In 1758 British forces captured Louisbourg and then cut the link between Canada and the Mississippi Valley by taking Fort Frontenac on Lake Ontario. This led to the fall of Fort Duquesne, renamed Fort Pitt. Meanwhile Robert Clive won a series of victories in India while Frederick the Great defeated the armies of France, Russia and Austria in Europe.

 KEY FIGURE

William Pitt (1708–78)
Pitt (the Elder), who entered Parliament in 1735, quickly established his reputation as a great orator. In 1757 he formed a ministry with the Duke of Newcastle and was largely responsible for British victory in the Seven Years' War.

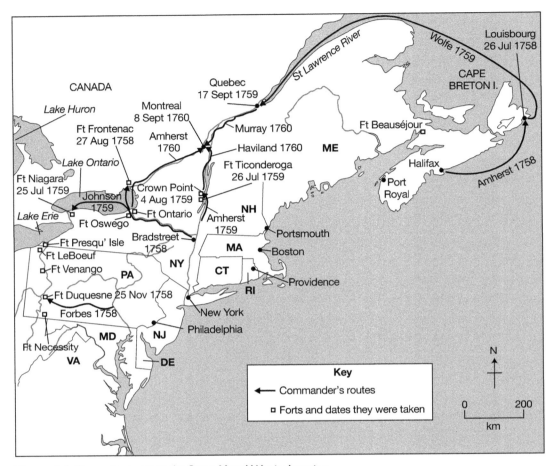

Figure 1.4 The main events in the Seven Years' War in America.

The greatest triumphs came in 1759 – the year of victories:

- Admiral Hawke smashed a French fleet at Quiberon Bay, southeast of Brest, thereby preventing France sending reinforcements to Canada.
- Britain captured Guadaloupe in the Caribbean.
- Britain launched a three-pronged attack on Canada. General Wolfe's defeat of Montcalm on the Plains of Abraham (12 September 1759) ensured the capture of Quebec, effectively destroying French power in Canada.

In 1760 Amherst took Montreal and the capture of Canada was complete. By the terms of the Peace of Paris (1763):

- Britain received Canada and all French possessions east of the Mississippi.
- Britain acquired most of France's Caribbean islands.
- Britain acquired Florida from Spain.
- France ceded Louisiana to Spain.

Other results of the Seven Years' War

- Britain was now the world's greatest imperial power, controlling North America, the Caribbean and much of India.
- The war gave training to men who later became senior officers in the American army.
- There was mutual contempt between some American and British soldiers. British officers tended to regard the Americans as a rabble. Americans, in turn, considered British officers haughty and incompetent.
- Americans, particularly those who lived near the frontier (in colonies like Virginia), expected to benefit from the expulsion of the French. A huge area of western land beyond the Appalachian mountains now seemed open for settlement.
- Ironically, the British triumph prepared the ground for the American Revolution. French elimination from North America weakened the colonists' sense of military dependence on Britain.

SOURCE C

Thomas Barnard, an American preacher in 1763, quoted in R.D. Brown, editor, *Major Problems in the Era of the American Revolution 1760–1791*, D.C. Heath, 1992, pp. 50–1.

America, mayest well rejoice, the children of New England may be glad and triumph in reflection on events past, and prospect of the future. Encompassed with native savages, our Fathers having escaped from oppression, deepest felt by pious minds, carried their lives in their hands, subjected to captivities, to inhuman cruelties and massacres; encompassed with crafty, faithless Europeans, who sought their ruin, what prospect could they have before them? … And if we their offspring, call to mind the idea which possessed us in the year 1756, with what exultation must we sing, 'The snare is broken and we are escaped.'

Now commences the era of our quiet enjoyment of those liberties which our fathers purchased with the toil of their whole lives, their treasure, their blood. Safe from the enemy of the wilderness, safe from the gripping hand of arbitrary sway and cruel superstitions: here shall be the late founded seat of peace and freedom. Here shall our indulgent mother, who has most generously rescued and protected us, be served and honoured by growing numbers, with all duty, love and gratitude, till time shall be no more.

Why, according to Source C, were Americans much better off in 1763 than they had been earlier?

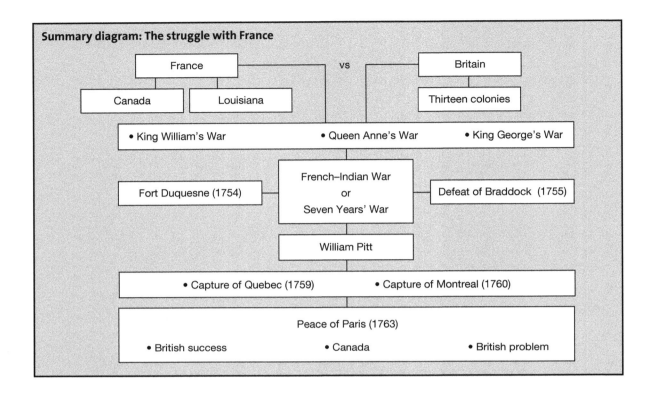

Summary diagram: The struggle with France

France vs Britain

Canada — Louisiana — Thirteen colonies

- King William's War
- Queen Anne's War
- King George's War

Fort Duquesne (1754) — French–Indian War or Seven Years' War — Defeat of Braddock (1755)

William Pitt

- Capture of Quebec (1759)
- Capture of Montreal (1760)

Peace of Paris (1763)
- British success
- Canada
- British problem

5 Britain by 1763

In 1763 Britain seemed a state of modernity, combining economic growth, political maturity and imperial strength.

The economic situation

Britain had a rising population, with 7.5 million people in 1760. Although more than half the British people were connected with farming, the **Industrial Revolution** was beginning to take effect, principally in the production of textiles, iron and steel. Cities like Birmingham and Manchester were rapidly growing. London, with 700,000 people, was the largest city in the world. Britain was the world's greatest trading nation.

The social situation

British society was hierarchical. Great landowners dominated society and politics. The nobility and their relations filled most of the high offices, whether in the ministerial departments, church or army.

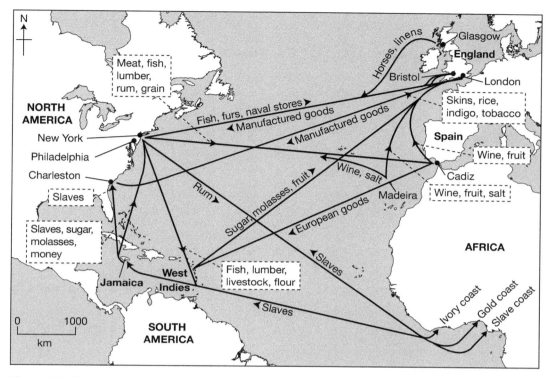

Figure 1.5 Colonial overseas trade.

Britain's rising middle class was essential to the growth of the economy and to Britain's social flexibility and stability. The middle class, diverse in both wealth and economic activity, was not a coherent group. There was a large gap, for example, between the great merchants, who often married into the aristocracy, and the small tradesmen and craftsmen who represented the backbone of commercial England.

At the bottom of society there were large numbers of agricultural and industrial labourers.

The political situation

Britain was a parliamentary monarchy. While **the Glorious Revolution** had reduced the monarchy's power, all government was – in theory – the king's. From the lowest official in the parish to the greatest minister of state, service undertaken was in the name of the monarch. George III (1760–1820) took an active part in government. Within limits, he chose the ministers who served him – the limits being essentially their ability to command parliamentary support.

 **KEY TERM**

The Glorious Revolution
In 1688 King James II fled from Britain. William III and Mary became joint monarchs. Parliament assumed greater control.

King George III

1738	Born, grandson of George II: he was the first Hanoverian king to be born and brought up in England
1760	Crowned king
1761	Married Princess Charlotte of Mecklenburg Strelitz
1783	Shared with Lord North the blame for the loss of the American colonies
Mid-1780s	Suffered periods of madness
1811	Became permanently insane; his son George became regent
1820	Died

In 1760, influenced by his former tutor, the Earl of Bute, George hoped to inaugurate a new era in politics by breaking the dominance of the Whigs and by ending the exclusion of the Tories from government, court and other office. Some Whig leaders, in consequence, accused George of plotting to enhance the power of the Crown and reduce Parliament to subservience. There is no evidence that Bute infected the future king with authoritarian intentions. Far from planning to reduce Parliament's powers, George III wanted to protect the constitution from the Whigs and the corruption which he imagined they employed to reinforce their power. While George had no wish to be a despot, he was determined to rule as well as reign. He thus did what he could to influence government policy.

George has generally had a bad press. Early twentieth-century historian Sir George Otto Trevelyan wrote that 'he invariably declared himself upon the wrong side in every conflict'. Historians today are somewhat kinder but most agree he was headstrong and obstinate. His political prejudices helped to cause the ministerial instability in the 1760s. If he had had greater perception or intelligence he might have steered Britain away from the disastrous policies of confrontation with the American colonies.

Parliament

Parliament consisted of the House of Lords and the House of Commons. The Commons' control of financial matters meant that it had ultimate power. But Britain was not democratic:

- In the 1761 election only 215,000 reasonably wealthy males were entitled to vote.
- Most of the growing cities were not represented in the Commons.
- Rich landowners usually determined who would stand as candidates and who would be elected.
- Few MPs were independent. A half owed their seats to patrons. Nearly a third held offices or honours under the government, usually voting as the government directed.

The political parties

In the early eighteenth century there were two major political parties: the **Whigs** and the **Tories**. After the **Hanoverian succession** in 1714, George I (1714–27) and George II (1727–60) were strongly committed to the Whigs. Between 1722 and 1762 there were only seven years in total in which the Whig **oligarchy** failed to provide Britain with stable and generally successful government. Politics after 1720 was dominated first by Sir Robert Walpole and then by the Pelhams: Henry Pelham and his brother the Duke of Newcastle.

Walpole and the Pelhams were adroit managers of the Commons, using government patronage to skilful effect.

In the late seventeenth century, the Whig Party had stressed government by consent of the people, resistance against arbitrary rule and the inviolability of the individual's fundamental rights. However, by 1760 Whiggism – indeed the Whig Party – had little real meaning. Everyone who mattered politically was a Whig. The Whigs were less a party than a broad-based political establishment with a few great Whig families at its core. The Tory Party had little influence, with many of its ambitious members joining Whig factions. In the absence of the Whig–Tory framework, politics became factionalised. Several powerful political leaders battled for control. Given the Whig feuding, ministries found it hard to command majorities. There was a constant shifting of support from one faction to another. The result was political instability in the 1760s.

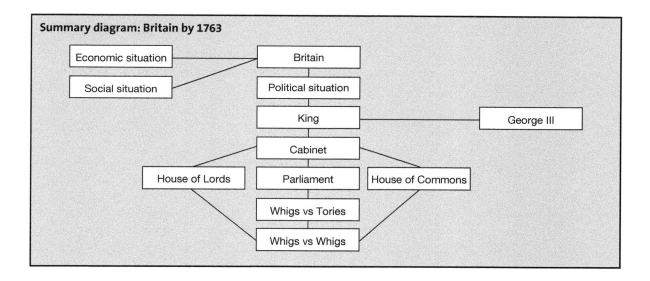

Summary diagram: Britain by 1763

6 Key debate

▶ *To what extent were there signs in 1763 that the colonies were likely to break their ties with Britain?*

Historians continue to debate the extent to which the American colonies were tied to Britain in 1763. It is possible to argue that the relationship between the two was weakening and would inevitably end. It is also possible to claim that the ties between Britain and its colonies were still very strong.

Signs of a weakening relationship

EXTRACT 1

From Robert Middlekauff, *The Glorious Cause: The American Revolution 1763–1789*, Oxford University Press, 1982, p. 26.

The colonies owed allegiance, and paid it, to the same king of England itself, but because their experience was different from the parent country's, this connection and those to imperial agencies of government did not restrict them. Distance from England and the slowness of communications helped keep the ties … slack. So also did the robust political institutions found in the mainland colonies – the provincial assemblies or legislatures and the county, town, and parish governments which gave order to their lives. Before 1776, the Americans had become almost completely self-governing.

Arguably, by 1763 the thirteen colonies were developing so rapidly that it was only a matter of time before they broke their ties with Britain. In all parts of America, there were tendencies at work that pointed to autonomy rather than to colonial dependency. The colonies' populations were rapidly growing and by 1763 colonists were aware of being something other than Britons. The mixing of diverse peoples in the colonies helped to forge a new identity. 'The standard culture retained its English cast but the presence of large bodies of non-English populations eroded its English texture', claims Robert Middlekauff.

By 1763 the colonies pretty well ran their own affairs. British governors complained throughout the early eighteenth century that they were dealing with an incipient or even fully matured spirit of independence. Unless Britain asserted its rights, the colonies were likely simply to drift away from British control. But if Britain tried to assert its rights, this was likely to cause ructions. According to historian Bernard Bailyn, the colonists' ideological outlook predisposed them to be acutely sensitive to all threats, perceived or real, to their liberty.

The colonists were also aware of their economic strength, and economic ties were beginning to pull the colonies together. British mercantilism, although not strictly enforced, rubbed the colonies up the wrong way.

The peace settlement of 1763 boded ill for future American–British relations. Once Canada was under British control, the colonies had nothing to fear from France and were thus less dependent on Britain.

Signs of a strong relationship

EXTRACT 2

From Maldwyn A. Jones, *The Limits of Liberty: American History 1607–1992*, Oxford University, 1995, p. 37.

At the close of the Seven Years War in 1763 hardly any of the American colonists are likely to have harbored thoughts of independence. For all their varied origins they were closely bound to Great Britain by ties of interest and affection. They were proud to be members of the British Empire and rejoiced in its great triumph over France. They cherished the British tradition of political liberty and, though chafing at certain aspects of the imperial economic system, were reasonably content with it.

Which of the two extracts provides the more convincing interpretation?

It is possible to argue that the colonial–British relationship was strong in 1763. For all the apparatus of regulation and control, the British imperial system was in practice easy-going. No other colonising nation conceded to its colonial subjects the degree of autonomy that the inhabitants of the thirteen colonies enjoyed. There were strong bonds of affection between Britain and the colonies, much of which stemmed from the colonists' pride in their British heritage and rights. Most Americans were loyal to Britain: during the Seven Years' War some 25,000 Americans had joined militias to fight against the French.

The strong relationship with Britain united the colonies rather than any inner sense of American unity. The only common institutions were those derived from Britain – notably the monarchy, common law, the English language and British culture. Moreover, Britain and the colonies were held together by a real community of economic interests within the mercantile system.

Pre-1763 the colonies showed no desire to attain unity. The word 'American' was mainly a geographical expression. People's loyalties were confined primarily to their own colony and then to Britain. Many customary features of nationhood were missing. The army, customs service and post office were British, and there was no single legal or monetary system. The thirteen colonies had different governments, different laws and different interests. There was a good deal of inter-colonial jealousy and squabbles over boundaries and land claims.

In 1763 virtually no American colonist sought or predicted the likelihood of separation from Britain. There was thus nothing inevitable about American independence. The argument that distance, population growth and nationalism would sooner or later have made separation inevitable is conjecture: the same factors did not make Canada in 1775 or later fight a war for independence.

Chapter summary

By 1763, it seemed that the development of Britain's colonies in North America had been hugely successful. The thirteen colonies had growing populations, thriving economies, and cultural and intellectual achievements. The colonies also had considerable political freedom and were far more democratic than Britain. Success against France in the Seven Years' War ensured that Britain was the dominant power in North America. But the conquest of Canada meant that the thirteen colonies were no longer militarily dependent on Britain. Historians continue to debate the strength of the colonies' ties to Britain.

 ## Refresher questions

Use these questions to remind yourself of the key material covered in this chapter.

1 Why did the American population grow so quickly in the eighteenth century?

2 What impact did immigration have on the thirteen colonies?

3 To what extent did the colonists govern themselves?

4 How democratic were the colonial governments?

5 How did British rule in the colonies operate?

6 Why were the American colonies so prosperous?

7 What were the effects of mercantilism?

8 How different were colonial and British societies?

9 How important was the Great Awakening?

10 Why did Britain win the struggle with France for control of North America?

11 What were the results of British success?

12 How strong were British–American ties in 1763?

 ## Question practice

ESSAY QUESTIONS

1 Which of the following was more responsible for British and American success in the Seven Years' War: i) American militia forces or ii) regular British troops? Explain your answer with reference to both i) and ii).

2 To what extent did the mercantilist system hinder the economic growth of the American colonies?

3 'Britain's success against France in the Seven Years' War weakened the American colonies' relationship with Britain.' Explain why you agree or disagree with this view.

4 'In 1763, the relationship between Britain and its North American colonies was strong.' Assess the validity of this view.

INTERPRETATION QUESTION

1 Read the interpretation and then answer the question that follows: 'The British mercantilist system may on balance have been economically advantageous to the colonies.' (Maldwyn A. Jones, *The Limits of Liberty, American History 1607–1992*, Oxford University Press, 1995.) Evaluate the strengths and limitations of this interpretation, making reference to other interpretations that you have studied.

SOURCE ANALYSIS QUESTIONS

1 With reference to Sources 1 and 2, and your understanding of the historical context, which of these two sources is more valuable in explaining the relationship between Britain and the American colonies in 1763?

2 With reference to Sources 1, 2 and 3, and your understanding of the historical context, assess the value of the sources to a historian studying the relationship between Britain and the American colonies in the early 1760s.

SOURCE 1

Thomas Hutchinson, a Bostonian and the last royal governor of Massachusetts, writing of the situation in Massachusetts in 1763.

Advantages in any respect enjoyed by the subjects in England, which were not enjoyed by the subjects in the colonies began to be considered in an invidious light and men were led to inquire, with greater attention than formerly, into the relation in which the colonies stood to the state from which they sprang … . It is well known in America that the people of England, as well as administration, were divided upon the expediency of retaining Canada rather than the islands [Guadeloupe and other French Caribbean islands] and it was also known the objection to Canada proceeded from an opinion that the cession of it by France would cause in time a separation of the British colonies from the mother country. This jealousy [suspicion] in England being known, it was of itself sufficient to set enterprising men upon considering how far such a separation was expedient and practicable.

SOURCE 2

James Otis (who later became a major opponent of Britain) speaking in the town meeting of Boston in 1763.

We in America have certainly abundant reasons to rejoice. The heathen are not only driven out, but the Canadians, much more formidable enemies are conquered and become fellow subjects. The British dominions and power may now be said, literally to extend from sea to sea … And we may safely conclude from his majesty's wise administration hitherto that liberty and knowledge, civil and religious, will be co-extended, improved and preserved to the latest posterity. No other constitution of civil government has yet appeared in the world so admirably adapted to these great purposes as that of Great Britain.

SOURCE 3

Reverend Andrew Burnaby, an Anglican minister, writing about his visit to America in 1760.

My first attachment, as it is natural, is to my native country [England]. My next is to America and such is my affection for both that I hope nothing will ever happen to dissolve that union, which is necessary to their common happiness … .

The province of Massachusetts Bay has been for some years past, I believe, rather on the decline, its inhabitants have lost several branches of trade which they are not likely to recover again … Their ship trade is considerably decreased, owing to their not having been so careful in the construction of vessels as formerly. Their fisheries too have not been equally successful … However, notwithstanding what has been said, Massachusetts Bay is a rich, populous and well-cultivated province.

CHAPTER 2

The causes of the American Revolution

In 1763 Americans seemed closely bound to Britain by ties of interest and affection. British actions after 1763 loosened those ties. Americans, fearing that their freedom was in jeopardy, vigorously resisted British efforts to tighten control over the colonies. Twelve years of controversy culminated in the likelihood of armed revolt. This chapter will examine the causes of the American Revolution (also called the War of Independence) by examining the following themes:

★ The situation in 1763–4

★ The Stamp Act controversy

★ The Townshend crisis

★ The impact of the Boston Tea Party

Key dates

1763		The Proclamation Line	1770	March	Boston Massacre
1764		The Sugar and Currency Acts		April	Repeal of Townshend duties
1765		The Stamp Act	1773	May	The Tea Act
1766		Repeal of the Stamp Act		Dec.	Boston Tea Party
1767	March	Townshend duties	1774	Spring	The Coercive Acts
	March	New York Restraining Act		Sept.	First Continental Congress

 ## 1 The situation in 1763–4

▶ *Why did Britain try to strengthen its control over the American colonies and with what result?*

Britain emerged from the Seven Years' War with a vastly increased empire in North America and a vastly increased **national debt** that had almost doubled between 1755 and 1763. The cost of the war in America had contributed greatly to the debt. For the most part, the American colonies had escaped paying for the war, although they greatly benefited from the defeat of France.

- They no longer faced a French threat from Canada.
- They hoped to be able to exploit the vast territories acquired in North America from France (see page 18).

Stronger imperial authority

It seemed evident to most British politicians in 1763 that imperial control over the newly extended North American empire should be tightened:

- Defence was a major concern. As colonial boundaries moved westwards, there was the likelihood of Native American attacks.
- Government had to be provided for 80,000 French Canadians, alien in language and religion.
- A coherent western policy was needed to reconcile the conflicting needs of land settlement, the fur trade and Native Americans.
- During the Seven Years' War it had become apparent that smuggling, with both Europe and the West Indies, was big business in America.

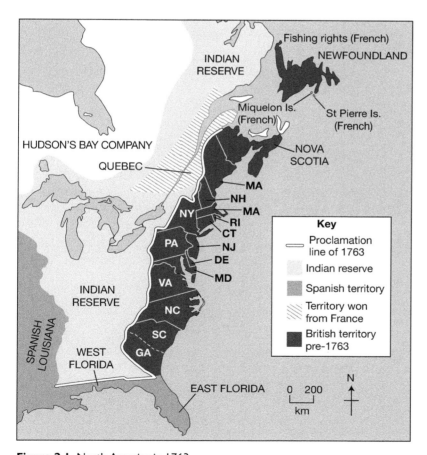

Figure 2.1 North America in 1763.

- Some politicians were angry that colonial governments had done little to contribute to their own defence during the war.

In February 1763 the new prime minister, the Earl of Bute, announced that 10,000 British troops were needed as a permanent army in North America and that the Americans should contribute something to the expense.

George Grenville

In April 1763 Bute was succeeded as prime minister by George Grenville, an experienced politician who had served ably in various ministries since 1744. Grenville's main concern was reducing the national debt, the annual interest of which was £4.4 million at a time when the government's annual income was only £8 million. (You probably need to add three noughts to get some notion of what these figures would mean in present-day terms.) Grenville had little option but to increase taxation and try to reduce expenditure. The cost of colonial administration and defence was a major worry: it had risen from £70,000 in 1748 to £350,000 in 1763. Still more money would be needed to maintain 10,000 troops in America. Grenville enthusiastically supported the notion that Americans should contribute to the cost of their own defence, particularly as they paid far less tax than the average Briton.

Pontiac's rebellion

Fearing (with good cause) further encroachments on their lands by white settlers, Ohio Valley tribes, led by the Ottawa chief, Pontiac, rose in revolt in May 1763. They destroyed every British post west of Niagara, except Detroit, killing or capturing hundreds of settlers in the process. Native American success was short lived. In August, British forces lifted the siege of Detroit. British officials used bribes to detach most of the Iroquois from Pontiac and to persuade the southern tribes to remain neutral. Although fighting continued into 1764, the serious Native American threat was over. The Native Americans were defeated by British soldiers paid for by Britain, confirming the view already held in London that the colonies were unable or unwilling to provide for their own defence and that there was thus a need for British troops.

The 1763 Proclamation

KEY TERM

Frontiersmen People who lived close to the colonial borders or in Native American territory and who were able to survive in what was often a hostile environment.

In October, Grenville's ministry issued the Proclamation of 1763. This declared that the boundary of white settlement was to be a line running along the crest of the Appalachians. All land claims west of the boundary were to be nullified (see Figure 2.1). Britain regarded the Proclamation Line as a temporary measure to minimise white–Native American conflict. The intention was not to curb white expansion permanently but to ensure that it was controlled.

The Proclamation Line angered some colonies (especially Virginia, which had claims to western lands) and many **frontiersmen** and land speculators.

However, it did not spark serious discontent. It was one thing for British politicians to draw a line on the map and proclaim that Native Americans should remain on one side and settlers on the other. It was quite another to enforce it. At least 30,000 American settlers ignored the restriction and moved west in the five years after 1763 in search of new lands. By 1768 Britain had accepted the breakdown of the Proclamation Line.

Grenville's anti-smuggling measures

Grenville hoped to use the trade laws (see page 10) to extract more revenue from the Americans. The problem was that the colonial customs service was inefficient: smuggling was rife and the customs officers were frequently corrupt. Americans thus evaded most of the customs duties.

In 1763 Britain introduced measures intended to reduce smuggling:

- Colonial customs officials had to reside in America rather than delegating their duties to deputies.
- To counter the leniency of colonial juries towards smugglers, jurisdiction in revenue cases was transferred from colonial courts to a vice-admiralty court in Halifax, Nova Scotia, where the judge alone would hand down the verdict.

The 1764 Sugar Act

Under the terms of the Sugar Act of 1733 Americans were expected to pay a duty of 6d. (six old pence; 2.5p) per gallon (4.5 litres) on molasses and sugar imported from non-British Caribbean colonies. This duty, largely ignored by American merchants and British customs officials, had yielded only £21,652 over 30 years. Grenville's Sugar Act, passed in April 1764, reduced the duty on foreign molasses from 6d. a gallon to 3d. The Board of Customs commissioners advised Grenville that the revised duty, strictly enforced, would yield £78,000 per year.

There was virtually no opposition to the act in Parliament. Most British MPs were complacent about and indifferent to the situation in the American colonies. There was no sustained American pressure group in Parliament and very few Americans: only five sat in the Commons between 1763 and 1783. Few British politicians anticipated much resistance to a measure that lowered duties. Moreover, it affected primarily just one region, New England (where distillers turned molasses into rum).

As part of the legislation associated with the Sugar Act, Grenville added products (including wine, silk and coffee) to the list of enumerated commodities. Among the new regulations of the Sugar Act and its companion legislation, any customs official convicted of accepting a bribe was subject to a £500 fine and disqualification from serving in any government post.

The Currency Act

The 1764 Currency Act placed a ban on colonial paper money. The act, aimed mainly at Virginia, which had issued a large amount of paper money during the Seven Years' War, appeased British merchants who insisted that colonial debts be paid in a more acceptable currency, for example, British sterling or Spanish dollars.

The American reaction

Grenville's measures angered many colonists and kindled their suspicions. New England merchants were especially aggrieved by the Sugar Act. The enforcement of customs legislation by vice-admiralty courts also represented a challenge to the colonial legal system.

The Currency Act could not have been passed at a worse time as far as the colonists were concerned. An economic depression had hit the colonies as the war ended and orders for supplies for the forces fell off. The **deflationary** effects of the Currency Act threatened some Americans with ruin.

American suspicions

Britain's right to regulate colonial trade had long been accepted as normal practice. However, the Sugar Act represented a fundamental revision in the relationship between Britain and the colonies. By imposing duties to raise revenue, Britain was essentially taxing Americans who were unrepresented in Parliament. Once it was accepted that Parliament could tax the colonies at will, where would it end, colonists asked?

By the mid-eighteenth century, the colonists regarded themselves as good Whigs. Their Whiggism, however, was not the same as the Whiggism prevalent in mid-eighteenth-century Britain (see page 23). American Whiggism in the 1760s was that of the first English Whigs who had come to prominence when England seemed to be sliding towards despotism under Charles II and James II. Americans were concerned with the old Whig issues of resisting **arbitrary power**, upholding popular rights and defending the integrity of representative institutions. The writings of early eighteenth-century British radical Whigs (in the 1720s), who condemned ministers for conspiring to undermine traditional freedoms, enjoyed wide support in the colonies.

Accordingly, many Americans were convinced of the need to guard against attempts to expand executive power by stealth. The position of influence attained by George's ex-tutor, the Earl of Bute, seemed to provide cause for alarm. Although Bute was no longer prime minister, many Americans feared that he was still a power behind the throne. There was also the fact that a large peacetime British army was being stationed in North America. The colonists had

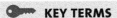

KEY TERMS

Deflation The situation resulting from a decreasing amount of money in circulation. People have insufficient money to buy goods or to invest.

Arbitrary power Power that is not bound by rules, allowing a monarch to do as he or she wishes.

not asked for that army and many were suspicious of it. Standing armies had long been seen as a potential threat to liberty.

The influence of John Wilkes

Many Americans identified with John Wilkes, a radical British MP and co-editor of the journal *North Briton*. Wilkes demanded freedom of the press and a more democratic Parliament. In 1763, after he had criticised the king and accused his ministers of being 'the tools of despotism and corruption', he was arrested and imprisoned. Although he was soon released, he was subsequently convicted of libel and fled to France. Wilkes became an American as well as a British hero. The British government seemed to be trampling on British – as well as American – liberties.

American opposition in 1764

By 1765 nine colonial assemblies had sent messages to London all arguing that Parliament had abused its power by introducing the Sugar Act. While conceding Parliament's right to regulate trade, they did not accept its right to tax in order to raise revenue in America.

It was not only the assemblies that objected to the Sugar Act. Some Americans took up their pens. James Otis, a member of a prominent Massachusetts family, published an influential pamphlet in 1764, *The Rights of the British Colonies Asserted and Proved*, in which he criticised Parliament's new aggressiveness towards the colonies and asserted that there should be no taxation in America without the people's consent.

Despite the objections of assemblies and pamphleteers, most Americans complied with the Sugar Act. Few were directly affected by it. This compliance gave Grenville the confidence to proceed with the Stamp Act.

SOURCE A

From James Otis, *The Rights of the British Colonies Asserted and Proved*, 1764, which attacked the Sugar Act.

The colonists being men, have a right to be considered as equally entitled to all the rights of nature with the Europeans, and they are not to be restrained in the exercise of any of these rights, but for the evident good of the whole community. By being or becoming members of society, they have not renounced their natural liberty in any greater degree than other good citizens and if it is taken from them without their consent, they are so far enslaved.

They have an undoubted right to expect that the best good will ever be consulted by their rulers, supreme and subordinate, without any partial views confined to the particular interest of one island or another.

What does Source A imply is wrong with the Sugar Act? **?**

Summary diagram: The situation in 1763–4

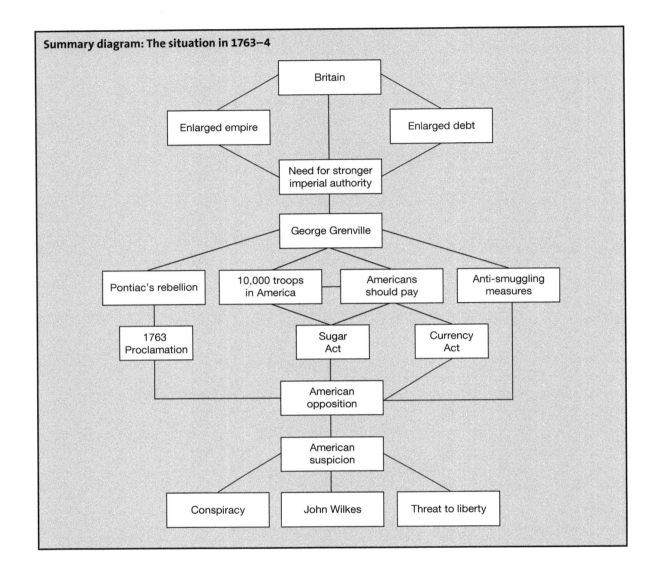

2 The Stamp Act controversy

▶ *Why did the Stamp Act provoke such a violent reaction in the colonies?*

In March 1764 Grenville let it be known that he was planning to bring in a **stamp duty** in America in 1765. It was possibly a mistake to give Americans a year's warning of the Stamp Act. The measure might have created less controversy had it been brought in more quickly. As it was, the colonies had time to prepare their opposition.

The Stamp Act

Ignoring messages of protest from American assemblies, Grenville introduced the stamp bill to Parliament in February 1765. The bill required stamps to be affixed to almost anything formally written or printed in the colonies. Fifty items, ranging from newspapers, legal documents, insurance policies, tavern and marriage licences, even playing cards, would be affected. The American stamp duties were much lighter than those in England, where they had been levied for over 70 years. The Treasury estimated that the new duty would raise £60,000 in its first year. The money, to be spent entirely in the colonies, would be only a quarter of the sum needed for colonial defence.

There was not much opposition to the stamp bill in the Commons. Most MPs agreed with Grenville that Parliament had the right to tax the colonies and that the Americans should contribute something to their own defence. The bill, having passed easily through Parliament, was given royal assent in March. It was to take effect on 1 November 1765.

The American reaction

News of the Stamp Act produced an intense reaction in America. Whereas the Sugar Act had affected only New England merchants, the Stamp Act applied universally, antagonising some of the most influential groups of colonists – lawyers, printers and tavern-keepers. The first direct tax levied by Parliament on the colonies, it was seen as a dangerous and unjustified innovation, and raised the issue of whether colonists could be taxed by a body in which they were not represented.

SOURCE B

An extract from a speech by Eliphalet Dyer of Connecticut, quoted in Hugh Brogan, *Longman History of the United States of America*, Longman, 1985, p. 111.

If the colonies do not now unite, and use their most vigorous endeavours in all proper ways, to avert this impending blow, they may for the future, bid farewell to freedom and liberty, burn their charters and make the best of thraldom and slavery. For if we can have our interests and estates taken away, and disposed of without our consent, or having any voice therein, and by those whose interest as well as inclination it may be to shift the burden off from themselves under pretence of protecting and defending America, why may they not as well endeavour to raise millions upon us to defray the expense of the last, or any future war?

The Virginia Resolves

On 29 May 1765 **Patrick Henry** introduced in the Virginia House of Burgesses (the Virginia assembly) seven resolutions attacking the Stamp Act and

Study Source B. Why, in Dyer's opinion, was it necessary for the colonies to unite against the Stamp Act?

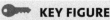 **KEY FIGURE**

Patrick Henry (1736–99)

A lawyer from Virginia, Henry was famous for his denunciation of the Stamp Act in 1765. A great orator, he served in the First Continental Congress. He later opposed the 1787 Constitution.

threatening resistance. Henry put forward his resolves at the end of the session when most members had left for home. On 30 May the remaining 39 burgesses, by no means unanimously, adopted the five mildest of Henry's resolutions:

- Colonists possessed the rights of Englishmen.
- Colonists rights were guaranteed by royal charter.
- Colonists could be taxed only if they had proper representation.
- Colonists had the right to give their consent to their laws.
- The House of Burgesses had the sole right to tax Virginians.

Since Henry's resolutions were printed in their entirety in many colonial newspapers, the impression was given that Virginia had rejected the Stamp Act and sanctioned open resistance if Britain tried to enforce it.

Most of the colonial assemblies had finished their spring sessions by the time news of the Virginia Resolves arrived. It was not until the autumn, therefore, that they discussed the Stamp Act. However, by the end of 1765 eight other assemblies had passed resolutions condemning the act and denying Parliament's right to tax the colonies. Most drew up petitions to the Crown and Parliament appealing for the act's repeal.

The Stamp Act Congress

In June 1765 the Massachusetts assembly suggested that an inter-colonial meeting be held in order to draft a set of resolutions which expressed a common colonial position. Accordingly, a Stamp Act Congress met in October in New York. Twenty-seven delegates from nine colonies attended – all men of high social standing. They denounced the Stamp Act as having 'a manifest tendency to subvert the rights and liberties of the colonies' and claimed that only their own legislatures could impose taxes on them. It was the duty of the colonies to seek the repeal of the Stamp Act, the abolition of vice-admiralty courts and 'of other late Acts for the restriction of American commerce'.

The ideological debate

Scores of pamphlets expressed similar views to the Stamp Act Congress. The colonists were not prepared to accept taxation without representation. This was a right that Americans, as Englishmen, believed was enshrined in the English Constitution. Direct American representation in Parliament was thought impracticable by most colonists because of the distance involved. A handful of American MPs, some colonists feared, would be worse than none. Their presence at Westminster would simply give Parliament the excuse to levy higher taxes on the colonies. The only proper way to raise money in America, colonists maintained, was through the assemblies.

Many Americans believed that government was by its nature oppressive, and that only constant vigilance could check its tendency to encroach on individual rights. The notion that the Stamp Act was evidence of a conspiracy to deprive the Americans of their liberties was thus widely disseminated. But who was conspiring? The ministry? Parliament? The king? Were they all in league against the Americans? No one suggested that they were. Indeed, George III was still well regarded and Parliament furnished the model of the colonists' own representative assemblies. Thus, the ministers – first Bute and now Grenville – were seen as the real villains. While the fears of covert designs against colonial liberty were misconceived, they seemed eminently reasonable to many Americans. Why did the British need a standing army in America unless it was to be used to force colonists to yield to such oppressions as unconstitutional taxes?

Popular protest

Colonial leaders could not have challenged British policy successfully without popular support. It was people in crowds who turned the situation from a debate into a movement. Crowd action was a fact of life in the eighteenth century. However, the sustained popular militancy that developed in most American towns in 1765 was something new.

Popular resistance to the Stamp Act originated in Boston among a group of artisans and shopkeepers known as the Loyal Nine. The group's most important leader was Samuel Adams (see page 43), who focused resentment on purported supporters of the Stamp Act. These included Andrew Oliver, the designated Massachusetts' stamp distributor, the Chief Justice (and Oliver's brother-in-law) Thomas Hutchinson, and Governor Francis Bernard. Adams turned to the North and South End gangs for support. These gangs, comprising unskilled workers, sailors and apprentices, had fought each other for years. They now agreed to unite against the act.

Mob action

On 14 August effigies of Oliver and Bute were hung from the **Liberty Tree** in Boston. Men stood by the tree, collecting a mock stamp duty from every passer-by. When Hutchinson ordered the effigies to be cut down, a crowd prevented the order being put into effect. Towards nightfall, a mob tore down Oliver's office and then destroyed his house. Oliver quickly resigned from the stamp distributor post.

On 26 August another Boston crowd damaged the houses of two British officials. The goal was the same: to force the officials to resign. (One rapidly did.) The crowd then attacked Hutchinson's mansion. There was an element of class resentment in the destruction. Oliver and Hutchinson were unpopular, not just because they were seen as British minions, but because they were wealthy. Social discontent was a latent ally of political rebelliousness. Indeed, many rich Bostonians feared that popular resentment at the Stamp Act had turned into an attack on property by the 'rabble'. Consequently, Governor Bernard, to his surprise, had no difficulty raising the militia and for several weeks was able

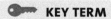

KEY TERM

Liberty Tree An actual (but also symbolic) tree in Boston, representing freedom from tyranny.

to maintain order. As news of events in Boston spread, so did crowd action, particularly in New York. Stamp distributors, fearing for their lives, resigned or fled in every colony.

The Stamp Act had been nullified by mob action. If no one was prepared to be a stamp distributor, the stamp duties could not be levied. Britain would have to use force if it was to maintain its authority. While Britain had 10,000 soldiers in America, most were stationed in Nova Scotia and on the western frontier. Only a few hundred men were garrisoned in New York and Philadelphia. Moreover, the army could only be called out to deal with civil disobedience if a governor made a request to the military commander. None did so.

The Sons of Liberty

By the autumn of 1765 the men directing the crowd action belonged to a semi-secret society known as the Sons of Liberty. The Sons included members of the elite as well as new men – small merchants, artisans and dissident intellectuals like Sam Adams. The Sons' influence has possibly been exaggerated:

- The organisation was far from united.
- The Sons had limited influence in the southern colonies.
- The Sons orchestrated an urban movement. But townspeople were less than five per cent of America's population.

Nevertheless, the organisation did ensure that political consciousness was kept high.

Economic sanctions

As the crisis deepened, the Sons of Liberty appealed to the public not to buy British goods. In October 1765 leading merchants in New York signed an agreement not to import goods from Britain until the Stamp Act was repealed. The boycott soon spread across the colonies. While merchants formed non-importation associations, many Americans simply boycotted British goods.

The repeal of the Stamp Act

In July 1765 Grenville was replaced by a new ministry led by the Marquis of Rockingham. Like Grenville, Rockingham wanted to see Parliament's authority upheld. But while Grenville thought that Parliament's right to tax the colonies had to be boldly asserted to avoid being lost, Rockingham believed that it was best not to exercise some rights, or at least to exercise them with discretion.

British opinion, inside and outside Parliament, was divided. Many MPs, horrified by the mob violence in America, were against repealing the Stamp Act, convinced that this would seem an act of weakness. They did not accept the American argument that because they were unrepresented Parliament could not legislate for them. The colonies were no more unrepresented than many British towns. There were MPs willing to speak for America just as there were MPs who could speak for Manchester and Birmingham. Most MPs believed that they represented not the interests of certain communities but the whole 'Commons of Great Britain' – and that included the Americans who were British subjects.

But British merchants and manufacturers, alarmed by the colonial boycott, campaigned for repeal of the Stamp Act. Rockingham was also informed by General Thomas Gage, commander-in-chief in the colonies, that the act could not be enforced without far greater military force than he possessed. Rockingham thus resolved to repeal the act.

The Commons debated the issue in January 1766. Grenville defended his measure, asserting that taxation was part of the sovereign power. He wanted a motion to declare the colonies in a state of rebellion. William Pitt, by contrast, declared that 'this kingdom has no right to lay a tax upon the colonies' and praised American resistance to the Stamp Act: 'Three millions of people, so dead to all the feelings of liberty, as voluntarily to submit to be slaves, would have been fit instruments to make slaves of the rest.' But some MPs wondered why anyone should expect Americans ever to pay taxes again if they escaped this one. Benjamin Franklin, appearing before a Commons committee, did his best to ease those fears. He made a distinction between internal and external taxes. The colonies, Franklin said (not quite correctly), objected only to internal taxes: they would willingly pay external duties on trade in return for the protection of the Royal Navy. The Stamp Act was repealed in March 1766 by 275 votes to 167.

The Declaratory Act

Most British MPs did not vote for repeal because they thought it was the right thing to do. They acted because they feared the colonies' ability to damage Britain's economy. Nor did they wish to incite rebellion. The British government, while abandoning a measure it could not enforce, did not surrender the constitutional principle of parliamentary sovereignty. At the same time as it repealed the Stamp Act, Parliament passed the Declaratory Act. This asserted that the colonies were subordinate to the 'Crown and Parliament of Great Britain' and that Parliament had full authority to make laws 'to bind the colonies and people of America … in all cases whatsoever'.

The effects of the crisis

In America news of the repeal was rapturously received. Non-importation was abandoned. The Sons of Liberty virtually disbanded. Most assemblies sent addresses of gratitude to the king. Nevertheless, the Stamp Act crisis marked a crucial turning point in British–colonial relations. As Grenville had recognised, there was more at stake in the controversy than revenue. The fundamental issue was Parliament's sovereignty over the colonies. In 1765 most Americans still believed that the Stamp Act was the problem, not British rule itself. Nevertheless, in denying Parliament the right to tax them, the Americans were implicitly denying Parliament's right to govern them. If not yet demanding independence in principle, they were demanding independence – or at least self-rule – in practice. Ruling out all British parliamentary interference in colonial internal affairs, they recognised a connection only with the king. This stance arose from the need to find a reason to deny Britain the right to impose a fairly modest tax. The response seemed out of all proportion to the provocation.

Britain had been caught unawares. British assumptions that the colonies were too self-interested to act together had been swept away. The Stamp Act had brought the colonists closer together than they had ever been before.

In several colonies, the Stamp Act crisis resulted in important shifts of power. Those factions who could be charged with supporting the Stamp Act lost control of the assemblies. In Massachusetts, for example, the Otis faction had no trouble in discrediting Governor Bernard and Thomas Hutchinson for supporting British policy. Consequently, in 1766, Bernard's supporters took a drubbing at the polls.

Both Americans and Britons learned important lessons from the crisis:

- Americans believed that they must remain vigilant in defence of their liberties.
- The crisis suggested that British authority could be defied if there was colonial unity.
- Many British politicians felt that they must reassert authority over the obstreperous colonies or they would become independent by default.

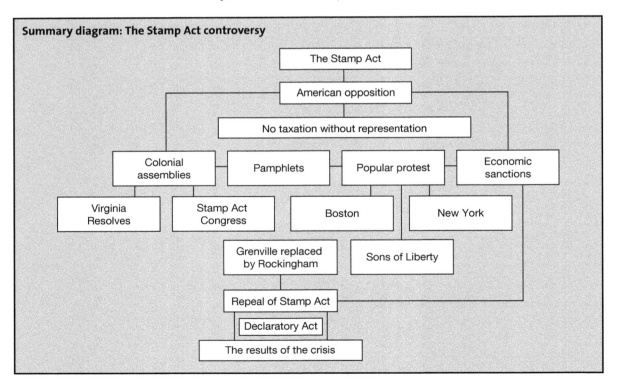

Summary diagram: The Stamp Act controversy

The Townshend crisis

▶ *What was the American response to the Townshend duties?*

In July 1766 Rockingham was replaced by national hero William Pitt, now given the title the Earl of Chatham. A passionate imperialist, Chatham did not want to see the British Empire undermined by provocative measures like the Stamp Act. However, in poor health, he passed responsibility to the inexperienced Augustus Henry Fitzroy, the Duke of Grafton.

Townshend's duties

In this situation, Chancellor of the Exchequer **Charles Townshend** dominated proceedings. Concerned that royal officials in America were dependent on colonial opinion, he was determined that they should be paid directly by Britain, not by the colonial assemblies. He also believed that the colonies should shoulder the burden of this expense.

In May 1767 Townshend introduced new duties on colonial imports of glass, wine, china, lead, paint, paper and tea. During the Stamp Act crisis Americans (like Franklin) had drawn a distinction between internal and external taxes, denying Parliament's authority to impose the former on them but conceding its right to regulate trade, even if such regulation produced revenue. Since Townshend's new duties were unquestionably external (and relatively light), he reasoned that the colonists could not logically object to them. Some MPs realised that Townshend's measures, which would raise only £40,000 per year, were a mistake. Edmund Burke, a prominent MP, pointed out that it no longer mattered to Americans whether taxes were external or internal: if they were levied by Britain they would oppose them. Nevertheless, Townshend had gauged the strong anti-American mood in the Commons and his measures easily passed.

To tighten trade enforcement, Townshend established an American Board of Customs Commissioners. Stationed in Boston, it was to be directly responsible to Britain and would give American customs officials more powers.

The New York Restraining Act

Townshend also took steps to enforce the Mutiny (or Quartering) Act of 1765. Designed to remedy the shortage of military accommodation, the act required colonial assemblies to make provision for quartering and supplying British troops. Most of the colonies had grudgingly complied but New York, the headquarters of the British army in America, had refused because the burden of the act fell disproportionately on the colony. Faced with this defiance, Townshend brought in the New York Restraining Act (March 1767). Under its terms, the New York assembly was prohibited from taking any legislative action until it complied with the Quartering Act. By suspending the assembly, Parliament had posed the problem of the constitutional standing of the colonial

 KEY FIGURE

Charles Townshend (1725–67)
An ex-president of the Board of Trade with extensive experience in colonial administration. A gifted man, he was nevertheless erratic in private and public conduct.

legislatures. Most colonists disliked the notion that Parliament could suspend or change them at will. However, the New York assembly, lacking support from the other colonies, now agreed to support the troops.

Townshend's death

It was ironic that an administration, nominally headed by the pro-American Chatham, approved Townshend's policies. It was also ironic that Townshend did not have to deal with the colonial response to his measures. He died suddenly in September 1767.

Colonial resistance

Colonial resistance to Townshend's measures developed more slowly than had been the case in 1765. Not all Americans were sure whether the new duties constituted a violation of colonial rights. Merchants, enjoying a period of economic boom, had no wish for another trade war. Nevertheless, it was soon clear that American resentment was widespread.

The intellectual response

John Dickinson wrote the most influential attack on Townshend's measures. His *Letters of a Pennsylvania Farmer* (1768) was printed in most colonial newspapers. Dickinson argued that while Parliament could regulate the colonies' trade, it did not have the right to tax them without their consent, through either internal taxes or external duties. He also condemned the suspension of the New York assembly as a blow to colonial liberty.

Other writers suggested that Townshend's measures would strengthen the executive and make colonial governments less accountable. Americans particularly feared that the new position of customs official would become a rich field of **patronage** at the disposal of the executive. Many feared that patronage power would in time corrupt a majority in the assemblies, making their members mere creatures of the British government.

The political response

In February 1768 the Massachusetts assembly sent out a **circular letter** denouncing the Townshend duties for violating the principle of 'no taxation without representation' and appealing to the other colonies for common action. The document, largely the work of Samuel Adams and James Otis, was branded as seditious by Governor Bernard. Despite efforts by other governors to prevent its endorsement, seven colonial assemblies quickly approved the letter. Virginia's House of Burgesses went further, issuing a circular letter of its own, advocating joint measures by the colonies against any British actions which 'have an immediate tendency to enslave them'. At a lower level, the Sons of Liberty movement was revived throughout the colonies in order to co-ordinate opposition.

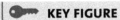

KEY FIGURE

John Dickinson (1732–1808)

A prominent Philadelphian lawyer, who wrote letters and pamphlets which were critical of British actions in the 1760s and 1770s. He was largely responsible for writing the Articles of Confederation.

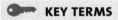

KEY TERMS

Patronage The right of bestowing jobs or offices – offices usually given to supporters, family or friends.

Circular letter A letter of which copies are sent to several people.

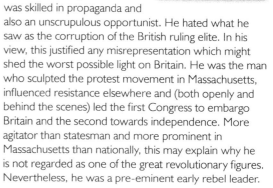

Samuel Adams

1722	Born in Boston
1740	After graduating from Harvard, he was apprenticed to a merchant who soon decided he had no aptitude for business
1748	Took over – not very successfully – the family malt business
1756	Elected tax collector in Boston
1765	Helped to co-ordinate the Stamp Act resistance in Boston
1768	Secured passage of the circular letter
1772	Helped to form the Committees of Correspondence
1773	Helped to plan the Boston Tea Party
1774	Led the opposition to the Coercive Acts
1774–81	A member of the Continental Congress
1794–7	Governor of Massachusetts
1803	Died

A radical idealist, Sam Adams was skilled in propaganda and also an unscrupulous opportunist. He hated what he saw as the corruption of the British ruling elite. In his view, this justified any misrepresentation which might shed the worst possible light on Britain. He was the man who sculpted the protest movement in Massachusetts, influenced resistance elsewhere and (both openly and behind the scenes) led the first Congress to embargo Britain and the second towards independence. More agitator than statesman and more prominent in Massachusetts than nationally, this may explain why he is not regarded as one of the great revolutionary figures. Nevertheless, he was a pre-eminent early rebel leader.

Economic resistance

In 1768 Boston led the way in organising a new economic boycott against Britain. Other towns followed, albeit slowly in some cases. Many merchants opposed non-importation, so the boycott was never totally watertight. Nevertheless, by 1769 every colony except New Hampshire had organisations pledged to boycott British goods. Complementing the non-importation agreements were decisions by individuals not to purchase British products. American housewives, for example, stopped serving British tea. As in 1765, non-importation spurred home manufacturing as an alternative to boycotted British goods.

Non-importation provided considerable scope for popular activity because it touched the lives of ordinary people, offering them a means of effective action. Unofficial bodies, usually called committees of inspection, were set up in most colonies to enforce non-importation. Those merchants who did not comply had their warehouses broken into and their goods damaged. Violators also faced the threat of violence, including being **tarred and feathered**.

As well as putting economic pressure on Britain, non-importation strengthened the moral resolve of the colonists. Some Americans were delighted to stem the tide of British luxury goods that were thought to be undermining the simplicity, virtue and independence of colonial life. 'The baubles of Britain,' says historian T.H. Breen, 'were believed to be threatening American liberty as much as were parliamentary taxation and a bloated customs service.'

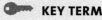 **KEY TERM**

Tarred and feathered
Victims were stripped naked, covered with hot tar and then rolled in goose feathers.

Unrest in Boston

Placing the American Board of Customs Commissioners in Boston proved to be a major error. From the time they arrived in November 1767 the commissioners were targets of popular wrath. Charged with tightening up the customs service, they faced an impossible task. There were far too few customs men to stop smuggling. Unable to carry out their duties, the commissioners sought help from the Royal Navy. In June 1768 the 50-gun warship *Romney* sailed into Boston harbour. Emboldened by this reinforcement, the commissioners seized the *Liberty*, a small vessel belonging to leading radical **John Hancock**. A mob soon marched to the wharf and a scuffle began with the customs men. Sailors from the *Romney* boarded the *Liberty* and took the boat out into the harbour. However, in the face of threats, the customs officials were forced to take refuge in Castle William, on an island in Boston harbour. By the summer of 1768 the Sons of Liberty controlled Boston.

The Wilkesite movement

In 1768 John Wilkes returned to England from France. He was promptly arrested, fined £1000 and sentenced to 22 months in prison. In May 1768 some 30,000 people gathered near the prison in London where Wilkes was incarcerated, demanding his release. Troops fired into the crowd, killing six and wounding twenty. While in prison, Wilkes was elected to Parliament three times: on each occasion he was expelled for libel. On the fourth try, the Commons illegally installed a rival. Wilkes' treatment, which was well reported in colonial newspapers, suggested to Americans that the British government was pursuing a concerted programme to suppress liberty on both sides of the Atlantic. Subscriptions for Wilkes' relief were taken in several towns. In 1769 South Carolina's assembly donated £1500 to Wilkes' cause.

The Secretary of State for America

In January 1768 Grafton created a secretary of state for colonial and American matters. Unfortunately, the Earl of Hillsborough, the first colonial secretary, lacked tact and political wisdom. One of his first acts was to order the Massachusetts assembly to rescind the circular letter it had sent out, on penalty of dissolution.

The situation in Boston

In Massachusetts, Governor Bernard did his best to obey Hillsborough's orders. When the Massachusetts assembly voted not to rescind the letter, he dissolved it. This only worsened matters. The Sons of Liberty now had another issue on which to campaign. To keep up popular enthusiasm, Otis and Adams organised marches and meetings while radical newspapers carried on an endless campaign against the British government and its servants. By 1768 Boston had a disciplined cadre of men who spent so much time and energy countering every British move that they were virtually professional revolutionaries. Not surprisingly, crowd trouble continued. Royal officials were threatened and the houses of customs commissioners damaged. Bernard was forced to ask for troops to try to restore order.

In late September, 600 British troops arrived in Boston. Far from ending the town's disaffection, they gave it another focus – themselves. The day-to-day presence of British troops became a constant aggravation:

- There were problems of barracking and quartering the men.
- Bostonians, accustomed to leading their lives with a minimum of interference, were harassed by British patrols.
- Off-duty soldiers sought to improve their meagre incomes by taking part-time jobs. The fact that they were prepared to work for less money than Americans increased tensions.

Boston newspapers reported (often fabricated) stories of brutality and debauchery among British troops. The army, goaded by a hostile population, had better cause to grumble. Brawls between troops and Bostonians were common. Troops resented the fact that they received severe treatment in local courts.

The Boston Massacre

In Boston tension increased:

- On 22 February 1770 a suspected customs informer killed an eleven-year-old boy during a riot. The Sons of Liberty turned the funeral into a political demonstration: 5000 Bostonians attended.
- On 2 March workers at a rope factory attacked some soldiers seeking jobs: a pitched battle ensued.

The climax came on 5 March. A detachment of British soldiers guarding the customs house was attacked by a mob hurling hard-packed snowballs. The troops, under extreme provocation, opened fire, killing five Bostonians. Sam Adams's political machine gave the impression that there had been a deliberate massacre – a version of events that was accepted by most Americans. The funerals of the dead were occasions for mass political demonstrations. The American cause now had martyrs.

Eight of the soldiers were eventually brought to trial. Six were acquitted after a skilful defence by their counsel John Adams, a cousin of Sam. Two, found guilty of manslaughter, were released after being branded on the thumb.

The situation by 1770

By 1770 the British government faced problems:

- There were insufficient troops in the colonies to impose order.
- Relations between British authorities and the assemblies had broken down.

SOURCE C

Paul Revere's engraving of the Boston Massacre.

? Why was Source C a masterful piece of colonial propaganda?

'The Americans,' wrote MP Edmund Burke, 'have made a discovery, or think they have made one, that we mean to oppress them. We have made a discovery, or think we have made one, that they intend to rise in rebellion against us … we know not how to advance, they know not how to retreat … some party must give way.' However, colonial unity was not total. Conservatives were alarmed at the resort to mob action. Nor was non-importation uniformly observed.

The repeal of the Townshend duties

The British government was concerned by events in the colonies. The Townshend duties, which had stirred up such a hornet's nest, made little financial sense. Not only were they failing to raise a significant revenue, they were also penalising British exports to the colonies. Grafton decided that the duties should be repealed. When he resigned in January 1770 the task of overseeing the repeal fell to the new prime minister, **Lord North**. In March, North secured the repeal of all the duties save that on tea. The decision to retain the duty on tea was taken in cabinet by a single vote, that of North himself. He saw the duty 'as a mark of the supremacy of Parliament'.

North's action divided conservative merchants from more radical agitators. New York quickly abandoned non-importation. As other ports followed suit, the crisis ended. Three years of comparative calm followed. Anglo-American trade resumed. As colonial prosperity returned, there was something of a conservative reaction against the radicals. In 1772 the Earl of Dartmouth succeeded Hillsborough as secretary for the colonies. Dartmouth believed in accommodation rather than confrontation.

Committees of correspondence

In 1771 the **Boston town meeting**, at Sam Adams's behest, created a Committee of Correspondence which was to communicate colonial grievances throughout Massachusetts. By mid-1773, 50 Massachusetts towns had their own committees. Other colonies followed suit, so much so that by February 1774 every colony except Pennsylvania and North Carolina had committees. In the event of another crisis, it was envisaged that the committees would ensure a rapid dissemination of information and a unified response. Although the committees did not do a great deal pre-1774, they at least communicated with each other and were a focus for radical activity in each colony.

American disunity

From Britain's point of view, the good news was that the colonists were far from united. Indeed, at times they seemed more intent on quarrelling among themselves than with Britain:

- There were disputes between colonies over boundaries and land claims, for example, between New York and New Hampshire over what (eventually) became Vermont.
- There were tensions between rich and poor in some colonies.
- In 1768 the so-called Regulator movement began in North Carolina and spread to South Carolina. Most of the participants were backcountry farmers who protested against the oppressions and corruption of Tidewater officials. After a period of virtual civil war the Regulators were crushed in 1771 at the battle of Alamance by eastern militia forces. Some 300 Regulators were killed.

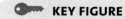

KEY FIGURE

Lord North (1732–92)

British prime minister 1770–82. A well-respected politician before 1775, North proved to be a poor war leader. He provided no firm unified direction and failed to ensure that his war ministers co-ordinated their activities.

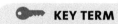

KEY TERM

Boston town meeting
The town council of Boston.

Summary diagram: The Townshend crisis

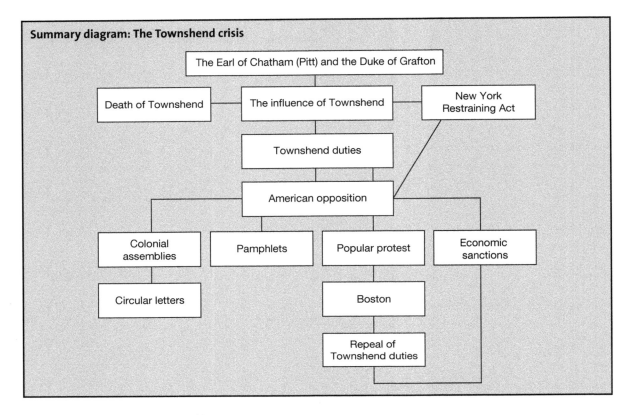

 The impact of the Boston Tea Party

▶ *Why was the Boston Tea Party so important?*

Despite three years of relative peace, unrest in the colonies continued to simmer. In 1773 Lord North's actions brought the simmering to the boil.

The 1773 Tea Act

 **KEY TERM**

East India Company
A powerful company that controlled much of Britain's trade with India.

In 1773 the British government reopened old wounds by introducing a Tea Act. The act was designed to save the near-bankrupt **East India Company** rather than assert parliamentary sovereignty over the colonies. It aimed to relieve the financial stresses of the company by permitting it to export tea to the colonies directly and retail it there, using its own agents. The Tea Act abolished British duties on the company's tea while obliging Americans to continue paying the duty levied under Townshend's legislation. Nevertheless, the tea sold by the company would be so cheap that it could undercut tea that was traded legitimately by American merchants and foreign tea that was smuggled in, usually by the same merchants. It seemed that:

- American consumers would benefit because tea would drop in price
- the East India Company would sell its vast stocks of tea in America at a healthy profit
- Britain would obtain increased duties.

But Lord North had miscalculated. It should have been clear to him that the colonists would not buy the tea until the duty was lifted. For a few pounds – the tea imported into America had netted only £400 in 1772 – North was risking the export of £2 million of tea and antagonising the Americans into the bargain.

The American reaction

Most Americans were convinced that the Tea Act was another attempt at parliamentary taxation and the destruction of the independence of their assemblies. The measure was bitterly attacked in newspapers and pamphlets. Philadelphians set the tone of the opposition and gave it direction in ways made familiar in the crises over the Stamp Act and the Townshend duties. Violence was threatened against those merchants importing East India Company tea. Tea sent to Philadelphia and New York was rejected and sent back to England. In all the major ports the **tea agents**, facing severe intimidation, were forced to resign.

 **KEY TERM**

Tea agents Men responsible for collecting tea duties.

The Boston Tea Party

On 28 November 1773 the ship *Dartmouth*, bearing 114 chests of East India Company tea, entered Boston harbour. Among the merchants to whom the tea was consigned were two sons of Governor Hutchinson. Hutchinson was determined that the tea be disembarked. Most Bostonians were equally determined that the *Dartmouth* should depart. Thousands gathered daily to prevent the tea from being unloaded. On 2 December the *Eleanor* joined the *Dartmouth*. Two weeks of discussion between Hutchinson and patriot leaders resulted in deadlock. On 15 December the *Beaver* arrived.

On 16 December 60 Sons of Liberty men, crudely disguised as Mohawk Native Americans and directed by Sam Adams, boarded the three tea ships and threw their cargoes – 342 tea chests worth about £10,000 – into the harbour. A huge crowd watched in silence. Admiral Montagu, the Royal Navy commander in Boston, could have ordered his nearest warship to open fire. Fearing that this might worsen the crisis, Montagu did nothing. Nor did the troops stationed at nearby Castle William.

John Adams wrote in his diary: 'This destruction of the tea is so bold, so daring, so firm, intrepid and inflexible, and it must have so important consequences and so lasting, that I cannot but consider it as an epocha [epoch or notable stage] in history.'

SOURCE D

Examine Source D.
What was the purpose of
the cartoon?

A British cartoon, printed in 1774.

The British reaction

When news of the Boston Tea Party reached London, the reaction was one of
outrage. In 1766 and 1770 colonial protest had brought about a reversal of British
policy. Confronted with colonial defiance for a third time, North's government
determined to take a hard line. North was convinced that Britain faced a
fundamental challenge to its imperial system, a challenge which could not be
ignored without imperilling national prosperity and security. Parliament was
either the supreme authority in the empire or it was not. Even staunch friends

of the colonists in Britain refused to defend the Tea Party. Chatham said it was 'criminal'.

The Coercive Acts

Concluding that Boston was at the centre of colonial troubles, North's ministry decided to punish it. In early 1774 Parliament passed four Coercive (dubbed by the colonists 'Intolerable') Acts:

- The Boston Port Act closed Boston to all trade until the destroyed tea had been paid for.
- The Massachusetts Government Act allowed the royal governor to appoint and remove most civil officials. Town meetings could not be held without his permission.
- The Impartial Administration of Justice Act provided for the transfer to Britain of murder trials.
- A new Quartering Act gave broader authority to military commanders seeking to house their troops.

Chatham and Burke spoke against the measures, warning of the consequences. Their eloquence had no effect. All passed with large majorities. Meanwhile, the commander-in-chief in America, General Gage, was made governor of Massachusetts.

The Quebec Act

Colonial sensibilities were further inflamed by the Quebec Act (June 1774). This ill-timed effort to solve the problem of governing the French inhabitants of Canada was seen by Americans as confirmation of evil British designs. The act placed authority in the hands of a governor without an elected assembly and limited trial by jury. This suggested to colonists that Britain intended to put the whole of North America under authoritarian forms of government. Moreover, the extension of the Quebec boundary south and west to the Ohio and the Mississippi looked like an attempt to check westward expansion by the thirteen original colonies.

The American reaction

While the Coercive Acts were intended to punish Massachusetts, especially Boston, most Americans believed that the measures were a threat to all the colonies. If Massachusetts could be dealt with in this way, no colony was secure. People in other colonies rallied to Boston's support, sending food and money to help the town's poor. In March 1774 New Yorkers found East India Company tea on board the *Nancy*. They set out to follow the Bostonians' example. While a party of 'Mohawks' prepared themselves, the main crowd surged on to the ship and disposed of the tea.

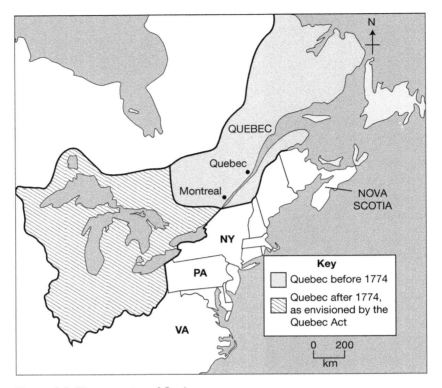

Figure 2.2 The expansion of Quebec.

The economic response

On 13 May the Boston Town Meeting asked all the colonies to boycott British goods until the Boston Port Act was repealed. The Boston Committee of Correspondence drafted a Solemn League and Covenant (5 June) committing itself to a British boycott. Many communities endorsed the document. However, not all merchants were convinced that this was the right course of action:

- A trade boycott would probably harm America more than Britain.
- Previous non-importations had shown that boycotts were difficult to enforce and that some merchants had made money from trade with Britain at the expense of others.

The political response

Colonial assemblies, town and country meetings, newspapers, clergymen and other men of influence denounced the actions of the British government. Propaganda, disseminated by the Committees of Correspondence, persuaded the colonists of the need for common action to defend American liberties. Royal governors dissolved assemblies that seemed ready to denounce the Coercive Acts and to support an economic boycott. Undeterred, the Virginian House of Burgesses passed a resolution on 24 May condemning the Coercive Acts. Two days later Governor Lord Dunmore dissolved the House. On 27 May, 89 of the 103 burgesses met at the Raleigh Tavern in Williamsburg. This body proceeded to adopt a non-importation agreement, pledged non-consumption of tea and denounced the Boston Port Act. It declared that 'an attack, made on one of our sister colonies, to compel submission to arbitrary taxes, is an attack on all of British America and threatens the ruin of all'. Accordingly, it proposed that an inter-colonial congress be called to seek redress of American grievances.

During the summer of 1774 seven other colonies, where royal governors had forbidden assemblies to meet, followed Virginia's example and set up extra-legal conventions. Meeting in open defiance of British authority, they assumed the role of government. Usually they were simply the assemblies meeting without sanction. But in some colonies the conventions had a broader membership than the old assemblies.

Newspapers and pamphlets

By 1775 there were 42 colonial newspapers, mainly concentrated in New England. All but two or three were radical in emphasis, their language incendiary and strident. Numerous pamphlets defended the rights of the colonies. In 1774 Thomas Jefferson (see page 71) published *A Summary of the Rights of British America*. In Jefferson's opinion, the British Parliament had no right to exercise authority over Americans. There was no reason why 160,000 electors in Britain should give laws to millions of Americans, 'every individual of whom is equal to every individual of them'.

By 1774 some pamphlets and newspapers openly discussed – and some supported – colonial independence. John Adams, under the pseudonym Novangulus, published twelve essays between January 1774 and April 1775 in the *Boston Gazette*. In one he declared, 'America is not any part of the British realm or dominions'.

The Continental Congress

In September all the colonies except Georgia sent at least one delegate to Philadelphia to a Continental Congress 'to consult upon the present unhappy state of the colonies'. Most of the 56 delegates (usually chosen by the extra-legal conventions) were men who had played prominent local roles in opposition to Britain over the previous decade. John Adams thought the Congress was almost equally divided between radicals, who favoured severing most ties with Britain, and moderates, who favoured retaining more ties. The most prominent radical figures were **Richard Henry Lee** and Patrick Henry of Virginia, and John and Sam Adams of Massachusetts. Leading moderates included John Dickinson and Joseph Galloway of Pennsylvania.

The Congress endorsed the Suffolk Resolves (17 September). These declared the Coercive Acts null and void and called on Massachusetts to arm for

 KEY FIGURE

Richard Henry Lee (1732–94)

A leading opponent of Britain in Virginia. He served as a delegate to Congress from 1774 to 1776. In June 1776 he moved that the colonies should declare themselves independent.

defence. Congress also called for non-importation of all British goods, starting on 1 December 1774, unless Parliament repealed the Coercive Acts. A ban on exports to Britain would begin in September 1775 (allowing planters time to sell crops raised in 1774). To promote the trade embargo, Congress called on colonists everywhere to form a Continental Association so that non-importation would be a united effort rather than merely local initiatives.

On 14 October Congress agreed on a Declaration of Rights and Grievances. While acknowledging allegiance to the Crown, the declaration denied that the colonies were subject to Parliament's authority. While accepting that Parliament could regulate trade for the good of the whole empire, Congress declared that it could not raise revenue of any kind from the colonists without their consent. It also proclaimed the right of each colonial assembly to determine the need for troops within its own province. Although the Congress had no coercive or legislative authority, it provided a useful unifying purpose. When it came to an end on 26 October, another Congress was called for May 1775.

The trade boycott

The ban on British imports boosted the radical cause by encouraging local production and pride in frugality. Indeed, non-importation and non-consumption again became the basis for a drive for moral regeneration in which the rejection of luxury items and a return to a simple rustic life played an important part. Even wealthy landowners tempered their aristocratic lifestyles so they were in tune with ordinary Americans.

Committees of Safety

In late 1774 Committees of Inspection (or Safety) were established across the colonies in accordance with the Continental Association. Some of these committees were organised by the old elite. Others involved new – poorer – men. The committees had a mandate to enforce the boycott. But many went much further than this, acting in place of the defunct local government. The committees had considerable powers. Functioning as quasi-courts, they investigated and punished those who broke the Continental Association's rules. By the spring of 1775 some 7000 colonists, many directly involved in politics for the first time, were serving either on Committees of Safety or in the extra-legal conventions.

The situation in Massachusetts

By late 1774 British authority had broken down completely in Massachusetts. In outlying areas those officials who were still loyal to Britain were terrorised by mob action and forced out of office. Outside Boston, effective authority resided in the Provincial Congress and a host of committees. As well as stopping trade with Britain, these bodies took on themselves the organisation of military resources. Across Massachusetts, militia units began to prepare for war.

General Gage found that his power extended only as far as British troops could march. Effectively besieged in Boston, where his relatively few troops were concentrated, all Gage could do was ask the British government for 20,000 extra soldiers. He was all for teaching the rebels a bloody lesson but had insufficient force to do so.

The situation in other colonies

By early 1775, in most colonies, extra-legal conventions and committees had expelled traditional authority. Arms and ammunition were stockpiled and militias drilled. Rhode Islanders and New Hampshire militiamen seized cannon, arms and munitions from British forts. However, not all Americans supported the rebel cause. New York, for example, remained predominantly loyal to Britain. Most Americans continued to hope that a solution to the troubles could be found within the framework of a continuing Anglo-American connection. Relatively few Americans sought total independence.

British determination

In November 1774 Gage wrote to North recommending the temporary suspension of the Coercive Acts. But neither North nor the king had any intention of backing down. Both men recognised that the colonies were in a state of rebellion. In the circumstances, North's military measures were remarkably lax: only 4000 extra troops were sent to Boston. North still failed to appreciate the scale of the military task facing them.

Some politicians tried to persuade the government to make concessions to the Americans:

- Chatham introduced a bill in February 1775 proposing the repeal of the Coercive Acts: it was rejected by 61 to 32.
- Burke, in the Commons, offered repeal of all legislation offensive to the Americans: his proposal was defeated by 270 votes to 78.

SOURCE E

An extract from a speech by Lord Camden in February 1775, from Hugh Brogan, _Longman History of the United States of America_, Longman, 1985, p. 169.

To conquer a great continent of 1,800 miles, containing three millions of people, all indissolubly united on the great Whig bottom of liberty and justice, seems an undertaking not to be rashly engaged in ... It is obvious, my lords, that you cannot furnish armies, or treasure, competent to the mighty purpose of subduing America ... [and] whether France or Spain will be tame, inactive spectators of your efforts and distractions, is well worthy of the consideration of your lordships.

Study Source E. Why did Lord Camden oppose military intervention in America?

North did introduce a Conciliation Plan but it promised merely that Parliament would 'forbear' to tax any colony paying the cost of its own civil administration and making a satisfactory contribution to imperial defence. This attempt at concession failed. Americans were no more inclined to accept North's small carrot than to bend to his equally small stick.

In February 1775 Parliament declared Massachusetts in a state of rebellion. In March it limited New England's commerce with Britain and the British West Indies. In April this restriction was extended to most colonies.

Meanwhile, in March, Dartmouth finally dispatched a letter telling Gage to move against the rebellion and to arrest 'the principal actors and abettors'.

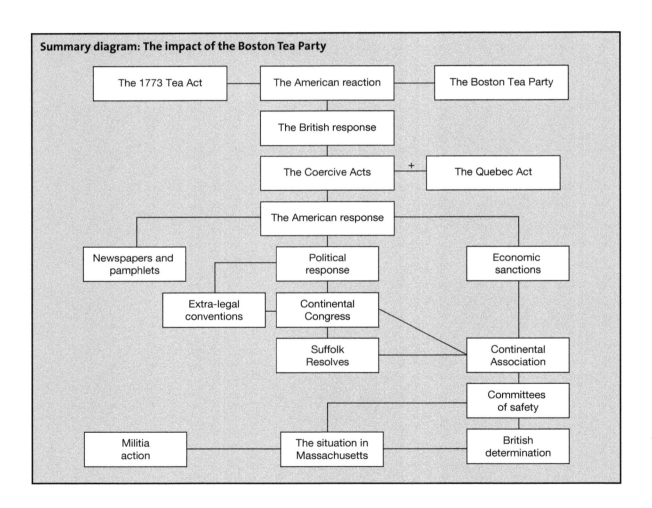

Summary diagram: The impact of the Boston Tea Party

Chapter summary

By 1775 American colonists, angered by British actions and fearful that these actions threatened their liberty, were on the verge of attempting to break away from Britain. American angers and fears were generated by Britain's efforts to tax colonists to help pay for the cost of the Seven Years' War. Most British MPs thought that Britain had the right to tax Americans: the proposed taxes were light by British standards. However, Americans resented taxation without representation in Parliament. British actions – Grenville's early measures, the Stamp Act, Townshend's duties, the Tea Act – were met by American resistance – political, intellectual, economic – and by acts of violence. By 1775 discontent had resulted in the breakdown of British authority, particularly in Massachusetts.

 ## Refresher questions

Use these questions to remind yourself of the key material covered in this chapter.

1 Why did Britain try to strengthen its control over the colonies?

2 To what extent did Grenville's western policies alienate Americans?

3 Why did many Americans oppose Grenville's 1764 measures?

4 Why did the Stamp Act provoke such a violent reaction?

5 Why did Britain repeal the Stamp Act?

6 Why did Townshend introduce his duties?

7 To what extent was American resistance between 1767 and 1770 similar to that in 1765?

8 What caused the Boston Tea Party?

9 What impact did the Coercive Acts have in America?

10 Were the colonies in a state of rebellion in 1774–5?

11 Why was the British government determined to stand firm in 1774–5?

 ## Question practice

ESSAY QUESTIONS

1 'The American reaction to the 1765 Stamp Act was fully justified.' Assess the validity of this view.

2 'Between 1766 and 1770 the American colonies became united in their opposition to Britain.' Explain why you agree or disagree with this view.

3 How important was the impact of the Boston Tea Party on relations between Britain and its American colonies?

4 How successful were the actions of Sam Adams and the Sons of Liberty?

INTERPRETATION QUESTION

1 Read the interpretation and then answer the question that follows: 'The attempt of the inefficient, ignorant, envious and indignant British government to deal with the intricate colonial problems that resulted from the [Seven Years'] war led to the American Revolution – a rebellion that was costly and unnecessary.' (John A. Garraty, *The American Nation: A History of the United States,* third edition, Harper & Row, 1979.) Evaluate the strengths and limitations of this interpretation, making reference to other interpretations that you have studied.

SOURCE ANALYSIS QUESTIONS

1   With reference to Sources 1 and 2, and your understanding of the historical context, which of these two sources is more valuable in explaining the reasons for animosity between Britain and its American colonies?

2   With reference to Sources 1, 2 and 3, and your understanding of the historical context, assess the value of these sources to a historian studying the Stamp Act crisis.

SOURCE 1

From George Grenville's speech in Parliament on the Stamp Act, 14 January 1766 (the Stamp Act had been passed a year earlier).

Protection and obedience go together. Great Britain protects America; America is bound to yield obedience. If this is not so, tell me when were the Americans emancipated? When they want the protection of this kingdom, they are always ready to ask for it. This nation has run itself into an immense debt to give them their protection. Now that they are called upon to contribute a small share towards the public expense (an expense incurred to their benefit) they renounce our authority, insult our officers and break out into open rebellion.

SOURCE 2

From William Pitt the Elder's speech in Parliament on the Stamp Act, 14 January 1766. Pitt was the Secretary of State who helped lead Britain to victory in the Seven Years' War. He was Grenville's brother-in-law.

I am no courtier of America: I stand up for this kingdom. Our legislative power over America is sovereign and supreme. When two countries are connected together, like England and her colonies, the greater must rule the lesser, but must so rule the lesser, as not to contradict the fundamental principles that are common to both. If the gentleman [Grenville] does not understand the difference between internal and external taxes, I cannot help it. The gentleman asks, when were the colonies emancipated? But what I desire to know is, when were they made slaves?

SOURCE 3

Benjamin Franklin facing examination before the House of Commons during the debates over the repeal of the Stamp Act in March 1766.

The colonies submitted willingly to the government of the Crown, and paid, in all their courts, obedience to acts of parliament. Numerous as the people are in the several old provinces, they cost you nothing in forts, citadels, garrisons or armies to keep them in subjection. They were governed by this country at the expense only of a little pen, ink and paper. They were led by a thread. They had not only respect, but an affection, for Great Britain, for its laws, its customs and manners, and even a fondness for its fashions, that greatly increased the commerce. Natives of Britain were always treated with particular regard; to be an Old-England man was, of itself, a character of some respect, and gave a kind of rank among us.

CHAPTER 3

Independence

The first gunshots of the American War of Independence were fired at Lexington in April 1775. Ironically, few Americans were fighting for outright independence from Britain in 1775. However, the fighting in 1775–6 and the failure to reach any sort of compromise meant that by the summer of 1776 many Americans sought independence. This chapter will examine the events of 1775–6 that culminated in the Declaration of Independence by examining the following themes:

★ The outbreak of war

★ The war 1775–6

★ The Declaration of Independence

The key debate on *page 72* of this chapter asks the question: What inspired the American colonies to declare independence?

Key dates

1775	April	Fighting at Lexington and Concord	1775–6		Failure of American invasion of Canada
	May	Second Continental Congress	1776	Jan.	Publication of *Common Sense*
	June	Battle of Bunker Hill			
	July	Olive Branch Petition		July	Declaration of Independence

 ## The outbreak of war

▶ *Why was the fighting at Lexington and Concord a disaster for Britain?*

Over the winter of 1774–5 General Gage sent spies through Massachusetts to assess the strength of colonial resistance and to discover where the rebels had stockpiled their weapons. In February 1775 he sent troops to Salem to seize munitions. Outnumbered by militiamen, Gage's men were forced to withdraw. Americans now not only defied parliamentary laws, they openly resisted British soldiers performing their duty.

Lexington and Concord

Gage received no help from Britain and no instructions until 14 April, when Dartmouth's letter ordered him to arrest rebel leaders and authorised him to use force to disarm the population. Gage, for so long patient despite serious provocation, was ready to act. On the evening of 18 April he sent 700 men from Boston under Colonel Smith to Concord, 26 km (16 miles) away, to seize rebel arms and to arrest leaders of the Provincial Congress. Unfortunately for Gage, the Massachusetts militia were informed of British intentions by Paul Revere, William Dawes and Dr Prescott – all members of the Boston committee of safety.

On 19 April the British troops found their path barred by 70 **minutemen** at Lexington. Shots were fired – it is still not clear who fired first – and eight colonists were killed. The British pushed on to Concord. Here they encountered a larger militia force and there was a heavy exchange of fire. After destroying the military stores but failing to arrest rebel leaders, Smith's troops turned back to Boston. On the return they were assailed by Americans firing from the cover of stone walls and woods.

? In what ways does Source A give a biased account of what happened to British troops on the march to Concord and back?

SOURCE A

A loyalist woman's account of the events at Lexington and Concord, quoted in R.D. Brown, editor, *Major Problems in the Era of the American Revolution, 1760–1791*, D.C. Heath, 1992, p. 147.

After daybreak a number of the people appeared before the troops near Lexington. They were called to, to disperse, when they fired on the troops and ran off. Upon which the light infantry pursued them and brought down about fifteen of them. The troops went on to Concord and executed the business they were sent on, and on their return found two or three of their people lying in the agonies of death, scalped and their noses and ears cut off and eyes bored out, which exasperated the soldiers exceedingly, a prodigious number of people now occupying the hills, woods, and stone walls along the road. The light troops drove some parties from the hills but all the road being enclosed with stone walls served as a cover to the rebels, from whence they fired on the troops still running off whenever they had fired, but still supplied by fresh numbers who came from many parts of the country … Lord Percy has gained great honour by his conduct through this day of severe service; he was exposed to the hottest of the fire and animated the troops with great coolness and spirit. Several of the officers are wounded and about 100 soldiers. The killed amount to near 50; as to the enemy we can have no exact account but it is said there was about ten times the number of them engaged and that near 1,000 of 'em have fallen.

Smith's troops might have had to surrender had it not been for the arrival of a relief force under Lord Percy, which held the militiamen at bay at Lexington. The British then resumed the retreat to Boston, galled all the way by American snipers. By the time they reached Boston, the troops had suffered 273 casualties;

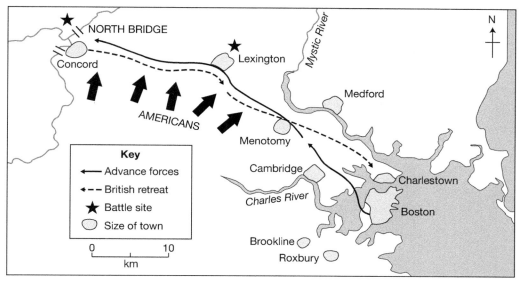

Figure 3.1 Lexington and Concord.

the Americans lost only 92 men. Within a week 20,000 New England militia besieged Boston.

The results of Lexington and Concord

The events of 19 April transformed the political dispute between the colonists and Britain into a military struggle. Lexington and Concord galvanised military preparations throughout the colonies. New York now threw itself behind Massachusetts and even the conservative Pennsylvania assembly voted to raise 4300 men. Militiamen, led by Ethan Allen and Benedict Arnold, seized Fort Ticonderoga (see Figure 3.3 on page 65) on 10 May. Crown Point, garrisoned by just nine men, fell two days later.

The Second Continental Congress

The first Continental Congress, meeting in September 1774, had been summoned to express and co-ordinate colonial opposition to the Coercive Acts. The second Continental Congress, meeting on 10 May 1775 in Philadelphia, faced a very different set of challenges. Sixty-five delegates attended, with men representing all thirteen colonies. Fifty had served in 1774, ensuring that there was an important degree of continuity. Newcomers included Benjamin Franklin and Thomas Jefferson. The Congress had little choice but to take charge of the conduct of the war, assuming responsibility for the army around Boston and impressing a quota on each colony sufficient to raise a Continental army of 20,000 men. In mid-June, Congress voted to issue $2 million in paper money to finance the force.

The appointment of George Washington

Congress unanimously appointed George Washington (see page 87) to command the Continental army. Washington at least looked the part. Six feet three inches (190 cm) tall and with natural aristocratic manners, he had worn his militia colonel uniform at all the congressional meetings, reminding congressmen of his military experience in the Seven Years' War (see page 27). Crucially, Washington was from Virginia. Placing a southerner in command of what was still a predominantly New England army was expected to help cement colonial unity. Moreover, the choice of a wealthy planter – Washington reputedly owned 35,000 acres (14,000 hectares) – would allay fears of radicalism.

Efforts at reconciliation

While Congress adopted the attributes of a national government, some of its members were reluctant to accept such a role. Most colonial conventions had instructed their delegates to seek reconciliation with Britain. On 6 July Congress adopted a Declaration of the Causes and Necessities of Taking up Arms, listing the colonial grievances. While asserting that Americans would rather die than be enslaved, it disclaimed any intention of 'separating from Great Britain and establishing independent states'. Congress also adopted the Olive Branch Petition (8 July). Professing attachment to George III, it begged him to prevent further hostile measures so that a plan of reconciliation might be worked out. The petition's purpose was to convince moderates that Congress did not intend

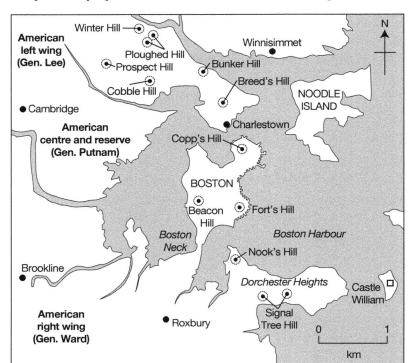

Figure 3.2 The Siege of Boston. The British held Boston but, as the map shows, were surrounded by American forces.

to pursue independence except as a last resort. John Adams described the Olive Branch as giving 'a silly cast to our whole doings'. In his view, the time for petitioning was past: 'powder and artillery are the most efficacious, sure and infallible conciliatory measures we can adopt'.

Disinclined to hear appeals from an illegal body which was waging war against his troops, George III refused to consider the Olive Branch Petition. Instead, on 23 August he called on all his loyal subjects to help suppress the rebellion.

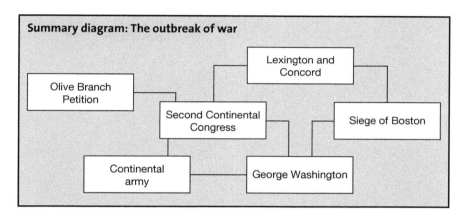

Summary diagram: The outbreak of war

2 The war 1775–6

▶ *Which side was most successful militarily in the first year of the war?*

While the Second Continental Congress deliberated, there was a spate of military action that made it more difficult for Britain and the colonies to reach a compromise.

The battle of Bunker Hill

In May 1775 British generals Howe, Clinton and Burgoyne arrived in Boston with a few thousand reinforcements. Gage now had a force of 6500 men. On 17 June American forces looked set to occupy Bunker Hill, which commanded Boston from the Charlestown peninsula (see Figure 3.2 opposite). When a rebel force of 1500 men occupied the neighbouring Breed's Hill (by mistake), General Howe launched a frontal attack on the rebel defences. He dislodged the Americans but lost over 1000 of his 2500 men in the process. American casualties were less than half that number.

The battle (always called Bunker rather than Breed's Hill) was the bloodiest engagement of the war. One-eighth of the British officers killed in the entire conflict died in the battle. Gage wrote to Dartmouth, 'the rebels are not the despicable rabble too many have supposed them to be, and I find it owing to a military spirit encouraged amongst them for a few years past, joined with an uncommon degree of zeal and enthusiasm'. One politician remarked that 'if we have eight more victories such as this there will be nobody left to bring news of them'.

SOURCE B

The Battle of Bunker's Hill, **a painting finished in 1786 by artist John Trumbull (who was not present at the battle). A British officer restrains a grenadier from bayoneting a fallen American officer.**

Look at Source B. Do you think this is a British or an American representation? Why? And does the source have any historic value?

Washington takes command

Washington assumed command of the Continental army in July. He was not impressed by what he found. Only 15,000 poorly trained, poorly equipped and poorly disciplined troops were fit for duty. The army had fewer than 50 cannon, hardly any powder, and few trained gunners. Far worse, in Washington's view, was the fact that the army lacked any kind of military order. The officers, most of whom had been elected by the men, failed to inspect their troops or supervise their food and quarters. Washington realised that he must transform what was essentially a militia force into a professional army, similar to that of the British. Improving the officer corps seemed essential. Convinced that sharp distinctions of rank were imperative, he determined to curb the army's democratic excesses. Incompetent officers and those guilty of misconduct were removed. Those who remained were distinguished from ordinary troops by special insignia. Washington also set about imposing discipline on the men. Offences from card playing to desertion were punished by flogging.

Boston 1775–6

Washington was eager to attack Boston but was restrained by politicians who feared the town's destruction. He was also discouraged by the strength of the British fortifications, by his own shortage of munitions and by the fact that many of his men went home to their families. By mid-winter, his army, suffering from dysentery, typhus and typhoid fever, had fallen in numbers so much that the reinforced British outnumbered their besiegers. But Howe, who had replaced Gage in October, did nothing. The Americans undoubtedly benefited from having the main British army – 9000 men – bottled up in Boston, taking no effective action. As historian Jeremy Black (1991) says, 'It is not difficult … to feel that opportunities were missed and that the British failed to make adequate use of their sea power' in 1775–6. British inaction gave the rebels time to consolidate their hold elsewhere.

The invasion of Canada

In 1775 Congress decided to invade Canada, hoping that the French population would join the rebellion. Richard Montgomery, with 1200 men, advanced up the Champlain waterway, while a second force under Benedict Arnold marched through Maine, intending to combine with Montgomery in an attack on Quebec.

Although wasting valuable time besieging Fort St John, Montgomery captured Montreal (defended by only 150 men) on 13 November. In December Montgomery joined Arnold, who had reached Quebec with 700 hungry and sickly men a few weeks before. Since most American enlistments expired at the end of the year, an attack on Quebec had to be made quickly.

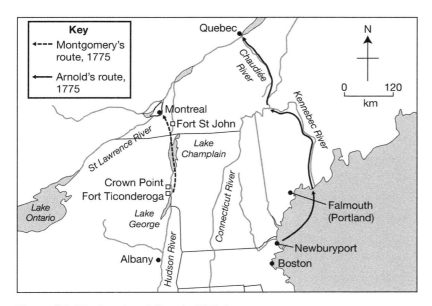

Figure 3.3 The invasion of Canada 1775–6.

General Carleton, the British commander, had 1800 men – French Canadian militia, seamen and marines from British ships and about 100 regular soldiers – to defend Quebec. The American assault, made in a snowstorm on 31 December, failed: Montgomery was killed and Arnold wounded. Over the next few weeks, the Americans suffered from a lack of supplies and from smallpox. Many deserted. The arrival of British reinforcements in the spring ended the siege. Montreal was abandoned as the Americans retreated from Canada in disorder.

War in the South

Lord Dunmore, with 500 loyalists and the assistance of several warships, launched raids on Virginian coastal towns. In November he issued a proclamation promising freedom to any slaves who fled their rebel masters and aided the British war effort. This was anathema to most white southerners, solidifying rebel support in Virginia.

In late 1775 intelligence from the royal governors suggested that co-ordinated operations by loyalists and (minimal) British forces could put an end to the rebellion in the Carolinas and Georgia. North Carolina was selected as the starting point. Backcountry settlers, many of whom had supported the Regulator movement (see page 47), resented the Tidewater elite (see page 9) and were ready to support Britain. But Carolinian loyalists acted too quickly and were defeated at Moores Creek (February 1776). General Clinton, with 1500 troops, did not sail south from Boston until February. Finding little support along the North Carolina coast, Clinton sailed to South Carolina and tried – unsuccessfully – to take Charleston. He then returned north.

The evacuation of Boston

By early 1776 Washington had overcome some of his difficulties around Boston. Thanks to Henry Knox's efforts, artillery from Ticonderoga was transported by sledge, boats and wagon more than 480 km (300 miles) to Boston, arriving in February. On 4 March the rebels – 17,000 strong – captured Dorchester Heights overlooking Boston. This made the British position untenable. On 17 March Howe's army, accompanied by more than 1000 loyalists, began evacuating Boston, sailing to Halifax, Nova Scotia – Britain's main naval base.

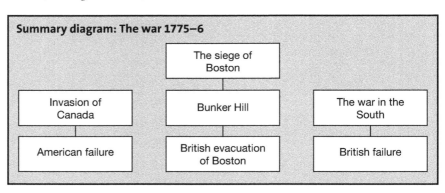

Summary diagram: The war 1775–6

- The siege of Boston
- Invasion of Canada → American failure
- Bunker Hill → British evacuation of Boston
- The war in the South → British failure

The Declaration of Independence

▶ *Why did Congress not declare independence until July 1776?*

Relatively few Americans talked of independence until early 1776. Americans had long thought of themselves as Britons overseas. Severing the emotional, political, economic and intellectual ties with Britain was no easy matter. By no means all Americans were convinced that their interests would be best served by independence:

- A large minority remained loyal to Britain.
- Others, while prepared to fight for colonial rights, continued to insist that they remained loyal to the Crown, hoping for a conciliatory royal gesture.

However, by early 1776 all hopes of reconciliation had faded:

- It was clear that George III, no less than his ministers, was bent on subjugation.
- Several months of fighting weakened the British–American ties.
- Southern support for separation was strengthened when Governor Dunmore of Virginia offered slaves their freedom.

By 1776 the political tide was moving towards independence. In the 1760s most Americans had blamed evil ministers for conspiring to destroy American liberty. But by 1776 many believed that the conspiracy included Parliament and the Crown.

Common Sense

Thomas Paine's pamphlet *Common Sense* expressed – and helped to mould – the developing mood. The 37-year-old Paine, arriving in America in November 1774, quickly involved himself in radical politics. In England, he had failed at everything – corset making, tax collecting, teaching, shop-keeping and marriage (twice: his second wife paid him to leave her home). *Common Sense* was far from a failure. Published in January 1776, it quickly sold 120,000 copies and had the greatest influence of all the pamphlets published during the 1770s.

Written in forceful, straightforward prose, *Common Sense* was readily accessible to most Americans. Paine argued that events made independence a foregone conclusion. Blood had been spilled and with its loss American affection for Britain had drained away. 'Reconciliation', he wrote, 'is now a fallacious dream.' He attacked the British constitution, not least the king – 'the Royal Brute' – and the whole concept of hereditary monarchy and aristocratic privileges. Rather than fear independence, Americans should welcome the opportunity to sever their ties with an oppressive system of government which had no basis in scripture or natural law. Paine called on Americans to establish a republic, based on a broad franchise and annual assemblies.

The situation in early 1776

Most Congressmen were convinced that foreign aid was essential to the American cause. (In November 1775 Congress had established a Committee of Secret Correspondence to carry on diplomacy with foreign nations and also sent Silas Deane, a delegate from Connecticut, to France to obtain military supplies.) Many believed that foreign aid would not be forthcoming until Americans declared independence.

By 1776 all royal governors had been replaced by makeshift rebel governments. Congress exercised sovereign powers: making war, issuing money and preparing to negotiate treaties. 'Is not America already independent?' Sam Adams asked in April 1776. 'Why then not declare it?'

Congress would have to be the body to formally declare independence. However, the delegations within Congress could not declare independence without prior authorisation from their colonial conventions. Therefore, the momentum for independence had to originate within the colonies. Between April and July 1776 various bodies and institutions debated the merits and risks of independence. Thus, independence was not foisted on the American people by a small group of radical Congressmen. Rather, throughout early 1776 local organisations urged Congress to declare independence.

Some bodies effectively declared independence before Congress made its decision. In May, for example, the Rhode Island legislature repealed legislation imposing new officials to take an oath of allegiance to the Crown and expunged all references to the king from its charter and laws.

In May, Virginia was the first colony to instruct its delegation to propose that independence be adopted. Other colonies followed suit. However, the Pennsylvania, Delaware, New Jersey, New York and Maryland legislatures instructed their delegates not to agree to separation.

The situation in Congress

On 7 June Richard Henry Lee introduced in Congress the Virginia convention's resolution 'that these united colonies are, and of right ought to be, free and independent states'. The following day Congress debated the proposal. Although most moderates had given up hope of reconciliation with Britain, their leaders argued that the time was not yet right for a declaration of independence because the middle colonies had not yet pronounced in favour. Recognising the need for unanimity, Congress delayed making a decision. In the meantime, a committee was set up to work on a draft declaration. The committee consisted of Thomas Jefferson (Virginia), John Adams (Massachusetts), Benjamin Franklin (Pennsylvania), Roger Sherman (Connecticut) and Robert Livingston (New York).

John Locke (1632–1704)

Locke was England's foremost political philosopher in the late seventeenth century. His book *Two Treatises of Government* (1690) greatly influenced Thomas Jefferson and his ideas figured prominently in the debates culminating in the Declaration of Independence. The *First Treatise* refuted theories of the **divine right of kings**. The more important *Second Treatise* set forth Locke's contract theory of government. According to Locke, people were endowed with certain natural rights – basically the rights to life, liberty and property. Without government, such rights could not be safeguarded. Thus people came together and by mutual agreement established governments. Kings were parties to such agreements and bound by them. When they violated the rights of the people, the people had the right to overthrow the monarch and change their government.

 **KEY TERM**

Divine right of kings The view that kings ruled by the authority of God rather than by the consent of the people.

The work of Thomas Jefferson

Jefferson, a 33-year-old Virginian planter, did most of the work (see page 71). He did not have to come up with new ideas or arguments. He drew from principles set forth by John Locke (see the box) and other Enlightenment writers, and from Virginia's Declaration of Rights. The case against the king he derived from two documents he had previously written – *A Summary View of the Rights of British America* (1774) and the 1776 draft of a Virginia Constitution – along with the petitions and declaration of Congress. Jefferson worked on the declaration of independence for two weeks, consulting with Adams and Franklin on its content. His draft was then discussed and approved by the full committee.

Declaring independence

In mid-June Delaware instructed its delegates to support independence. In New Jersey radicals ousted Governor William Franklin (son of Benjamin) and sent a new delegation to Congress with instructions to support independence. In Pennsylvania the conservative assembly was overthrown by a radical Committee of Safety, which authorised Pennsylvania's delegates to vote for independence. Maryland's delegates received similar instructions. However, New York's provincial assembly refused to instruct its delegates to support independence.

Jefferson submitted the draft declaration to Congress on 28 June. Congress considered the question of independence on 1 July:

- Nine colonies voted in favour.
- South Carolina and Pennsylvania voted against.
- The two-man Delaware delegation was split.
- The New York delegates abstained.

SOURCE C

This painting of the Declaration of Independence by John Trumbull was begun in 1786 and not completed until the 1820s. It shows, standing in the centre from left to right: John Adams, Roger Sherman, Robert Livingston, Thomas Jefferson and Benjamin Franklin.

? Given that Trumbull did not witness the signing of the Declaration, to what extent is his painting a reliable source?

Anxious for unanimity, Congress decided to return to the question the next day. Over the next few hours:

- A third Delaware delegate rode to Philadelphia to support independence.
- South Carolina's delegates changed their minds and decided to vote for it.
- Pennsylvanians John Dickinson and Robert Morris, who opposed independence, decided not to attend the next day's session, while James Wilson changed his vote.

Consequently, on 2 July, twelve of the thirteen colonies voted in favour of independence: New York still abstained. (Its assembly endorsed Congress's decision a week later.) It was the 2 July vote, rather than the adoption of the Declaration of Independence on 4 July, that proclaimed the birth of the United States of America. Arguably, for over 200 years Americans have been celebrating their country's birthday on the wrong day.

The Declaration

Having voted to declare independence, Congress turned its attention to the declaration itself. Although Jefferson claimed that Congress 'mangled his manuscript', the final document was probably improved by congressional editing.

Thomas Jefferson

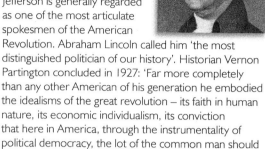

Principal author of the Declaration of Independence, Jefferson is generally regarded as one of the most articulate spokesmen of the American Revolution. Abraham Lincoln called him 'the most distinguished politician of our history'. Historian Vernon Partington concluded in 1927: 'Far more completely than any other American of his generation he embodied the idealisms of the great revolution – its faith in human nature, its economic individualism, its conviction that here in America, through the instrumentality of political democracy, the lot of the common man should somehow be made better.' More recently historian Gordon Wood has described Jefferson as one of 'the greatest and most heroic figures in American history'.

1743	Born in Virginia: his father was a rich planter
1769	Elected to the House of Burgesses
1772	Married Martha Skelton
1774	Published *A Summary View of the Rights of British America*
1775	Represented Virginia in the Second Congress
1776	Drafted the Declaration of Independence
1779–80	Elected governor of Virginia
1785–9	US minister to France
1790–3	Secretary of state under Washington
1796	Elected vice president
1801	Inaugurated president
1809	Retired from the presidency
1826	Died on 4 July: the fiftieth anniversary of the Declaration of Independence

An American aristocrat, Jefferson had a breadth of cultivated interests that ranged perhaps more widely in science, the arts and humanities than those of any contemporary. He read or spoke seven languages, was an able musician, and his house at Monticello and the University of Virginia are monuments to his architectural talent.

Not all scholars are so fulsome in their praise. Jefferson has been criticised for his harsh treatment of Native Americans, his unsuccessful tenure as governor of Virginia, his disloyalty under presidents Washington and Adams, and his continued ownership of hundreds of slaves, in conflict with his stated views on freedom. In fairness to Jefferson, he was a man of his age, a slaveholder and a politician who recognised the importance of pragmatism. Indeed, arguably he was a man ahead of his age, his ideas resonating to future generations of Americans.

The Declaration's purpose was to furnish a moral and legal justification for the rebellion. The preamble, a lucid statement of the political philosophy underlying the colonists' assertion of independence, was the document's most significant part.

SOURCE D

Preamble to the Declaration of Independence.

We hold these truths to be self-evident, that all men are created equal; that they are endowed by their creator with certain unalienable rights; that among these are life, liberty and the pursuit of happiness. That, to secure these rights, governments are instituted among men, deriving their just powers from the consent of the governed; that, whenever any form of government becomes destructive of these ends, it is the right of the people to alter or to abolish it, and to institute new government, laying its foundation on such principles, organising its powers in such form, as to them shall seem most likely to effect their safety and happiness.

Study Source D. Which truths did Jefferson believe were 'self-evident'?

Having asserted that the American people had a right to change their government if it violated their rights, the Declaration went on to list the wrongs committed against the colonists since 1763, charges ranging from interfering in colonial government to waging war against the colonies. All the charges were laid squarely, if unfairly, at the door of George III, who was accused of seeking to establish an 'absolute tyranny over these states'.

The Declaration of Independence was formally adopted by Congress on 4 July. Over the next few weeks the document was read to troops and public gatherings. However, it was one thing to declare independence; it was another thing to win it. While Congress was in the process of declaring independence, Britain had 32,000 troops ready for a major assault.

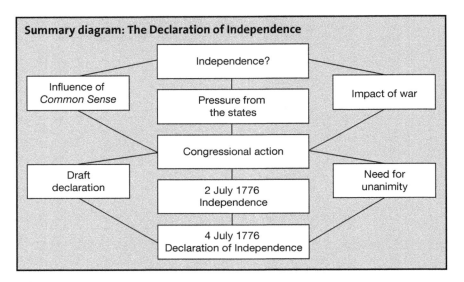

Summary diagram: The Declaration of Independence

 ## 4 Key debate

▶ *What inspired the American colonies to declare independence?*

In 1763 virtually all white colonists considered themselves loyal British subjects. By 1775–6 most sought to end the relationship with Britain. Why had this come about? Who was to blame?

How important were economic factors?

EXTRACT I

From Louis M. Hacker, *The Triumph of American Capitalism* (1940), quoted in J.C. Wahlke, editor, *The Causes of the American Revolution*, D.C. Heath, 1962, p. 1.

The struggle was not over high-sounding political and constitutional concepts over the power of taxation or even, in the final analysis, over natural rights. It was over colonial manufacturing, wild lands, and furs, sugar, wine, tea and currency, all of which meant simply, the survival or collapse of English mercantile capitalism within the imperial-colonial framework of the mercantilist system.

Historians like Charles Beard and Merrill Jenson emphasised the importance of economic factors in bringing about the American Revolution, stressing the irksome Trade and Navigation Laws and oppressive customs duties. But few scholars today believe that commercial issues were a major cause of the revolution. Trade grievances were mentioned only once in the Declaration of Independence. Americans realised that they benefited from the mercantilist system. Indeed, trade relations were a factor pulling Britain and the colonies together rather than dividing them. Nor was the revolution caused by high taxes. Americans were among the most lightly taxed people on earth. The unpopular taxes/duties, proposed by Britain in the 1760s and 1770s, were low and the colonists could easily afford to pay them. Principle, not economic hardship, was the cause of opposition to the taxes and duties.

How important was ideology?

EXTRACT 2

From Thad W. Tate, 'The Coming of the Revolution in Virginia' (1974), quoted in R.D. Brown, editor, *Major Problems in the Era of the American Revolution 1760–1791*, D.C. Heath, 1992 p. 186.

What remains as the fundamental issue in the coming of the Revolution, then, is nothing more than the contest over constitutional rights. None of the other potential issues seems to have applied in Virginia as the opening of the struggle. Perhaps after all the Virginians had stated their grievances reasonably accurately. In 1763 there was a tradition of jealously guarded rights and privileges, but no lingering issues capable in themselves of instigating new conflicts. The Revolution did not open in force until the announcement of the Stamp Act. From then until the beginning of armed conflict with Dunmore in the fall of 1775 political or constitutional issues were the occasion for every outbreak of protest within the colony.

Which extract provides the more convincing explanation of the causes of the War of Independence?

Historians today are more likely to stress the importance of ideology in bringing about revolution. American political ideology owed much to English constitutional thought, which emphasised the rights and liberties of free-born Englishmen and the limitations of royal power. Repeatedly the colonists insisted they were Englishmen, entitled to all the rights granted by the English Constitution. If Englishmen could not be taxed without their consent, as given by their representatives in Parliament, the same applied to Americans. Influenced by eighteenth-century English radical writers, many Americans believed (wrongly) that a small clique of evil British ministers aimed to destroy American liberties. This view was sufficiently strong among influential Americans in the decade before 1775 to invest almost every British action with a sinister intent.

To what extent were British policies to blame?

British policies brought about American demands for independence. After 1763, British ministries, in an effort to squeeze money from America, devised a series of irritations which propelled the colonies towards independence. In 1764, 1765, 1767 and 1773 British governments forced the issue of Britain's power over the colonies. Parliament's first attempt (1764) was ambiguous, as was the American response. But on the other three occasions the result was confrontation. Twice Parliament backed down, repealing the Stamp Act and the Townshend duties. By bowing to American pressure, Parliament undermined its claim to exercise control over the colonies.

After the Boston Tea Party, North's ministry chose to stand firm, expecting that a show of force would be sufficient to subdue Massachusetts. But Britain had too few forces on hand at the start to overawe the rebels. The colonists may not have been so headstrong if Gage had had 24,000 troops rather than 4000.

In defence of British policies

While it is possible to blame a blundering generation of British politicians for causing the war, in fairness to the politicians:

- It is understandable that Britain failed to anticipate that the colonists would rebel against the nation that had nurtured the liberty they prized so highly.
- In 1765 there was little indication of the anger to be aroused by the Stamp Act.
- Britain came to be demonised by Americans without good cause. The notion that British ministries were bent on reducing the colonies to a state of slavery was nonsense. With the possible exception of Townshend, no British minister had any deliberate wish to diminish American liberty.
- Successive ministries acted in a manner consistent with their understanding of the British Constitution, in which Parliament was the Empire's supreme governing body. If Parliament was sovereign then it must have the power to tax. Giving up the right to tax was to surrender Parliament's supremacy – the equivalent to recognising American independence.
- Britain's determination to hold on to the American colonies was understandable. They were a valuable source of raw materials and a major market.
- Although the Americans talked lofty principles, there was a sordid side to what occurred. Some rebel leaders were unsavoury characters, acting ruthlessly to enforce their control – beating, tarring and feathering and publicly humiliating their opponents.

Chapter summary

The outbreak of war in 1775 was almost an accident. However, it was an accident waiting to happen. Once the first shots had been fired at Lexington and Concord, it proved difficult to stop the shooting. The Second Continental Congress took charge of the conduct of the war, appointing Washington to command American forces. In 1775–6 the Americans had some military success (for example at Bunker Hill) but also some failures (especially in Canada). The fighting made it more difficult for Britain and the colonies to reach agreement. By 1776 many Americans, influenced by Thomas Paine's *Common Sense*, favoured a complete break with Britain. Congressmen reflected that opinion. In July 1776 they agreed to a Declaration of Independence. Historians continue to debate why exactly this had come about.

 Refresher questions

Use these questions to remind yourself of the key material covered in this chapter.

1 Why was the fighting at Lexington and Concord a disaster for Britain?

2 Why was Second Continental Congress important?

3 Why were Britain and the colonies unable to reach a settlement in 1775?

4 Why was the battle of Bunker Hill important?

5 What were Washington's main problems in 1775?

6 Why did the Americans fail to conquer Canada?

7 Why did Britain not have more success in the southern colonies?

8 Why was there increasing support for independence by 1776?

9 How did the Declaration of Independence come about?

 Question practice

ESSAY QUESTIONS

1 'The outbreak of war in 1775 was inevitable.' Explain why you agree or disagree with this view.

2 How successful were American forces in 1775–6?

3 Assess the reasons for the signing of the Declaration of Independence in 1776.

4 'Thomas Paine's book, *Common Sense*, was essential in persuading Americans to support independence.' Assess the validity of this view.

INTERPRETATION QUESTION

1 Read the interpretation and then answer the question that follows: 'Independence was probably inevitable by the end of 1775.' (John Garraty, *The American Nation: A History of the United States*, Harper & Row, 1984.) Evaluate the strengths and limitations of this interpretation, making reference to other interpretations that you have studied.

SOURCE ANALYSIS QUESTIONS

1 With reference to Sources 1 and 2, and your understanding of the historical context, which of these two sources is more valuable in explaining the attitudes in the American colonies towards war against the British government?

2 With reference to Sources 1, 2 and 3, and your understanding of the historical context, assess the value of these sources to a historian studying the attitudes of American colonists towards British rule in the years 1775–6.

SOURCE 1

From an address to the New Jersey Assembly by Governor William Franklin, 13 January 1775. The governor was Benjamin Franklin's son.

Gentlemen of the Council and Gentlemen of the Assembly: You now have pointed out to you, two roads – one evidently leading to peace, happiness and a restoration of the public tranquillity; the other inevitably conducting you toward anarchy, misery and all the horrors of a civil war. Your wisdom, your prudence will be best known when you have shown to which road you give preference. I shall say no more at present on this disagreeable subject, but only to repeat an observation I made to a former Assembly: 'Every breach of the British Constitution, whether it proceeds from the Crown or from the people, is, in its effects, equally destructive to the rights of both'.

SOURCE 2

An extract from *Common Sense*, written by Thomas Paine. Published in 1776, it became a bestseller in America.

I challenge the warmest advocate for reconciliation to show a single advantage that this Continent can reap by being connected with Great Britain … But the injuries and disadvantages which we sustain by that connection, are without number; and our duty to Mankind at large, as well as to ourselves, instruct us to renounce the alliance; because any submission to, or dependence on, Great Britain, tends directly to involve this Continent in European war and quarrels, and set us at variance with nations who would otherwise seek our friendship, and against whom we have neither anger nor complaint … Every day wears out the little remains of kindred between us and them, and can there be any reason to hope, that as the relationship expires, the affection will increase, or that we shall agree better, when we have ten times more and greater concerns to quarrel over than ever … Now! Now! Now! At this very moment must these uncorrupt and democratic colonies throw off the trammels of an effete and vicious monarchy.

SOURCE 3

From the 'Testimony of the people called Quakers', at a meeting held in Philadelphia, Pennsylvania, 24 January 1775.

As our religious principles lead us to live peaceably and to discourage any disloyalty to the King and the British government, such as seen in recent declarations, we feel a sense of duty to declare our complete removal of them as contrary to the Gospel and destructive of peace, and we fear disruptive protests are likely to jeopardise the liberty of conscience for which our ancestors came to Pennsylvania. We must therefore publicly declare our opposition to unlawful resistance to our British colonial government, and to any associations planning rebellion, as we are led by God's law.

CHAPTER 4

The War of Independence 1776–83

The fact that the War of Independence lasted so long suggests that its outcome was far from a foregone conclusion. In 1775 George III and his ministers assumed that British victory in America was certain. Indeed, Britain arguably should have won the war in 1776. But the war was eventually lost. This chapter will consider how that came about by focusing on the following themes:

★ The situation in 1776

★ Military operations 1776–7

★ The extension of the war

★ American victory 1778–83

The key debate on *page 102* of this chapter asks the question: Did Britain lose or America win the War of Independence?

Key dates

1776	July	British forces landed in New York	1779	Spain joined the war
1777	Sept.	Howe captured Philadelphia	1781	Cornwallis surrendered at Yorktown
	Oct.	Burgoyne surrendered at Saratoga	1782	Resignation of Lord North
1778		American alliance with France	1783	Peace of Paris

 # The situation in 1776

▶ *Which side seemed more likely to win in 1776?*

While Congress was in the process of declaring independence, it seemed likely that Britain would crush the rebels.

British strengths

At the start of the war most Britons were confident of victory:

- Britain had 8 million people; the colonies had 2.5 million, of whom nearly 500,000 were slaves.
- Most Britons fully supported the war.
- Britain had the support of at least 500,000 American loyalists (see page 119).
- Most Native Americans supported Britain.
- Britain had a 50,000-strong regular army.
- In 1775–6 Britain hired 18,000 soldiers from several German principalities including Hesse. More **Hessians** were hired in 1777. They provided Britain with trained troops who could immediately be sent to America.
- The Royal Navy, with over 300 ships in 1775–6, ruled the waves. Naval superiority enabled Britain to reinforce and supply its forces, move men along the American seaboard, and blockade and attack American ports. Given the fact that 75 per cent of Americans lived within 120 km (75 miles) of the sea, British naval strength was a crucial advantage.
- Lord Sandwich, first lord of the Admiralty, had ability and drive. He embarked on a major shipbuilding programme that ensured that Britain retained command of the sea, even when France and Spain joined the war (see page 92).
- Britain had much great financial and manufacturing strength.
- Lord George Germain, who replaced Dartmouth as colonial secretary in November 1775, co-ordinated the British war effort to good effect.
- Britain had several bases close to the thirteen colonies – Canada, Newfoundland, Florida, West Indian islands – from which to launch attacks.

American problems

The Americans had a number of serious problems:

- They lacked unity. For the most part America remained thirteen separate states, each state guarding its own interests.
- In 1775 America had to build an army from scratch. Given that many states were slow to furnish their quota of troops, filling the ranks of the Continental army was a constant problem. Moreover, many troops enlisted for only a short time. Washington's army never exceeded 20,000 men; much of the time he had barely 5000.
- The state militias were less impressive as a fighting force than most Americans hoped. Militiamen generally enrolled for only a few weeks and often went home before their terms expired.
- The Americans had no navy worthy of the name. Eventually some 50 vessels were commissioned into the Continental navy, and almost as many into state navies. But most were converted merchantmen, not **ships of the line**, and posed no real threat to Britain. Congress never appointed an overall naval commander because there was no proper navy to command.

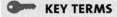

KEY TERMS

Hessians German auxiliaries who fought for Britain.

Ships of the line The great wooden battleships employed from the seventeenth to the mid-nineteenth centuries.

- The Americans lacked an effective national government. The Articles of Confederation, adopted by the Continental Congress in 1777, conferred only limited powers on the central government (see pages 116–17). Though empowered to make war, it lacked the means to wage it effectively.
- The American economy was disrupted by the war. The demands of the various armies plus the British blockade meant there was a shortage of many goods, affecting both the army and civilians. Americans troops were often short of firearms, munitions, provisions and suitable clothing. Supply shortages caused serious morale problems.
- Unable to levy taxes, Congress could finance the war only by printing and issuing paper money. The states did just the same. As the quantity of paper money increased, its value declined and prices rose.

SOURCE A

George Washington, writing in November 1775, quoted in Christopher Hibbert, *Redcoats and Rebels: The War for America 1770–1781*, Grafton Books, 1990, page 68.

Could I have foreseen what I have experienced and am likely to experience, no consideration on earth would have induced me to accept the command … I have already broke one colonel and five captains for cowardice and for drawing more pay and provisions than they had men in their companies … . In short, they are by no means such troops as you are led to believe of them from the accounts which are published … I daresay the men would fight very well (if properly officered) although they are an exceedingly dirty and nasty people.

According to Source A, what were the main problems with the Continental army at the start of the war?

American strengths/advantages

The American **patriots** did have some advantages:

- Most Americans were committed to (what many called) the 'glorious cause'.
- Although the Continental army was relatively small, the militia turned out in large numbers in areas where the fighting took place. Despite the fact that Washington distrusted them, the militiamen played a vital role. They served as a kind of political police, intimidating people loyal to Britain. They also contributed as a fighting force, both in battle and in skirmishes. Over 100,000 Americans served at some time in the militias.
- Britain did not entirely rule the waves. Congress and the states commissioned about 2000 **privateers**, which inflicted heavy damage on British merchant shipping.

British problems

- Britain was fighting a war 4800 km (3000 miles) away from home. It took two to three months for reinforcements and supplies to cross the Atlantic. By the time they arrived the situation that they had been intended to deal with had often changed out of all recognition.

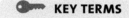

KEY TERMS

Patriots Americans who supported independence.

Privateers Privately owned vessels granted permission by a government to capture enemy ships.

- To wage war in a huge, unfriendly territory was a formidable task. Co-ordinating land and sea operations was particularly difficult. The terrain, and supply problems, made it hard for British forces to go more than 24 km (15 miles) from a navigable river or the sea.
- The British army was under-strength in 1775. Its real strength was more like 36,000 than its paper strength of 50,000. It had not been seriously tested in action since 1763. A quarter of the infantry in 1775 was made up of men with less than a year's service.
- The Royal Navy had been allowed to decay after 1763. Lord North was reluctant to provoke the French by a full-scale naval mobilisation. Not until October 1776, after reports that France was increasing its naval forces, did Britain start putting the navy on a war footing.
- The presence of Hessian troops, who quickly established a reputation for rapacity, convinced many neutral colonists to support the patriots.
- The fact that Native Americans supported Britain may have spurred many colonists to join the patriot side.
- British martial law, requisitioning of supplies and seizure of property to accommodate troops alienated potentially friendly Americans.
- Lord North was not an inspired or inspiring war leader.
- There was always the likelihood that France and Spain would join the war to settle old scores with Britain.

British strategic problems

British leaders, who had to find the right strategy to win the war, faced major problems. First, British troops faced a generally hostile population. The British army was thus dependent on Britain for obtaining most of its supplies. Crucially, the army had to protect American ports under British control, employing many troops in garrison duty. Thus, only a part of the army was available for field operations. Second, there was no necessary political or economic centre for British armies to capture. The occupation of territory by British forces brought no lasting advantage. The moment the British moved away from a town or region, rebellion flared up in their rear. The task for British forces was, according to historian Eric Robson, like 'trying to hit a swarm of flies with a hammer'.

Some British leaders favoured a seaboard strategy – a concentration of effort on gaining control of American ports and blockading the rest of the coast. This would minimise the problems of operating and fighting inland in difficult terrain. However, a fully developed seaboard strategy was not followed for several reasons:

- Such a policy would betray loyalists and lose loyalist support.
- The seaboard strategy had failed in New England in 1775 (see page 65).
- There was pressure in Britain for a speedy and decisive victory. A seaboard strategy would be long and drawn out.

From Britain's perspective, the destruction of the Continental army was more important than the possession of towns and territory. British leaders hoped that military success would make possible the resumption of British rule. They realised, however, that they must achieve some kind of reconciliation with the Americans. Restoration of the colonies to royal control would serve little purpose if the embers of rebellion smouldered among a discontented population and a large army was needed to maintain order. This would simply result in a substantial tax burden that would have to be borne by Americans and Britons alike. Given the need to reach a political solution, a war of unlimited destruction was ruled out. Finding the right blend of firmness and conciliation was no easy matter.

American strategy in 1776

Washington had three main options in 1776:

- He could fight a purely **guerrilla war**.
- He could fight what was called a 'War of Posts', fighting a series of tactical engagements and withdrawals designed to wear down the enemy.
- He could adopt an offensive strategy, confronting the British army with his entire force and fighting a major battle.

Washington rejected the guerrilla option (urged by his second in command, Charles Lee) in favour of conventional European warfare. He realised that guerrilla warfare, by itself, could not defeat the British. He thus tried to create a traditional army, consciously emulating British methods.

For much of 1776 Washington opposed a War of Posts. Such a defensive strategy would acknowledge the superiority of British arms. It also meant sacrificing New York, Philadelphia and wherever else the British chose to march. British occupation of swathes of American territory would damage American morale and encourage the loyalists.

Instead, Washington preferred taking on the British army in battle. According to historian Joseph Ellis (2004), 'He regarded battle as a summons to display one's strength and courage; avoiding battle was akin to dishonourable behaviour.' Washington welcomed the opportunity to demonstrate his contempt for what he saw as British pretensions of superiority. Like many Americans, he hoped that courage combined with the rightness of the cause would compensate for inferior numbers and inexperience.

The loyalists

The War of Independence pitted Americans against Americans as well as against Britons. John Adams estimated that one-third of the population were active rebels, one-third were loyalists (or Tories) and one-third were neutral. Historians today suspect that two-fifths of the population were active rebels, one-fifth active loyalists and two-fifths sought neutrality. By either estimate,

KEY TERM

Guerrilla war Warfare by which small units harass conventional forces.

a majority of Americans did not support the rebellion. By 1783 some 19,000 Americans had enlisted in the British army. Thousands more had joined loyalist militias.

Who were the loyalists?

Far from being an upper-class phenomenon, as historians once believed, loyalism drew adherents from all ranks of society. Ownership of great estates or mercantile wealth provided no adequate guide to political allegiance. (In Virginia, for example, the great planters overwhelmingly supported and led the patriot cause.) Many loyalists possessed strong links with Britain, especially those who were recent immigrants. Loyalists also tended to be drawn from minority groups who had little in common with the majority patriot population. These groups included southern backcountry farmers who resented the dominance of the Tidewater elite, Anglicans in New England, and Germans and Dutch in New York.

The geographical distribution of loyalism was uneven. There were more loyalists in the southern and middle colonies than in New England. In only a few areas (for example, New York city) did the loyalists comprise a majority.

Many African Americans supported Britain, in return for promises of freedom. Britain might have made more military use of black people. However, British leaders were aware that large-scale recruitment of slaves would jeopardise white support.

Loyalist problems

The varied backgrounds and motivations of the loyalists meant that they did not constitute a coherent opposition to the patriots. While the rebels had a clear idea that they were fighting for independence and republican self-government, the loyalists knew only that they stood against these things. Often motivated by local concerns, they were unable to organise themselves on a national level. Instead, they relied on the British to provide them with leadership and protection. Thus, while Britain placed great hopes on loyalist assistance, significant loyalist activity required the presence of British forces. Once those forces departed, loyalists were left exposed to the wrath of their patriot neighbours. During the war, tens of thousands of loyalists, real and suspected, were imprisoned, driven from their homes, deprived of land and property, and sometimes killed by patriots.

The nature of the war

Some historians, like Stephen Conway (1995), regard the War of Independence as the first modern war, anticipating what happened in Europe in the French Revolutionary and Napoleonic Wars (1792–1815):

- Unlike earlier eighteenth-century wars, this was not a dynastic war, waged for a strip of territory. Many American soldiers were motivated by the political ideals embraced by the new republic.
- The war was one of the first instances of the nation-in-arms. Nearly every free male of military age was eligible for service. By 1781, 200,000 American males, from across the social spectrum, had engaged in some kind of military service – about one in three of the men of military age. Continental army soldiers, both officers and privates, were essentially civilians, not regular soldiers.
- To a much greater extent than any other army of the time, the Continental army embodied the principle of careers open to talent. Many of its officers rose from the ranks.
- Guerrilla war was an important feature of the conflict. Militia forces made life difficult for small units of the British army.
- Americans are thought to have made good use of the rifle, a weapon that was accurate at up to 200 metres, twice the range of the ordinary musket.
- After 1778 Britain was involved in a world war. One in seven Britons of military age may have participated in the conflict – a higher mobilisation of manpower than in any previous war in which Britain had been engaged.

However, other historians, like Piers Mackesy (1964), portray the contest as essentially traditional:

- Nationalism was well developed in eighteenth-century Europe. Thus, soldiers often fought for ideological 'causes' well before the War of Independence.
- The notion of a nation of citizen soldiers putting aside their ploughs and picking up their guns was not really true. After an initial burst of enthusiasm, most men went back to their farms. Only about one in three Americans of military age fought in the war. Most of those who fought joined state militias, serving for a very limited term.
- The state militias were not very successful. The Continental army did the bulk of the fighting.
- The Continental army was similar to its European counterparts. Most of its officers were substantial landowners. The rank and file were drawn mainly from the poorest sections of society who joined the army mainly because they had no better prospects.
- The Continental and British armies fought essentially in the traditional manner. There was little innovation in the technology of war. The rifle's importance can be exaggerated. Most American soldiers were armed with the ordinary musket.

Arguably, the most that can be said is that the American war anticipated some of the features of the French Revolutionary War.

Summary diagram: The situation in 1776

British strengths	American strengths
• British Army • Population • American loyalists • American bases • American disunity • Weakness of American forces • American morale • British commitment • Native Americans • Royal Navy • Financial strength • Lord George Germain • Weak American government • British economic strength	• Difficult terrain • Distance from Britain • Lord North • American commitment • British policy in 1775 • British martial law • British strategic problems • Opposition to Indians • Opposition to Hessians • American privateers • Neglect of Royal Navy • Weakness of British army • France and Spain

---

 # Military operations 1776–7

► *Why did Britain not win the war in 1776–7?*

General William Howe, a second cousin of George III, commanded the British troops in America in 1776. He had fought with success in America in the Seven Years' War (pages 17–18), helping Wolfe to capture Quebec. Howe, who had declared in 1774 that he was against a policy of coercion, was fond of Americans. His military role in America in 1776–7 is much debated. By August 1776 he commanded 32,000 men – the largest trans-oceanic expedition ever previously sent from Britain. Had Howe fought with more determination, it is conceivable that Britain would have won the war.

The impact of General Howe

Following his withdrawal to Halifax in March 1776, Howe planned an assault on New York city, potentially an excellent base. He began landing his army at Staten Island in July. He hoped to lure Washington into battle, defeat him and negotiate an end to the rebellion. His army was supported by a fleet commanded by his elder brother, Admiral Lord Richard Howe, who was in overall command of British forces in America. Like William, Richard had some sympathy with the Americans and favoured a policy of conciliation rather than coercion.

New York

Washington, with only 20,000 men, would have been best abandoning New York. Given British command of the sea, the place was indefensible. But Washington had to fight, if only because Congress insisted he did so. At the battle of Long Island (27 August) Howe defeated the Americans, who suffered

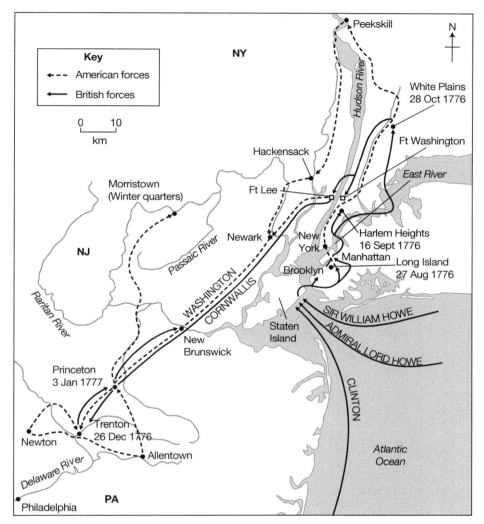

Figure 4.1 New York–New Jersey campaigns 1776–7.

2000 casualties, six times as many as the British. (Asked to explain the defeat, John Adams said: 'In general, our generals were out generalled.') Thanks to Howe's inertia, Washington, under cover of a dense fog, managed to withdraw his army to the mainland on 29 August.

Rather than continue the military momentum, Howe now sought to negotiate peace. In September Lord Howe met representatives of Congress: Benjamin Franklin, John Adams and Edward Rutledge. The Declaration of Independence proved to be the stumbling block. Lord Howe was not empowered to discuss a treaty between Britain and an independent America.

American retreat

In mid-September General Howe's troops landed at Kips Bay in Manhattan, between the two halves of Washington's army. Howe's caution again gave

SOURCE B

Washington crossing the Delaware, Christmas Day, 1776, ahead of his victory at Trenton. This painting by Emanuel Leutze was completed in 1851.

? How useful is Source B as a source for events in December 1776?

Washington time to withdraw. Several weeks of stalemate followed. Rather than attack well-entrenched positions, Howe preferred to turn the Americans' flank. Washington retreated slowly across New Jersey.

On 16 November British forces captured Fort Washington, taking nearly 3000 American prisoners and immense quantities of weapons and supplies – a shattering blow for Washington. For the next three weeks the American army was in full retreat. Many militiamen returned home and when the army crossed the Delaware River into Pennsylvania in December, it had dwindled to 3000 men.

Lord Howe now issued a proclamation offering all who would take an oath of allegiance to the king a 'free and general pardon'. Thousands applied for pardons. In December British forces seized Newport, Rhode Island. A disconsolate Washington wrote, 'I think the game is pretty near up.'

Trenton and Princeton

Instead of marching on Philadelphia – his for the taking – General Howe went into winter quarters, throw away another opportunity to destroy American morale. The respite gave Washington time to regroup. Reinforced by militia units and recognising the need to end the campaign with a victory, he recrossed the Delaware with 1600 men on 25 December. Attacking the unsuspecting garrison at Trenton, New Jersey, on 26 December, he captured more than 1000 prisoners. American casualties were four wounded. Washington followed this

George Washington

1732	Born to a Virginian planting family
1748	Worked as a surveyor/speculator in the West
1754	Led an unsuccessful military expedition into the Ohio country
1755–59	Colonel of the Virginia militia, in charge of the western frontier
1759	Married Martha Custis, a wealthy widow
1759–74	Managed his plantation at Mount Vernon and served in the House of Burgesses
1774	Elected to the First Continental Congress
1775–83	Led the Continental army
1783	Gave up his commission and returned to Mount Vernon
1787	Served as president of the Philadelphia Convention
1789	Elected first president of the USA
1792	Re-elected as president
1796	Stood down as president
1799	Died

Washington was by no means a military genius. He lost more battles than he won. In fairness, he struggled with a lack of supplies and men. His greatest talent was somehow holding the Continental army together. He learned from (bad) experiences and never gave up. Whatever his military failings, he did win the last major campaign, forcing General Cornwallis to surrender at Yorktown in 1781. Without his leadership, the Americans might well have lost the war. He was also the very model of the proper citizen soldier. He always acknowledged the supremacy of the civilian branch over the military, refrained from open criticism of Congress and kept Congress fully informed of his plans.

up with a similar coup at Princeton (3 January 1777). These counterstrokes forced Howe to relinquish most of his gains in New Jersey. More importantly, they breathed new life into the American cause. Taking up winter quarters at Morristown, Washington rebuilt his army.

Washington's change of strategy

Over the winter of 1776–7 Washington came to accept that he must adopt a more defensive strategy. He began to realise that the way to win the war was not to lose it. Never again did he risk his entire army in one decisive battle. He had to face what he called 'the melancholy truth' – his Continental army could not compete on equal terms on a conventional battlefield with the British army. Moreover, the terms were far from equal: Howe commanded more men than Washington. Although Washington's main priority was preserving his army, he was still determined to harass Howe whenever possible.

British plans in 1777

The situation for Britain in early 1777 was much better than it had been twelve months previously. Canada was secure. New York had been captured. Britain thus had great hopes of winning the war. In 1777 there were two large British armies in North America, one (in New York) commanded by General Howe, the other (in Canada) by General Burgoyne. Burgoyne aimed to drive down the Hudson Valley, isolating New England from the other colonies. Although

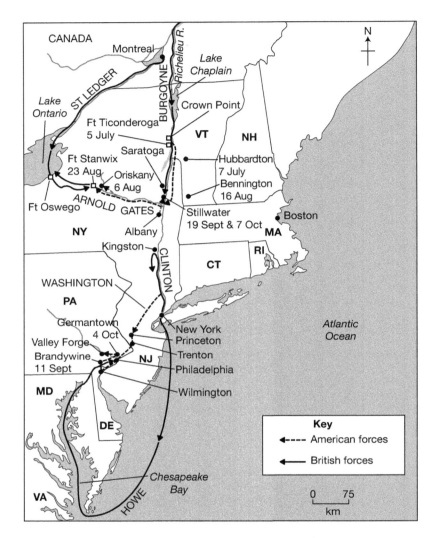

Figure 4.2 Saratoga and Philadelphia campaigns 1777.

Lord Germain had instructed Howe to co-operate with Burgoyne, Howe's main concern was to capture Philadelphia. Thus, what was perceived in London as a co-ordinated operation became two separate campaigns.

The capture of Philadelphia

Howe commenced his move on Philadelphia in July. Rather than march across New Jersey, he moved his 15,000-strong army by sea. After six weeks crammed on board transports, the sickly soldiers landed at the head of Chesapeake Bay, barely 64 km (40 miles) closer to Philadelphia than they had been when they left New York.

On 11 September Howe defeated Washington at Brandywine Creek. The Americans lost 1200 men, the British half that number. Howe again missed an opportunity to destroy Washington's army. After another victory at Paoli

(21 September), Howe captured Philadelphia (26 September). This appeared to be a major triumph. However, Philadelphia's fall did not lead to the rebellion's collapse. Although it had some symbolic importance, Philadelphia had no strategic value. Congress simply moved to Lancaster. As long as Washington commanded an army, the rebellion would continue.

Washington launched a counter-attack at Germantown (4 October) but his plan was too complicated and he lost more than 1000 casualties – twice as many as the British. In November Howe forced the Americans to evacuate the forts on the Delaware River, allowing British naval access to Philadelphia. Washington now withdrew to the desolate plateau of Valley Forge to the northwest of Philadelphia. Rather than attack, Howe spent the winter in Philadelphia. He had again failed to win a decisive victory.

Burgoyne's campaign

Leaving Canada in June, General Burgoyne's 9000-strong army sailed down Lake Champlain, recapturing Ticonderoga (5 July). Rather than sailing down Lake George and following a road already cut to Fort Edward, Burgoyne headed south through inhospitable terrain. Encumbered by an enormous baggage train, his army found movement difficult as patriot militia blocked roads, destroyed bridges and attacked stragglers. It took Burgoyne three weeks to cover the 37 km (23 miles) to Fort Edward.

Burgoyne's hope that loyalists would flock to his army did not happen. In fact, the presence of British forces did much to create rebels out of neutrally inclined Americans. Burgoyne's Native American allies did not help. During the advance, Iroquois warriors attacked outlying farms, killing several families. Political considerations took second place to racial enmity. The murder and scalping of Jane McCrea particularly alienated those who had been sympathetic to Britain. When Burgoyne demanded that his allies surrender the culprits, the Iroquois refused and most went home.

Burgoyne now spent a month collecting supplies. Six hundred troops on a foraging mission were killed or captured at Bennington (15–16 August) by New Hampshire militia. A relief party of similar strength suffered the same fate. More bad news reached Burgoyne's army. A diversionary force of 1600 British and Iroquois under St Leger had moved down the St Lawrence, and then along the Mohawk, intending to join Burgoyne. However, St Leger's column, while besieging Fort Stanwix, was checked at Oriskany (6 August) by local militia. The Native Americans, unhappy at the siege, left St Leger's camp. Short of men and supplies, St Leger retreated to Canada.

Saratoga

Burgoyne determined to press on to Albany. The Americans were ready for him. In mid-August General Horatio Gates replaced the unpopular General Schuyler as commander of the northern forces. Aided by some able subordinates, especially Benedict Arnold, Gates prepared defensive positions north of Albany. American successes in August encouraged New England militiamen to join Gates. By mid-September he had 7000 men, as did Burgoyne.

The two forces clashed at Freeman's Farm (19 September). Failing to defeat the rebels, Burgoyne found himself in a perilous position, 320 km (200 miles) from Canada, short of supplies and facing a well-entrenched and growing army. However, news that General Clinton was pushing northwards from New York gave Burgoyne renewed hope.

Given that there was no significant American force threatening New York, Clinton might have marched north sooner. In the event, he did not leave the city until 3 October with 3000 men. Capturing a clutch of forts in the New York highlands region, he drew close to Albany. Burgoyne hoped that Clinton's campaign would force Gates to deplete his army. On 7 October Burgoyne attacked the American defences on Bemis Heights. Thanks largely to Arnold's heroism, Burgoyne's attack failed. He lost another 400 men, the Americans only 150.

Burgoyne now retreated to Saratoga. His hope that Clinton might come to his rescue proved forlorn. Surrounded by twice as many troops, Burgoyne began negotiating with Gates on 14 October. The latter, worried by Clinton's advance, was keen to settle. Thus, Burgoyne (apparently) got good terms. His 5895 troops were to lay down their arms, march to Boston and embark on British ships on condition they did not again serve in America. However, Congress rejected Gates's terms, ensuring that Burgoyne's troops remained prisoners of war until 1783.

Who was to blame for the British defeat?

The American heroes were Arnold and the regulars of the Continental army. Gates's role and that of the militia were exaggerated at the time and since. But who was to blame on the British side?

- Howe did little to help Burgoyne.
- Burgoyne underestimated the enemy and the terrain.
- With hindsight, Germain should have ordered Howe to co-operate with Burgoyne. But Germain could not formulate too rigid a plan. He was dependent on the generals in America acting rationally in the light of the circumstances.

The results of Saratoga

- For the first time the rebels had defeated the British in a major campaign. This was a great morale booster.
- On hearing of Burgoyne's surrender, Howe wrote to Germain offering his resignation.

- Concerned about the situation in Pennsylvania, Howe ordered Clinton to send reinforcements. Clinton was thus forced to abandon the Highlands. Clinton believed the loss of Burgoyne's army might have been accepted as a necessary sacrifice had British forces retained this crucial area.
- In December, two days after news of Saratoga reached London, Lord North dispatched a secret agent to Paris to contact American commissioners Benjamin Franklin and Silas Deane with a view to exploring the possibilities for ending the war.
- In February 1778 Parliament passed North's Conciliatory Propositions. Britain agreed to repeal the Coercive Acts (see page 52) and renounce the right to tax Americans.
- A Peace Commission was appointed to try to negotiate an end to the war. The commissioners could accept the withdrawal of British forces from America and grant the Americans representation in Parliament. However, Britain's denial of American independence wrecked any hope of successful negotiations.
- Saratoga had important international consequences (see next section).

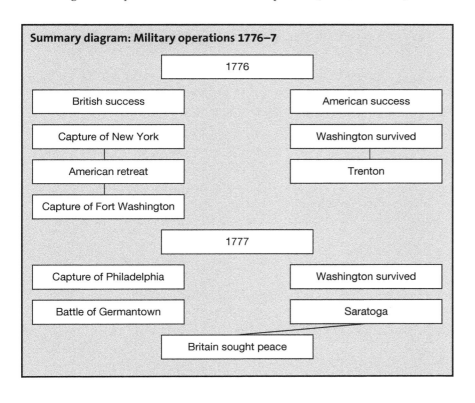

Summary diagram: Military operations 1776–7

1776

British success	American success
Capture of New York	Washington survived
American retreat	Trenton
Capture of Fort Washington	

1777

Capture of Philadelphia	Washington survived
Battle of Germantown	Saratoga

Britain sought peace

The extension of the war

 ► *Why did France join the war?*

In 1778 the war from Britain's point of view became a world war rather than just a rebellion. This had important consequences for America.

The French alliance

From the start of the war, the Americans had realised the importance of France's help, even if its Catholicism and **absolutist system of government** made the country less than a natural ally. French King Louis XVI had no love of rebellion or republicanism. Nevertheless, his government realised that the war offered an opportunity to avenge the humiliating outcome of the Seven Years' War (see pages 18–19) and weaken Britain's power. Accordingly, France was ready to supply the Americans with arms and gunpowder and to encourage army officers to place their service at America's disposal. (They included the Marquis de Lafayette, who became one of Washington's favourite officers.) However, Louis XVI had withheld formal recognition of American independence while the outcome of the war was in doubt. His treasury was so depleted that some ministers believed that France should avoid war at all costs.

In an effort to persuade France to join the war, Congress sent Benjamin Franklin as head of a diplomatic mission to Paris in 1776. He proved an inspired choice. His (apparent) simplicity and straightforwardness won French admiration.

Saratoga ended French fears of an American collapse. By prompting North to make fresh concessions, it allowed Franklin to play on French fears of a possible Anglo-American reconciliation. France may well have entered the war in 1778 even without Saratoga, as its government apparently was already committed to war and was simply waiting for completion of its naval preparations. However, Saratoga helped to overcome any last doubts and made French intervention certain.

On 6 February 1778 France and America signed two treaties, one a commercial agreement, the other a defensive alliance to take effect when France eventually went to war with Britain – as it did in June 1778. By the alliance's terms, both countries promised to wage war until American independence was 'formally or tacitly assured' and undertook not to make peace separately.

Spain and the Netherlands

In April 1779 Spain entered the war against Britain. It did so as an ally of France, not of America. As a great imperial power, Spain had good reason to be wary about encouraging colonial rebellion. It joined the war to regain possessions lost to Britain: Florida, Minorca, Gibraltar and Jamaica. In 1780 Britain declared war on the Netherlands, which was aiding France and Spain.

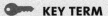 **KEY TERM**

Absolutist system of government Government by a ruler with unrestricted power and usually with no democratic mandate.

The League of Armed Neutrality

In 1780 Russia, Sweden and Denmark formed the League of Armed Neutrality. Its aim was the protection of neutral rights, given Britain's blockade of America. Prussia, Portugal and Austria joined in 1781. Although it accomplished little, the League bolstered the USA's international position.

The results of French and Spanish intervention

After 1778 America became something of a sideshow for Britain. Its main concern was now France. France's population (25 million) was twice that of Britain. Its army was over 150,000 strong and it had tried to construct a fleet capable of challenging British naval supremacy. As well as facing the threat of French invasion, British forces had to defend Gibraltar, Minorca and possessions in Africa, India and the West Indies (considered by many Britons as more vital to Britain's prosperity than the American colonies).

French intervention produced a national war effort in Britain that the American rebellion had not aroused. By 1782 Britain had an army of 150,000 troops, while the Royal Navy had 100,000 sailors and more than 600 ships. But Britain could no longer devote most of its military resources to North America. In 1778, 65 per cent of the British army was in North America; only 29 per cent was there in mid-1780. In 1778, 41 per cent of British ships were in American waters; only thirteen per cent were there in mid-1780.

Fortunately for Britain, its European opponents were not as strong as they seemed. British financial and military strength ensured that it was able to hold its own around the world and also continue the war in America. While Americans benefited from additional assistance in arms, material and money, their allies were more concerned with promoting their own interests than

SOURCE C

John Sullivan, a member of Congress, writing to George Washington in May 1781, http://founders.archives.gov/documents/Washington/99-01-02-05888

The reinforcements from France though far short of what was intended will (I trust) enable us to undertake offensive operations by land and sea. The generous donation of his most Christian Majesty with the measures adopted by Congress and by our financier will enable us to pay and supply our army. The clothing arrived and now on its passage will enable us to clothe our army. The measures adopted by the French court will furnish us with the necessary munitions of war … .The scrupulous adherence of his Christian Majesty to the terms of the alliance; the favourable disposition of the Spanish court; and the interest which the powers of Europe have discovered in our becoming an independent nation promise us everything in a negotiation which our exertions and their political interest may dictate.

According to Source C, how did France assist the American war effort?

they were with aiding America. Although a French naval squadron arrived in American waters in 1778, it soon departed for the Caribbean, bent on capturing British sugar islands. France sent fewer than 10,000 troops to America.

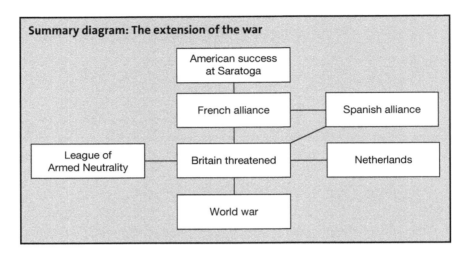

Summary diagram: The extension of the war

 4 # American victory 1778–83

▶ *How did the Americans win the war?*

In 1778 both sides continued to commit most of their military resources to the struggle for control of the middle colonies/states. Both sides found victory elusive.

Washington's problems in 1777–8

Although Saratoga boosted American morale, the winter of 1777–8 was one of trial and tribulation for the patriots. Gates's victorious army disintegrated as his militiamen returned home. Meanwhile, Washington's army, lacking food, fuel and shelter, endured great privations at Valley Forge. More than 3000 men died and many more deserted.

Even Washington's own position seemed in jeopardy. There is no evidence of an organised conspiracy against him – although he and his aides believed otherwise – but both in and out of Congress there was an undercurrent of criticism. Some feared that military dictatorship might result from what John Adams called 'the superstitious veneration that is sometimes paid to George Washington'. Others questioned Washington's military abilities, contrasting his sorry record with that of Gates. Matters came to a head in November 1777 with the publication of a letter written to Gates by General Conway expressing the hope that Gates would replace 'the weak general'. Gates, if not the organiser of a plot against Washington, was certainly ready to intrigue against him. Washington survived. So did his army – just. However, in early 1778 Washington's fortunes began to mend. His army increased to some 12,000 men and was re-equipped. Friedrich von Steuben, a German soldier of fortune, ensured that the American soldiers were better trained. By 1778 Washington was surrounded by a number of foreign military 'experts', few of whom had much expertise. More importantly, he had a small corps of battle-hardened American junior-grade officers and men who had been bloodied in combat.

Clinton's problems in 1778–9

In February General Howe was replaced by General Henry Clinton. Lord Germain told Clinton that Britain's main military effort was to be directed against French possessions in the Caribbean. Stripped of 5000 troops, Clinton was ordered to evacuate Philadelphia and concentrate his forces in New York.

Clinton set off for New York in mid-June 1778 with 10,000 soldiers and a 20-km (12 mile) long baggage train. An American attack on the British rearguard at Monmouth Court House (28 June) failed. Washington blamed the failure on his second in command, General Charles Lee. Lee insisted on a **court martial** to vindicate his conduct. Washington, who disliked Lee, complied. The court martial found Lee guilty of disobeying orders and he was suspended from command. Meanwhile Clinton's army reached New York without further hindrance. Washington lacked the strength to threaten the city's strong defences.

The 4000 French troops, conveyed by Admiral d'Estaing, besieged but failed to capture Newport, Rhode Island (July–August 1778). D'Estaing then sailed to the Caribbean, bent on capturing British islands.

In 1778–9 Clinton made some efforts to force Washington to fight a major battle by sending troops into New Jersey. But Washington would not be drawn. Clinton was similarly cautious.

Britain's position in America was by no means hopeless. It held a number of coastal enclaves, had opportunities in the South (see below), was able to launch offensives into the interior and might yet defeat Washington's army. It was conceivable that American war-weariness would lead to an upsurge of loyalist support and that Britain might still win the war.

American problems in 1779–81

In 1779 Washington faced difficulties which prevented him from taking the offensive. His greatest problem was lack of troops. Many deserted or refused to re-enlist. Popular enthusiasm for the war had long since diminished. Washington's encampment at Morristown over the winter of 1779–80 was worse than the winter at Valley Forge. Death and desertion reduced his army to 8000 men, of whom a third were not fit for duty.

 **KEY TERM**

Court martial A court held by officers of the army or navy for the trial of offences against service laws.

In 1780 Benedict Arnold, one of America's war heroes, resentful of real and imagined slights at the hands of Congress, plotted to turn over the fortress of West Point to Britain. The plot miscarried when Clinton's emissary, Major Andre, was captured with incriminating evidence. Andre was hanged as a spy but Arnold escaped to fight (with some success) for Britain. His action seemed to symbolise the crumbling of the American ideal.

In July 1780 a French army of 6000 troops, commanded by the Comte de Rochambeau, landed in Rhode Island but achieved little. The French fleet remained in the Caribbean.

Why, according to Source D, was Washington worried about the supply situation in August 1780?

SOURCE D

George Washington, writing to all the states, August 1780, quoted in R.D. Brown, editor, *Major Problems in the Era of the American Revolution 1760–1791*, D.C. Heath, 1992, pp. 225–6.

I am under the disagreeable necessity of informing you that the Army is again reduced to an extremity of distress for want of provisions. The greater part of it had been without meat from the 21st to the 26th. To endeavor to obtain some relief, I moved down to this place, with a view of stripping the lower parts of the county of the remainder of its cattle … Military coercion is no longer of any avail, as nothing further can possibly be collected from the country … without depriving the inhabitants of the last morsel. This mode of subsisting … besides being in the highest degree distressing to individuals, is attended with ruin to the morals and discipline of the army … It has been no inconsiderable support of our cause, to have had it in our power to contrast the conduct of our Army with that of the enemy, and to convince the inhabitants that while their rights were wantonly violated by the British troops, by ours they were respected. This distinction must unhappily now cease, and we must assume the odious character of the plunderers instead of the protectors of the people, the indirect consequence of which must be to alienate their minds from the Army and insensibly from the cause.

In January 1781 the Pennsylvania Line regiment mutinied. The mutiny resulted from long-smouldering discontent. Food and clothing were inadequate and pay was months in arrears. The mutineers, meeting with representatives of Congress, refused to return to duty until they were promised redress of their grievances. The promise was given. This encouraged the New Jersey Line to mutiny. Washington nipped this second rising in the bud, executing some of the ringleaders. In February Massachusetts and New Jersey troops clashed with each other in a serious riot at Princeton. For much of 1781 the Continental army was in no position to threaten Clinton. It remained badly supplied and paid.

The war in the West

The War of Independence saw a racial conflict between white people and Native Americans. Most of the 100,000 or so Native Americans who lived south of the Great Lakes and east of the Mississippi River chose to fight alongside the British. Various tribes saw the war as an opportunity to drive back the American settlers. Britain hoped that the Native American threat would prevent western settlements from sending support to the Continental army, and it might even force the rebels to divert precious troops and supplies westwards.

Western state governments kept up a constant pressure for assistance against Native American attack. However, the Native Americans were a mixed blessing as far as Britain was concerned:

- They were unreliable.
- They were divided.
- Savage attacks antagonised neutrals and loyalists.

The southern phase 1778–81

In 1778 Britain decided to mount a campaign in the South, where there were reputed to be large numbers of loyalists. The hope was to take control of Georgia and the Carolinas and then advance northwards. Conceivably, war-weariness might lead to an upsurge of loyalist support and to American surrender.

Georgia

In late 1778 Clinton sent a 3000-strong expedition under Colonel Campbell to thinly populated Georgia. In December Campbell captured Savannah, losing only three dead and taking over 500 American prisoners. Augusta fell in January 1779. Recognising the importance of winning support, Campbell prohibited his troops from ill-treating the Georgians, who responded by flocking to join a newly organised loyalist militia. In March the British defeated patriot forces at Briar Creek. The Americans lost 400 casualties and most of the survivors went home rather than rejoining General Lincoln's patriot army in South Carolina.

Nevertheless, Britain's position in Georgia remained precarious:

- Georgia's population remained divided, half loyalists, half patriots.
- General Lincoln's forces outnumbered those of the British.
- In September 1779 Admiral d'Estaing returned from the Caribbean and a combined Franco-American force besieged Savannah. After a bloody attack that cost the French–Americans 1500 casualties, the siege collapsed in mid-October. D'Estaing sailed away and Lincoln returned to Charleston.

The Carolinas

In February 1780 Cornwallis with 7600 men besieged Charleston, the largest town in the southern colonies. General Lincoln surrendered in May. The British took 5000 American prisoners, 343 artillery pieces and 6000 muskets. For the Americans this was the worst military disaster of the war.

British forces now moved into South Carolina's interior. Colonel Banastre Tarleton and 300 dragoons defeated 350 Virginians at Waxhaw Creek

Figure 4.3 The war in the South and Yorktown.

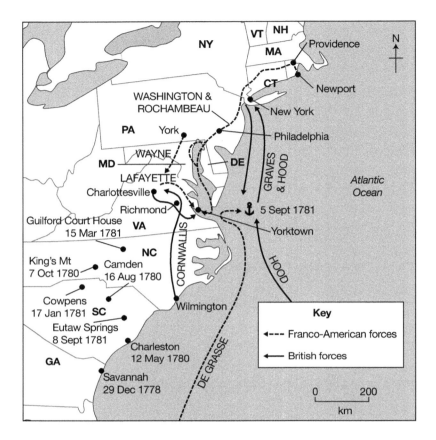

(29 May). Tarleton's men butchered many of the Virginians even after they had tried to surrender, 'If warfare allows me I shall give no quarter', Tarleton declared. 'Tarleton's quarter' – that is, take no prisoners – became a rallying cry of southern patriots. Warfare in the Carolinas was thus more savage than elsewhere.

For a time it seemed that South Carolina had been brought under British control. Its government fled and many people took an oath of allegiance to the Crown. Clinton, fearing a French–American attack on New York, returned north, leaving General Cornwallis in command of 4000 men in the South. Before departing, Clinton issued a proclamation which required that all adult males should openly support Britain or be treated as rebels. Neutrality was thus impossible. Many Carolinians, while ready to take an oath of allegiance, were reluctant to fight for Britain.

Initially, the coastal communities of South Carolina gave Cornwallis no trouble. However, the interior of the Carolinas was another matter. Here there were fierce divisions between loyalists and patriots. Ferocious fighting during the summer of 1780 resulted in success for patriot forces in North Carolina.

In August Horatio Gates, now commander of Continental forces in the South, led an army of over 3000 men into South Carolina. Beaten at Camden (16 August) by a 2000-strong British force, Gates's army sustained 1800 casualties while British losses were just over 300. It was, as Cornwallis reported, 'a most complete victory', destroying Gates's military reputation and opening the way for a British invasion of North Carolina. On 18 August Tarleton's dragoons defeated patriot militia at Fishing Creek, inflicting over 500 casualties. British casualties were 22.

Cornwallis began his invasion of North Carolina in September. Gates's army at Hillsboro was in no condition to fight. However, patriot militia harassed British foraging parties and once Cornwallis advanced into North Carolina, South Carolina rose behind him. On 7 October a 1000-strong loyalist force was wiped out by patriots at King's Mountain. Cornwallis, abandoning his invasion of North Carolina, returned south.

Over the winter of 1780–1 patriot and loyalist militias turned the backcountry regions of Georgia and the Carolinas into a wasteland of plunder and slaughter, both sides routinely torturing prisoners and hanging enemies. Protecting loyalist areas proved a major problem for Britain. Cornwallis, short of men, was dependent on loyalists to make up numbers for his field army. The loyalists themselves were dependent on British military support.

General Nathanael Greene

In late 1780 General Nathanael Greene, Washington's choice of successor should he die, took command of the Continental army in the South. Rather than risk his troops in a major battle, Greene divided his forces and relied on hit-and-run attacks, supported by patriot militia:

- Daniel Morgan was sent with 700 men to probe British defences in the South Carolina backcountry.
- Other troops co-operated with militia in attacks on British coastal positions.

In January 1781 Tarleton was defeated at Cowpens by Morgan. Undeterred, Cornwallis determined to drive Greene out of North Carolina. Their two armies met at Guilford Court House (15 March). Cornwallis won a costly victory, losing over 500 men, a quarter of his force. While Cornwallis' army recuperated, Greene marched into South Carolina. In April Lord Rawdon defeated Greene at Hobkirk's Hill. However, Rawdon was unable to follow up his victory and patriot forces continued capturing scattered British outposts. By mid-1781 only Charleston, Savannah and the remote Fort Ninety-Six remained in British hands in South Carolina and Georgia.

Yorktown

In April Cornwallis, rather than return to South Carolina to deal with Greene, headed north towards Virginia, reaching Petersburg on 20 May.

The situation in Virginia

Until 1780 Virginia had largely escaped the ravages of war. However, over the winter of 1780–1 Benedict Arnold led a series of raids into the state, inflicting major damage. In March General Phillips arrived in Virginia with 2000 more men. Cornwallis's junction with the British forces already in Virginia gave him command of an army of 8000 men. This military presence led to several counties proclaiming support for Britain. However, most Virginians were committed to driving out the British.

Having failed to destroy an American detachment led by Lafayette, Cornwallis moved towards the sea to maintain communications with Clinton in New York. In August he began to construct a base at Yorktown. If his army could be supplied by the Royal Navy, it could cause mayhem in Virginia. Unfortunately for Cornwallis, a French fleet with twenty ships of the line, commanded by Admiral de Grasse, now appeared in American waters. Admiral Rodney failed to send sufficient ships from the Caribbean to deal with the threat.

Cornwallis's surrender

In May 1781 Washington learned that de Grasse's fleet was on its way. Initially, he planned to use American and French forces to attack New York. But Rochambeau persuaded him that Cornwallis was a better target. In a well-conceived and well-timed operation, for which Washington deserves much credit, the combined French–American army, 16,000 strong, reached Virginia in early September, confronting Cornwallis with a force twice the size of his own and trapping him on the Yorktown peninsula. The repulse of a British fleet on 5 September gave the French vital control of Chesapeake Bay. Delay in dispatching a relief expedition from New York sealed Cornwallis's fate. By October, his army at Yorktown, in a weakly fortified position and short of supplies, was trapped. On 19 October, after a three-week siege, Cornwallis and his 8000-strong army surrendered. The British troops marched out of their positions to the tune of 'The World Turned Upside Down'.

The results of Yorktown

The news of Cornwallis's surrender came as a shock to most Britons. When North heard the news, he said, 'Oh God, it is all over.' Cornwallis's surrender need not have been decisive. Britain still controlled New York, Charleston and Savannah and still had over 30,000 troops in America. The immediate aftermath of Yorktown did not see the collapse of the British position. American and French forces failed to co-operate in an attack on Charleston. Instead, de Grasse sailed for the West Indies. Without French naval support the Americans could achieve very little. However, Yorktown was a crucial victory. After Cornwallis's surrender the British government discontinued offensive operations in America and it was clear that public and Parliament were sceptical about continuing the war. In February 1782 the Commons, to George III's chagrin, resolved to end military measures against the Americans. A month later North resigned. He was replaced by the Marquis of Rockingham. The Earl of Shelburne, who became colonial secretary, wanted peace.

Peacemaking

In April 1782 Rockingham's ministry ordered the evacuation of New York, Charleston and Savannah. (Savannah was evacuated in July 1782; Charleston and New York were not evacuated until December 1782 and November 1783, respectively.) On Rockingham's death in July 1782, Shelburne became prime minister.

Peace negotiations

American representatives entered into informal talks with British officials in Paris in April 1782, months before the formal peace negotiations began in September. By now France was also keen on peace. The Royal Navy again ruled the waves and French finances were in a hopeless mess.

Shelburne, intent on separating France and the USA, was prepared to be generous to the Americans. While John Jay and John Adams, the leaders of the American peace delegation, were suspicious of British motives, they also distrusted the French Foreign Minister Vergennes, suspecting – with good reason – that he was ready to support the Spanish claim to the **trans-Appalachian region** – an area Americans were determined to control. Without consulting either Franklin or the French, Jay and Adams opened separate discussions with Britain. After protracted negotiations, the American commissioners signed a preliminary peace treaty with Britain in November 1782. The terms of the treaty were accepted provisionally in January 1783. Britain proclaimed an end of hostilities in February. The Treaty of Paris was signed by Britain, the USA, France, Spain and the Netherlands on 3 September 1783.

 **KEY TERM**

Trans-Appalachian region The land west of the Appalachian mountains.

The Treaty of Paris

By the terms of the treaty:

- Britain recognised American independence and agreed that the boundaries of the USA should extend west to the Mississippi River, north to the St Lawrence River and the Great Lakes and south to the thirty-first parallel, the northern boundary of Florida.
- Americans were granted the 'liberty' to fish the Newfoundland Banks and to dry and cure fish in Nova Scotia and Labrador.
- The USA agreed that British merchants should meet with 'no lawful impediment' in seeking to recover their pre-war American debts and that Congress should 'earnestly recommend' to the states the restoration of confiscated loyalist property.
- Britain ceded Florida to Spain.

For the Americans the settlement was a major triumph. Especially surprising was Britain's willingness to concede the Mississippi boundary. In 1783 the British still controlled most of the trans-Appalachian area. But Shelburne considered this and other sacrifices to be worthwhile. He hoped that a generous peace might lay the foundation for an Anglo-American commercial alliance and eventually even some form of political reunion.

Summary diagram: American victory 1778–83

Main events			
1778	**1779**	**1780**	**1781**
• Valley Forge • Conspiracy against Washington • Battle of Monmouth Court House • French threat • Britain abandoned Philadelphia	• Lack of troops • No decisive battle	• Arnold's treachery • British success in Carolinas • Britain took Charleston • Battle of Camden • Guerrilla war in South	• Mutinies • Yorktown • Fall of Lord North • Peace negotiations • Treaty of Paris • French naval supremacy

---

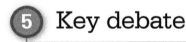

5 Key debate

▶ *Did Britain lose or America win the War of Independence?*

At many times in the war Britain seemed close to victory. As late as April 1781, with the American army and economy in disarray, American victory still seemed unlikely. So why did the war end in British defeat and American victory? Not surprisingly, historians stress different factors.

British failure

Fighting a war in America was never going to be easy. Nevertheless, Britain's leaders did themselves no favours. North's government made some important miscalculations early in the war, overestimating loyalist support and assuming that the rebellion was localised in Massachusetts. Better British diplomacy in the 1770s might have prevented France and Spain from entering the war. It may be that the British government also failed to direct and energise its generals. North was not a great war leader – although he did appoint some able men, Germain and Lord Sandwich, for example – to key positions. Inevitably, much had to be left to the discretion of the generals and admirals. The main mistakes were made in America, not in London.

Criticism can be directed both at individual commanders and at the overall calibre of British generalship. Howe was too cautious, missing several opportunities to destroy Washington's army in 1776–7. Clinton was equally timid. Other generals, especially Burgoyne, were overconfident. British officers – military and naval – did not co-operate particularly well. British admirals also made mistakes. Rodney, who failed to send sufficient ships to New York in 1781, bore some responsibility for Cornwallis's surrender at Yorktown.

Perhaps the employment of Hessian troops was unwise. As well as alienating Americans, arguably they were not totally committed to the British cause. During the war some 5000 deserted. However, Britain would have found it hard to have waged war without them: by 1778 they provided a third of British strength in America. Most of those who deserted did so after 1781 when the war was already lost.

Having failed to nip the rebellion in the bud in 1775–6, the British were unsuccessful in gaining local support. Indeed, they frequently offended neutral opinion or let down the loyalists. While both armies often behaved badly towards civilians, the British were notably worse. More importantly, British generals had a bad habit of moving into an area, rallying support and then leaving their supporters without adequate support. If they ever had a chance of holding a population loyal to the king they squandered it by neglecting the southern colonies until 1779.

American success

EXTRACT 1

From Joseph Ellis, *His Excellency George Washington*, Faber & Faber, 2004, p. 270.

In effect there were two distinct creative moments in the American founding, the winning of independence and the invention of nationhood, and Washington was the central figure in both creations. No one else in the founding generation could match these revolutionary credentials, so no one else could plausibly challenge his place atop the American version of Mount Olympus. Whatever minor misstep he had made along the way, his judgement on all the major political and military questions had invariably proved prescient, as if he had known where history was headed; or, perhaps, as if the future had felt compelled to align itself with his choices … His genius was his judgement.

American success was not just the result of British failure; it owed much to American endeavour. Some 200,000 men fought at various times in Continental or militia armies. Eight thousand American troops died in battle, a further 25,000 dying from disease and wounds. (This was 0.9 per cent of the population, compared with 0.28 per cent losses in the Second World War.) While British forces captured important towns and won most pitched battles, this success did not subdue the population. Whenever the British army moved out of an area, the people invariably reverted to the patriot cause.

George Washington's role

George Washington's contribution to American victory was important. He had a difficult job. For most of the war the Continental army was short of everything, men as well as supplies. During the course of the war at least one-third of the army deserted. But Washington kept it in being and improved its quality. The army was his creation. For many Americans his army *was* America. He did not like the defensive war he had to fight for most of the war but realised the necessity of fighting it. He had – and has – his critics. He never defeated the main British army in the open. He tended to make plans beyond the capacities of his army and also chose some bad locations to give battle. Sometimes he permitted personal jealousies and emotional weaknesses to intrude on tactical, strategic and personnel considerations.

But Washington's strengths outweigh his failures. Dealing with a host of state officials and Congress required enormous skill and tact. His attack on Trenton in 1776 showed efficiency and daring and the march to Yorktown in 1781 was a superb feat. Perhaps his greatest achievement was to keep his army in being through a long succession of dark days. In the end to survive was to triumph.

American military achievement

The Continental army, withstanding defeat and privations, became a reasonable fighting force. While Washington held them in contempt, the militia units served a useful purpose. The militia's ability to control most of the country not actually occupied by the British gave the Americans a huge advantage.

American heroes

- Washington apart, there were a (limited) number of other talented American officers. Benedict Arnold was probably the best (before he deserted to the British).
- American diplomats – Franklin, Jay and Adams – turned European rivalries to America's advantage and produced a series of diplomatic victories, starting with the French alliance (1778) and ending with the Treaty of Paris (1783).
- No congressman played a more important role than John Adams in ensuring that, as he later remarked, the 'thirteen clocks were made to strike together'.

Foreign intervention

EXTRACT 2

From 'The Wars of the American Revolution' by E. Wayne Carp,
http://revolution.h-net.msu.edu/essays/carp.html

It is probably not going too far to say that America owes its independence to foreign intervention and aid, especially from France. The French monarchy sent arms, clothing and ammunition to America. It also sent soldiers and the French navy. Most importantly, the French kept the United States' government solvent by lending it the money to keep the Revolution alive. The magnitude of French support of the American Revolution can be glimpsed at the battle of Yorktown. There the majority of George Washington's 15,000 Continental army were French soldiers.

Assess the Extract 1 (page 103) and Extract 2. Which provides the better explanation for British defeat and American victory?

Arguably, the war's outcome was determined neither by British mistakes nor by American prowess. The entry of France and Spain swung the struggle decisively in America's favour. The reallocation of British military and naval resources, caused by the broadening of the conflict, had important implications for America. France and Spain joined the war because they had old scores to settle with Britain, not because of brilliant American diplomacy.

Conclusion

Ultimately, the war was lost by the British rather than won by the Americans, and it was lost to the American landscape as much as to the Americans. All the British generals had to wage war in a difficult country with poor communications. Even if they had destroyed the Continental army and occupied all thirteen colonial capitals, the British army would still have had to control a widely scattered and hostile population. Nevertheless, British defeat was not inevitable. If North had sent more troops to America earlier in the war, or if Howe had been less cautious, British troops might have won a decisive victory which could have been fatal to the patriot cause.

The British army, often against the odds, won virtually every major battle in the war. But it was unable to deliver a knockout blow. Once France joined the war, it became less likely that Britain would conquer all the areas in rebellion. However, that did not mean that the success the Americans achieved in 1783 was inevitable. Cornwallis's surrender at Yorktown, which tipped the scales in favour of a peace settlement, was something of a fluke. It occurred after the sole significant French victory over the Royal Navy since 1690. If Yorktown had not occurred, it is hard to predict what would have happened. By 1782 Britain was better able to wage war than its European enemies. Before Yorktown a compromise peace between Britain and America was a real possibility. After Yorktown Britain had had enough of the American war.

Chapter summary

Britain had plenty of advantages in the war, not least the support of large numbers of Americans. If General Howe had been less cautious in 1776–7 and General Burgoyne more able in 1777, British forces might have won decisive victories. Once France joined the war, it became more likely that the Americans would win. Nevertheless, Britain still had some success in the southern states in 1780–1. Washington's victory at Yorktown in 1781 proved decisive. British Parliament and public alike decided that the time had come to make peace. The Treaty of Paris in 1783 was a triumph for the Americans who, epitomised by George Washington, had won the war by not abandoning the struggle.

 # Refresher questions

Use these questions to remind yourself of the key material covered in this chapter.

1 Which side had the greater advantages in 1776?
2 To what extent was the war a civil war?
3 Was the War of Independence the first modern war?
4 Why did Britain not win the war in 1776?
5 What were Britain's main military mistakes in 1777?
6 Why were the British defeated at Saratoga?
7 What was the effect of French intervention?
8 Why was there no decisive battle in the period 1778–81?
9 Why did both sides find it hard to win decisively in the South?
10 Why did Cornwallis surrender at Yorktown?
11 How successful were the Americans at peace-making?
12 Did Britain lose or America win the War of Independence?

 # Question practice

ESSAY QUESTIONS

1 How successful was Washington as a military commander?
2 Assess the reasons for American victory in the War of Independence.
3 How far was General William Howe to blame for Britain's failure to win the War of Independence?
4 'French sea power was the decisive factor in the outcome of the American War of Independence.' Assess the validity of this view.

SOURCE ANALYSIS QUESTION

1 With reference to Sources 1, 2 and 3, and your understanding of the historical context, assess the value of these sources to a historian studying the American armed forces in the War of Independence.

SOURCE 1

Congress calls on the states to support the Continental army, 24 September 1776.

You will perceive by the enclosed resolves that they [Congress] have come to a determination to augment our Army, and to engage the troops to serve during the war. As an inducement to enlist on these terms, the Congress have agreed to give, besides a bounty of twenty dollars, a hundred acres of land to each soldier; and in case he should fall in battle, they have resolved that his children, or other representatives, shall succeed to such land …

The heavy and enormous expenses consequent upon calling for the militia, the delay attending their motions, and the difficulty of keeping them in the camp render it extremely improper to place our whole dependence upon them. Experience hath uniformly convinced us of this, some of the militia having actually deserted the camp, at the very moment their services were most wanted … .

Without a well-disciplined army, we can never expect success against veteran troops; and it is totally impossible we should have a well-disciplined army, unless our troops are engaged to serve during the war. To attain therefore this most desirable end, I am to request you will at once, and without a moment's delay, bend all your attention to raise your quota of the American army.

SOURCE 2

General Armstrong, writing to Pennsylvanian President Wharton in November 1777.

Many, too many of the militia, are a scandal to the military profession, a nuisance in service and a dead weight on the public; yet it is equally true that taken as a body, they have rendered that service that neither the state nor the army could have dispensed with. They have constantly mounted guards, formed many and direct pickets, performed many occasional pieces of labour, patrolled the roads leading to the enemy by day and by night – they have taken a number of prisoners, brought in deserters, suppressed Tories, prevented much intercourse betwixt the disaffected and the enemy – met and skirmished with the enemy as early and as often as others, and … have had a proportional share of success, hazard and loss of blood.

SOURCE 3

Peter Oliver, a distinguished merchant from Massachusetts, asked a wounded American lieutenant, captured at Bunker Hill (1775), how he had come to be a rebel.

The case was this Sir! I lived in a Country Town; I was a Shoemaker & got my living by my Labor. When this Rebellion came on, I saw some of my Neighbors get into Commission, who were no better than my self. I was very ambitious, & did not like to see those Men above me. I was asked to enlist, as a private Soldier. My Ambition was too great for so low a Rank; I offered to enlist upon having a Lieutenants Commission; which was granted. I imagined my self now in a Way of Promotion: if I was killed in Battle, there would be an end of me, but if my Captain was killed, I should rise in Rank, & should still have a Chance to rise higher. These Sir! were the only Motives of my entering into the Service; for as to the Dispute between great Britain & the Colonies, I know nothing of it; neither am I capable of judging whether it is right or wrong.

CHAPTER 5

The American Revolution

The American War of Independence is also called the American Revolution. Like any long war, it had significant consequences, not least the creation of the USA. But did those consequences amount to a revolution? This chapter will examine the results of the war and the notion of an American Revolution by focusing on the following themes:

★ Political developments within the states

★ National government

★ The social and economic impact of the war

The key debate on *page 126* of this chapter asks the question: How revolutionary was the American Revolution?

Key dates

1776	June	Virginian Declaration of Rights	1777	July	Vermont abolished slavery
	July	Articles of Confederation drafted	1780		Pennsylvania abolished slavery
1777	Jan.	Vermont declared itself an independent state	1781		Articles of Confederation ratified

1 Political developments within the states

▶ *To what extent did political revolution occur in the thirteen states that made up the USA?*

Arguably, the American rebels had not intended revolution. 'I say again,' said John Adams, 'that resistance to innovation and to unlimited claims of Parliament, and not any new form of government, was the object of the revolution'. Whatever the intent, Adams clearly thought that revolution was the result. In political terms, revolution usually means rapid, fundamental change as one set of power relationships and institutions collapses and another takes its place. Did this occur in the American states?

Republicanism

The controversy between Britain and the colonies produced a new political philosophy: republicanism. Thomas Paine's *Common Sense* gave the terms republican and republicanism wide currency in America. Paine defined the word republic as 'the public good or the good of the whole'. In Paine's view, rule by nobility, oligarchy or faction was no more compatible with republicanism than rule by a king. The idea of republicanism was not yet interchangeable with the idea of democracy but it did imply a form of government which represented the whole people. Republicanism, essentially, was government by the consent of the governed.

In many ways America was well suited to republicanism. By 1763 the colonial assemblies had substantial power and most white men could vote. Colonial politics had become even more democratic by the 1770s. As the gentry passed resolutions against British tyranny in the assemblies, men of lesser rank took to the streets to intimidate stamp distributors and royal officials. The Sons of Liberty (see page 38), which contained many artisans and small merchants, helped to raise the political consciousness of Americans generally. The Committees of Safety which spread across the colonies in 1774–5 brought many new men into politics.

Once allegiance to the Crown was repudiated, republicanism became the only acceptable system of political values, providing philosophical underpinning and offering legitimacy for government and authority. Application of republican principles rested on the central proposition of **popular sovereignty**. In the words of the Virginia Declaration of Rights: 'All power is vested in, and consequently derived from, the people … magistrates are their trustees and servants, and at all times amenable to them.'

KEY TERM

Popular sovereignty The idea that political power should be held by the people.

? Look at Source A. What did Adams think was the essential meaning of the American Revolution?

SOURCE A

John Adams, writing in 1818, http://teachingamericanhistory.org/library/document/john-adams-to-h-niles/

But what do we mean by the American Revolution? Do we mean the American war? The Revolution was effected before the war commenced. The Revolution was in the minds and hearts of the people; a change in the religious sentiments of their duties and obligations. While the king, and all in authority under him, were believed to govern in justice and mercy according to the laws and constitution derived to them from the God of nature … they thought themselves bound to pray for the king and queen, and all the royal family, and all in authority under them, as ministers ordained of God for their good; but when they saw those powers renouncing all the principles of authority, and bent upon the destruction of all the securities of their lives, liberties, and properties, they thought it their duty to pray for the Continental Congress and all the thirteen State congresses.

After 1775 Americans grappled with the implications of republicanism. What form should a republican government take? What rights should a republican government guarantee? Who should have the right to vote and hold office?

The transition from colonies to states

As British authority collapsed in 1774–5, most colonial assemblies reconstituted themselves as provincial conventions. Establishing a legal foundation for these makeshift governments seemed an urgent necessity to American leaders, who were deeply concerned for the rule of law and who feared the spread of civil disorder.

Congress dithered in 1775 when asked whether it would recommend colonies (soon to be states) drawing up new constitutions. Some states changed their constitutions before Congress decided. However, in May 1776 Congress adopted a resolution by John Adams calling on all states that did not have a permanent constitution based on popular sovereignty to adopt one. Congress discussed the possibility of drafting a uniform model constitution, but Adams's view – that each state should be entitled to draft its own constitution – prevailed.

Between 1776 and 1780 all but two states adopted new constitutions. (The exceptions were Rhode Island and Connecticut, which merely revised their colonial charters, deleting all reference to royal authority.) The new constitutions embodied the principles of republicanism. That these principles were contested is reflected in the different constitutional arrangements adopted by the various states. Each state constitution reflected the balance of political power at the time of its writing, as well as an honest attempt by men of good faith to find the best way forward. Given the imperatives of the war, Americans wanted effective government. But they were also concerned about the dangers of excessive authority, as demonstrated by the British government, which they had convinced themselves was conspiring to destroy their liberty.

Elitists vs democrats

After 1775–6 the struggle about home rule was transformed into one about who should rule at home. Americans had to decide what type of government the new states should have and who should be allowed to vote and hold office. These issues were debated in newspapers, pamphlets, legislative chambers, committee rooms, pubs and homes. Broadly speaking, Americans divided into two camps: elitists and democrats.

The elitists were often men who had led the assemblies. They felt that while governments should maintain liberty, they must also preserve order. They feared that too much democracy might generate unstable governments, which could result in anarchy. They thus sought to design republics in which the people would exercise their **sovereignty** by choosing the best men to govern and then standing aside to let them do so. They sought to create governments along the lines of the former colonial system, whereby:

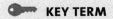

KEY TERM

Sovereignty Ultimate power.

- the franchise would be limited to property holders
- there would be (high) property qualifications for office holding
- the right to vote would be exercised relatively infrequently
- there would be a two-housed (bicameral) legislature, one representing the people, the other the elite
- governors would have wide powers.

The democrats were often men from humble backgrounds. They tended to favour:

- a broad franchise (although no one advocated giving slaves or women the vote)
- no – or low – property qualifications for office holding
- frequent elections
- one-housed (unicameral) legislatures: they felt there was no need for an aristocratic second chamber
- a weak **executive**.

The state constitutions

Most of the new constitutions were drawn up and put into effect by state legislatures without specific authorisation from the electorate. A few were the work of specially elected conventions. While varying in detail, the constitutions resembled each other in many respects and were broadly patterned on the colonial model:

- All agreed that sovereignty ultimately resided with the people.
- All were concerned about the **separation of powers**. Virginia was the first state to spell out explicitly the proposition that 'the legislative, executive and judiciary departments shall be separate and distinct'.
- The usual provision was for a legislature consisting of two houses. (The only exceptions were Pennsylvania and Georgia.) The lower house was seen as directly representing the people. The upper house (or Senate) was seen as representing 'gentlemen'.
- All the original states required property ownership or payment of taxes to vote. However, property qualifications for voting were generally low. In most states over two-thirds of white men over the age of 21 had the right to vote.
- Qualifications for office holding remained much the same as under the colonial governments.
- Every state (except Pennsylvania) had a single executive head – the governor – who was usually chosen by the legislature. The deep suspicion of executive authority (one of the legacies of the colonial past) resulted in governors being denied many of the powers enjoyed by their royal predecessors. Ten states set one-year terms for governors, most of whom were little more than figureheads.

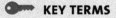
KEY TERMS

Executive The power or authority in government that carries the law into effect; a person (or persons) who administer(s) the government.

Separation of powers A system of government in which power is shared between the legislative, the executive and the judiciary, ensuring that no branch can become dominant.

Bills of Rights

Although most constitutions affirmed the principle of the separation of powers, authority was in practice largely concentrated in the legislatures, particularly in the lower houses. But the power of the legislatures was limited, first by the (usual) requirement to hold annual elections and second by the inclusion in most constitutions of declarations (or bills) of rights. The Virginia Declaration of Rights (1776) provided the model. It enumerated those fundamental English liberties which Americans had come to regard as their own: freedom of expression, worship and assembly, the subordination of military to civil power, the right to jury trial, protection against cruel and unusual punishments and guarantees against self-incrimination, against arrest without knowing one's accuser and against search warrants. The constitutions thus set out not only governments' powers but also their limits.

Elite vs new men

In most states the new arrangements were hardly models of democracy. The constitutions reflected the eighteenth-century belief that political rights should be confined to property holders. A man without property, it was held, was not sufficiently independent to be entrusted with political power. Property qualifications restricted the electorate in virtually every state and, for office holding, were sometimes so high as to exclude all but the really wealthy. In some states, for example South Carolina and Virginia, the elites retained their power.

Nevertheless, the suffrage, already extensive in America pre-1775, was widened further as nearly all states reduced property qualifications for voting. Thus, most state governments became more responsive to popular opinion. The departure of many loyalist office holders created vacancies for new men, often of modest means. The enlargement of the legislatures and the better representation in them of frontier districts also led to a change of personnel.

According to historian Jackson Turner Main (1978), the state legislatures after 1775 were significantly different from those before. Pre-1775 voters overwhelmingly selected representatives from among the rich. By 1783 the proportion of men from old elite families in the legislatures had dropped from 46 to 22 per cent. Pre-1775 small farmers and artisans had accounted for only about a fifth of assembly members; afterwards they constituted a majority in some northern legislatures and a sizeable minority in the South. While the wealthy continued to dominate politics, ordinary folk had a far greater voice in affairs.

Cosmopolitans vs localists

The assumption had been that the main division in American politics would be between the rich and the many. In the event this division proved to be only one of several. Main claimed that the primary division was that between agrarian–

localist interests on the one side and commercial–cosmopolitan interests on the other.

In the North the cosmopolitans came from commercial areas. In the South they comprised large property owners. Most lived along navigable rivers, had connections in towns and with large-scale commerce, were wealthy and, above all, had wide interests and experience and a broader outlook than their fellow citizens. They welcomed activist government and supported conservative monetary policies (see page 136). In contrast, the localists were predominantly rural, owned small properties, lived in remoter interior areas and had narrower intellectual, economic and social horizons. They were suspicious of government, banking and urban interests.

Whatever the divisions, it should be noted that there was no real party system in place by the mid-1780s and very little orchestrated campaigning.

Politics in the states

For most of the period from 1775 until 1787 the individual states remained the main stage for political activity. While Congress directed the war, it possessed little further authority. Each state controlled its own finances, trade and economic policy and dealt with a host of political and social issues. Critics of the new constitutions complained that they were dangerously democratic and not conducive to good government. However, according to historian Colin Bonwick (1991), the states' record of effective administration was 'far better than contemporary, and later critics have allowed'.

Many problems facing the states flowed directly from the processes of becoming independent. Some states had difficulty asserting their authority throughout their territory. Two New York counties – Gloucester and Cumberland – formed themselves into a separate state of Vermont in 1777. While the state did not receive official recognition until 1791, its existence from 1777 was a reality that even New York could not ignore.

The war created other problems. The operations of both armies often made civil administration difficult and sometimes impossible. The occupation by the British of New York city (1776–83), Philadelphia (1777–8) and Charleston (1780–2) made things difficult for New York, Pennsylvania and South Carolina, respectively. Financial problems were particularly severe. The states had no option but to increase taxation. In every case the revenue raised was insufficient. The states were thus forced to finance the war by issuing paper currency. This led, inevitably, to inflation. By the 1780s state finances were a major problem.

States also had to deal with the problem of loyalism. Every state required men to take oaths of allegiance to the state. Those who refused to take the oath could be barred from practising their trade or profession, had to pay extra taxes, and in some states could be banished or imprisoned. All states had laws for confiscation of loyalist property.

Freedom of religion

Pre-1775 most colonies possessed established churches (see page 14). After 1775 states debated whether religious establishment was consistent with individual liberties. New York, New Jersey, Delaware, Maryland, North Carolina, Georgia, South Carolina, Pennsylvania and Virginia prohibited established churches. In Virginia, James Madison and Thomas Jefferson worked to ensure that religion would become entirely a private matter. In 1786 Jefferson's Act for Establishing Religious Freedom was finally approved by the state legislature. It prohibited all forms of state intervention in religious affairs. No church was to enjoy privileges denied to others and no man was to suffer any formal disadvantages because of his religion. Nevertheless, the triumph of religious freedom did not occur everywhere. All the New England states except Rhode Island continued to require taxpayers to support 'public Protestant worship'.

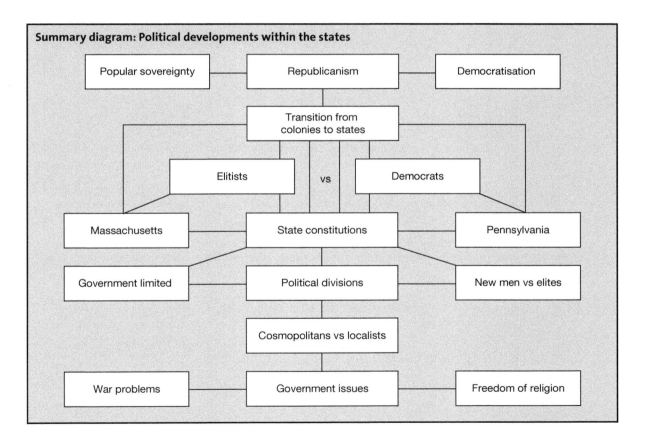

Summary diagram: Political developments within the states

National government

> ▶ *How strong was the Articles of Confederation?*

While opposition to British policy after 1763 stimulated continental unity and the outbreak of fighting made collaboration imperative, any sense of American nationality was, at most, embryonic. Most Americans thought of themselves as Virginians or New Yorkers first and Americans second. The colonies had rebelled against Britain in order to control their own internal affairs. Moreover, the struggle with Britain had bred a distrust of central authority. Since a strong national government would necessarily diminish the states' authority, many Americans resisted it as being a repudiation of the revolution itself. In the midst of a war to check tyranny, Americans had no wish to create a new one.

The Articles of Confederation

Congress, which began in 1774 as an extra-legal protest body, was poorly fitted to exercise national authority. It consisted of delegates from states eager to load it with responsibility but reluctant to cede it effective power. It functioned more as a conference of the states' representatives than as an autonomous government.

In June 1776 Congress appointed a committee of thirteen (with one man from each state) to draw up a constitution. A month later the committee produced a draft constitution – the Articles of Confederation. Largely the work of John Dickinson, the Articles provided for a central government with limited powers:

- Congress, which would act as the central government, was composed of one body in which each state, whatever its size of population, had one vote. State delegations consisted of two to seven people. Congressmen were elected annually and limited to three terms in six years.
- There was no provision for a national executive or a national judiciary.
- Congress could declare war, raise an army and navy, borrow and issue money, conclude treaties and alliances, apportion the common expenses among the states, settle interstate boundary disputes, regulate Native American affairs, make requisitions on the states for money and men (in case of war), set standards for weights and measures, and establish and regulate post offices.
- Important measures, such as treaties, needed the approval of at least nine states.
- The Articles themselves could not be amended without the consent of all thirteen states.
- All powers not specifically granted to the Confederation were reserved to the states. Crucially, Congress had no power to levy taxes, regulate trade or enforce financial requisitions.

The Confederation, in Dickinson's view, was little more than a 'firm league of friendship'. However, such was the hostility towards centralised authority, even of so limited a kind, that the Articles did not obtain congressional approval until November 1777. They would come into force only when ratified by all the states.

After Congress submitted the Articles to the states, its members acted on the assumption that they would be ratified and behaved as if the new constitution was in force. In fact, **ratification** proved difficult (largely because of disputes over western lands) and the unanimous consent of the states was not obtained until Maryland ratified in March 1781.

National government problems

Throughout the war, the USA had only a rudimentary central government. To make matters worse, Congress was in session only intermittently and had no fixed abode. Its members often found better things to do than attend its sessions. It only just managed to get a **quorum** to ratify the Treaty of Paris in 1783.

Nevertheless, Congress conducted national affairs, implementing as well as formulating policy. Gradually it devised a system of administration, operating through committees of its own members established to deal with particular subjects. The Secret Committee of September 1775, for example, arranged for imports of munitions and other military supplies. Other committees, founded in 1776, dealt with military, naval and financial matters. Major decisions, however, remained the responsibility of Congress itself.

Military matters were a crucial concern. At first, Congress implemented policy through state committees and assemblies that were called on to raise troops, requisition supplies and put the country on a war footing. But from 1777 it created small executive boards to run the war. Congress exercised close supervision over military affairs in part to enforce the principle of civil supremacy over military commanders, a task made easier by Washington's acceptance of the principle.

Unlike the states, Congress enjoyed no authority to impose taxes. It tried to pay for the war by:

- issuing paper money (which caused huge inflation)
- leaning on the states to provide money: the states, given their own financial problems, did not provide enough.

In 1780 Congress, virtually bankrupt, required the states to share in guaranteeing a new federal currency. The plan failed. By 1781 there was no effective national currency.

In 1783 the Articles faced a problematic future:

- The Confederation had been established by the states, not by the people: there was no element of direct popular election.
- The war had been a powerful unifier: peace diminished one of the most powerful imperatives to union.

 **KEY TERMS**

Ratification Official approval and sanction.

Quorum A minimum number of members necessary for transaction of business.

According to Source B, what were Washington's concerns? Why did his opinion matter?

SOURCE B

George Washington, writing in 1783, quoted in E. Latham, editor, *The Declaration of Independence and the Constitution*, D.C. Heath, 1962, p. 96.

The experience, which is purchased at the price of difficulties and distress, will alone convince us that the honor, power, and true interests of this country must be measured by a Continental scale, and that every departure therefrom weakens the Union, and may ultimately break the band which holds us together. To avert these evils, to form a Constitution that will give consistency, stability, and dignity to the Union and sufficient powers to the great Council of the Nation for general purposes, is a duty which is incumbent upon every man who wishes well to his Country, and will meet with my aid as far as it can be rendered in the private walks of life.

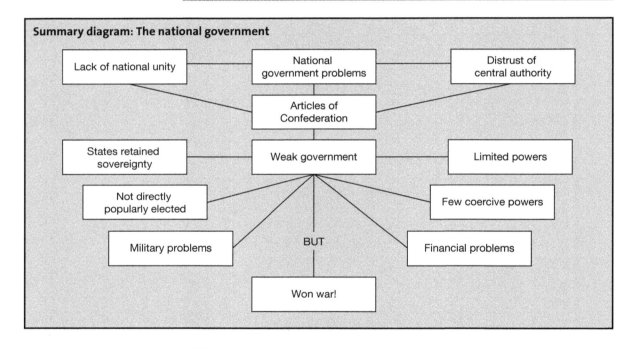

Summary diagram: The national government

3 The social and economic impact of the war

▶ *Was there a social revolution in America?*

Historians disagree about the extent to which the structure of society was affected by the American Revolution. The main debates concern the effect of loyalist emigration, whether the USA became a more equal society, and the war's impact on slaves, women and Native Americans. There is also debate on the revolution's economic effects.

The effect of loyalist emigration

By 1783 some 80,000 loyalists had left their homes and gone into exile in Britain, Canada, Nova Scotia or the West Indies. Historians once thought that this exodus had levelling effects, providing new men with land and opportunities. However, it is now accepted that loyalists came from all social classes; they were not simply the elite. The American Revolution was not, in historian Esmond Wright's phrase (1995), one of 'Nobs versus Mobs'. Thus, American society was not decapitated by the loyalists' departure. In so far as there was now more room at the top, it was quickly occupied, not by the poor but by the already well-off. During the war, state governments confiscated huge amounts of land from loyalists. The imperatives of war finance made it essential to sell the land quickly. Consequently, confiscated land was usually sold as a unit and at prices which ordinary men could not afford. Great patriot landowning families, who could obtain credit, were able to expand their estates substantially.

A more egalitarian society?

Some historians are convinced that the American Revolution profoundly changed society, resulting in more equality:

- After 1776 most Americans opposed hereditary privilege in all its forms, from monarchy down. Two states forbade the creation of titles of nobility. Many states prohibited hereditary office holding.
- New men, of lower social status, now sat in state legislatures. These men challenged the social and political supremacy of the old elite. They believed that they were entitled to share in the direction of a nation they were helping to create and demanded that their interests be considered even if they conflicted with those of the rich. The outcome was a significant realignment of relations between the elites and their social inferiors, with the latter showing less deference towards their 'betters'.
- Many ordinary Americans became officers in both the Continental army and militia units as a result of merit, not status.
- Some of the outward marks of social deference disappeared. Republican simplicity decreed less ceremony in the law courts. Judges no longer wore wigs and scarlet robes in the English fashion.
- The acquisition of territory west of the Appalachians created opportunities for landless Americans to acquire farms.
- Some states abolished slavery (see page 122).
- Arguably, women gained more equality (see page 123).
- Indentured servants almost disappeared as a result of the war. Many gained freedom through their military service while immigration traffic in contract labour ceased during the war.

However, it may be that the war did not profoundly disturb the social fabric:

- Virtually all American leaders accepted that class distinctions were natural and inevitable. They made no attempt to redistribute wealth or to promote social equality.
- Social classes did not change in significant ways. Except for its loyalist component, the old colonial aristocracy survived the war intact.
- In most states, the general pattern of land holding remained unchanged.
- Indentured service had been declining before the war.
- The war had a limited effect on slavery and the status of women (see page 124).
- America had been, and remained, a land of self-sufficient farmers.

The impact of the war on slavery

Prior to 1775 most white colonists had taken slavery for granted as part of the natural order of society. However, the Revolution represented a fundamental challenge to the institution of slavery:

- At the heart of the revolution was the belief in human liberty.
- It was difficult to reconcile the Declaration of Independence's assertion that 'all men are created equal' with the fact that one in six Americans was slave.

SOURCE C

What seems to be the nature of the slaves' work in Source C?

Slaves at work in the late eighteenth century.

Slavery during the war

Some slaves saw the war as an opportunity to secure their freedom. In pursuing that objective, black males were willing to align with whichever side offered them the best chance for success. For most, Britain seemed to offer the best hope. One of Washington's first acts as commander of the Continental army was to ban all black people from service – a move endorsed by the Continental Congress in November 1775. That same month, Lord Dunmore promised freedom to any Virginian slave who fled a rebel owner to serve the British. Accordingly, it made sense for Virginian slaves to become loyalists.

SOURCE D

The 1790 census (showing the number of slaves).*

State	Free white	All other free persons	Slaves	Total
Vermont	85,268	255	16	85,539
New Hampshire	141,097	630	158	141,885
Maine	96,002	538	None	96,540
Massachusetts	373,324	5,463	None	378,787
Rhode Island	64,470	3,407	948	68,825
Connecticut	232,374	2,808	2,764	237,946
New York	314,142	4,654	21,324	340,120
New Jersey	169,954	2,762	11,423	184,139
Pennsylvania	424,099	6,537	3,737	434,373
Delaware	46,310	3,899	8,887	59,096
Maryland	208,649	8,043	103,036	319,728
Virginia	442,117	12,866	292,627	747,610
Kentucky	61,133	114	12,430	73,677
North Carolina	288,204	4,975	100,572	393,751
South Carolina	140,178	1,801	107,094	249,073
Georgia	52,886	398	29,264	82,548
Total	3,140,205	59,150	694,280	3,893,635

* Data excerpted from the US Census Bureau (1978), *First Census of the United States* (Baltimore).

> According to Source D, which four states probably had a) most and b) least interest in the preservation of slavery?

Before undertaking the southern campaign in 1779, General Clinton issued a proclamation in which he declared that any slaves captured in service to the rebels would be sold, but that those who deserted the rebels and served Britain would receive 'full security to follow within these lines, any occupation which [they] shall think proper'. Although not an explicit promise of freedom, southern slaves interpreted it as such. Thousands – perhaps one in six of the South's slaves – fled to the British lines. The runaways were generally welcomed by the British, who employed them as labourers and servants (but rarely as soldiers).

At the end of the war, Britain transported some 20,000 black loyalists out of America:

- Most were resettled in the West Indies.
- Others, who had taken up arms, were absorbed into the British army.
- Some 3000 were given land (and freedom) in Nova Scotia.

Some slaves did fight for American independence. By tradition, New Englanders allowed slaves to serve in the militia in times of crisis. Thus, despite the Continental army ban, a few black people served in northern militias. By 1777

Washington and Congress bowed to chronic manpower shortages and accepted black people in the Continental army's ranks. Enlisted slaves expected to receive their freedom in exchange for their service.

Northern opposition to slavery

Even before the war, some white Americans, particularly Quakers, had begun to denounce slavery. In 1771 the Massachusetts assembly banned the slave trade with Africa. Rhode Island and Connecticut followed suit in 1774. As the revolutionary crisis heightened awareness of ideological principles, so the anti-slavery movement gathered strength in every northern state.

The task of abolishing slavery in the North was relatively simple since there were relatively few slaves: only three per cent of New England's population and six per cent of the middle states' populations were slaves. Vermont banned slavery in its 1777 constitution. In 1780 Pennsylvania adopted a law requiring gradual emancipation of slaves when they became adults. In 1784 Connecticut and Rhode Island passed similar measures. Between 1781 and 1783 Massachusetts courts ended slavery in the state by a series of decisions in response to suits brought by slaves who sought their freedom based on the state's 1780 constitution, which declared all men free. New Hampshire courts followed Massachusetts' example. However, in New York and New Jersey, opposition was sufficiently strong to delay the passage of gradual emancipation laws until 1799 and 1804, respectively. Even then the process of emancipation took decades to work itself out, and slavery was not officially abolished in New York until 1827 and in New Jersey until 1846.

The situation in the South

Nearly ninety per cent of slaves lived in the southern states. Most southern whites were determined to maintain slavery, which they saw as an instrument for increasing production and keeping black people 'in their place'. Anti-slavery agitation had little impact in most southern states. Nevertheless, a few southerners acknowledged that slavery was a moral evil. The most significant change to the slave system in the South after 1783 was the liberalisation of the **manumission laws**. Some planters, motivated by revolutionary ideology, took advantage of these laws to free their slaves. (Many simply used the legislation to free their children who had been born to slave women.) After 1783 there was a dramatic increase in the number of free black people, particularly in Maryland and Virginia: between 1782 and 1810 the number of free black people in Virginia rose from 2000 to 30,000. However, in Georgia and the Carolinas far fewer slaves were freed.

In addition to liberalising manumission, Virginia (1778) and Maryland (1783) banned participation in the trans-Atlantic slave trade. However, these actions were motivated more by economic interest than by humane considerations or revolutionary concern for liberty. By closing the African slave trade, Virginian and Maryland planters hoped to maintain the value of their slaves.

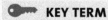 **KEY TERM**

Manumission laws Laws that allowed owners to free their slaves.

Once cotton became a profitable crop in the 1790s, the demand for slaves massively increased. From 1790 to 1807 more slaves were imported into North America than during any other similar period in colonial times.

Free black people

In 1790 there were some 60,000 free black people in the USA. Most white northerners held similar racist attitudes to those of white southerners. Consequently, free black people, North and South, suffered from discrimination and segregation. Economically they had the most menial jobs. But the free black community, by its very presence, was a challenge to the slave system. In the face of white intolerance, ex-slaves worked hard to construct their own cultural life, forming their own churches and voluntary organisations.

Conclusion

The war did something to weaken slavery. Most slaves who had fought against Britain were given their freedom at the end of their army service. All the New England states, realising that slavery seemed incompatible with revolutionary ideology, acted to free their slaves. After 1783 slavery no longer went unchallenged or unquestioned.

But arguably the Revolutionary generation was remarkable for its failure to take more action against slavery:

- The overwhelming majority of slaves remained slaves.
- Abolition in parts of the North was so gradual as to allow slaveholders to sell their slaves in the South if they so wished.
- The framers of the Constitution in 1787 were unwilling to take any meaningful action against slavery for fear of destroying the Union (see page 146).

The impact of the war on the status of women

Women of all races, regions and classes endured hardship during the war. Some were made homeless. Some were raped. Many lost loved ones. However, for some women, the war presented opportunities to exercise greater control over their lives. As many as 20,000 women served with the military forces in an ancillary capacity: as cooks, laundresses and prostitutes. Moreover, women replaced absent husbands as temporary heads of households. Some historians insist that the war greatly affected women's lives:

- Mary Beth Norton (1980) claims that women moved from submission into a world over which they had some control. Women, she believes, were no longer content to be 'good wives' and ignorant of the larger world. Instead, they read newspapers, discussed politics and ensured that their daughters had the best education possible.
- Historian Harry Ward (1999) claims that ordinary American families became less patriarchal. Just as the colonies had repudiated royal paternalism, Americans came to believe that the family should be founded on mutual trust and respect, without a domineering head.

However, it is easier and less speculative to claim that the revolution produced no significant changes or benefits for American women. They were still expected to confine themselves to the traditional domestic sphere: homemaking, childrearing, feeding and clothing their families. They were not allowed to vote or hold public office. Nowhere was there any significant improvement in their legal status. Most women remained in a subordinate position within a patriarchal social order.

The impact of the war on Native Americans

The war had disastrous consequences for Native Americans. According to historian Edward Countryman (1985), the transformation of power relations between white people and Native Americans in the trans-Appalachian west was among the most radical changes wrought by the war. After Britain's defeat, most Native American tribes had little option but to sue for peace. In 1784 the USA concluded treaties at Fort Stanwix (New York) and Hopewell (South Carolina) in which it won concessions of land from the Iroquois, Choctaws, Chickasaws and Cherokees. The new republic had little sympathy for Native Americans. As well as losing huge amounts of land, the Native Americans were largely excluded from the rights and privileges of citizenship.

Some tribes in the northwest – the Delawares, Shawnees, Miamis, Chippewas, Ottawas and Potawatomis – continued to resist. Covertly armed by Britain, they proved a serious obstacle to American settlement.

The economic impact of the war

The economic effects of the war were generally – but not totally – negative.

Negative effects

- Those areas that experienced significant military operations suffered. Property was destroyed or stolen by troops from both sides.
- Large numbers of American merchant ships were seized by the Royal Navy.
- American trade was devastated by the British blockade and by the fact that America was no longer part of the British mercantilist system. Tobacco production, for example, was reduced to a third of the pre-war levels.
- The New England fishing industry was temporarily destroyed.
- Hyper-inflation, the result of a shortage of goods and the printing of vast quantities of paper money, damaged day-to-day economic activity.
- Military requisitioning of wagons had a disruptive effect on internal transport.
- The plantation economies of the southern states were disrupted by the flight of slaves seeking British protection.

Positive effects

- Freed from the constraints of the Navigation Acts, Americans could export directly to European markets.

- Privateering was a risky but potentially very profitable operation for some towns and some individuals. American privateers captured British vessels worth about £18 million.
- The sharp reduction in imports of manufactured goods from Britain had a stimulating effect on the American iron, textile, paper, pottery and shoe-making industries.
- Military demands boosted domestic production of uniforms, munitions and guns.
- Farmers outside the immediate war zones profited from selling food to the various armies.
- British-held areas, especially New York city, boomed during the war.
- Some traders, for example, Robert Morris, who won contracts for military supplies, made huge profits.

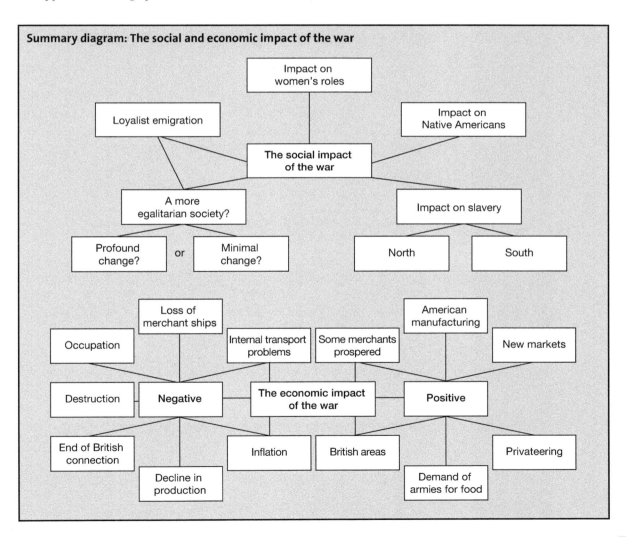

Summary diagram: The social and economic impact of the war

Key debate

▶ *How revolutionary was the American Revolution?*

During the congressional debate over independence, John Adams wrote, 'We are in the very midst of a Revolution, the most complete, unexpected and remarkable of any in the history of nations.' But historians continue to debate just how revolutionary the American Revolution was. In fact, there is little agreement about what the revolution actually was:

- Was it simply the decision of the thirteen colonies to declare independence?
- Did it arise from the strains of war?
- Did its significance lie in the replacement of monarchy by a republican government?
- Did it take place in Americans' mentality and ideology or in the real world of social and political relationships?
- Was it an enormous transformation that bound together many separate changes?

Historians do not even agree about how long the revolution lasted. Did it start in 1763, 1765 or 1775? When did it end? In 1781 with Britain's surrender at Yorktown? In 1783 with the Treaty of Paris? In 1787 with the drawing up of the Constitution? In 1788–9 with the inauguration of the Constitution? Or even later?

Non-revolutionary?

EXTRACT I

From Maldwyn A. Jones, *The Limits of Liberty: American History 1607–1992*, Oxford University Press, 1995, p. 58.

It [the American Revolution] had none of the cataclysmic quality associated, say, with what happened in France in 1789 or in Russia in 1917. It was limited, decorous, even prosaic, with little social upheaval or class conflict, no radical reorganization of government or the economy, no challenge to existing religious beliefs, no bloodthirsty mobs, no carnivals of pillage, no descent into anarchy or dictatorship, no reign of terror … . One might be forgiven for concluding, as Burke did at the time, that there was no real revolution in America, but simply a successful war of independence which ended British rule but otherwise left things pretty much as they had been.

Arguably, the revolution hardly deserves its name. The events which led to the creation of the USA can be seen as merely the culmination of political, economic and social trends at work in the thirteen colonies long before independence. The Americans in 1775 were struggling for political independence, not for social revolution. American republicanism was not synonymous with egalitarianism and the USA did not immediately become a democratic society. The new states looked very similar to the old colonies in government terms. Rich supporters of independence retained much of their power. Many white men were still excluded from participation in politics. Women and black people scarcely benefited from the revolution politically or socially. The conservative elite who created the revolution remained in control of what they created. Thus, it is possible to conclude that the American Revolution was simply a successful war of independence which ended British rule but otherwise left things pretty much as they had been.

In social and economic terms, the America of the mid-1780s was not far removed from that of 1760. Most Americans continued to work on the land. Only three per cent of the population lived in the six towns of more than 8000 people (Philadelphia, New York, Boston, Charleston, Baltimore and Salem). Philadelphia, with 40,000 people, remained the largest city. There was little by way of manufacturing industry.

Revolutionary?

EXTRACT 2

From Edward Countryman, *The American Revolution*, Penguin, 1991, p. 244.

The year 1776 saw the collapse of virtually all old political relations. It inaugurated a search – energetic, frantic and hopeful – for new relations to take their place. The search was necessary because people who had once been content to stand to the side now insisted on coming to the centre. People began to say that a private was as good as a colonel, a baker as good as a merchant, a ploughman as good as a landlord and that was no small change. Some began to think and say the same about blacks and women and that was considerably more.

Assess both extracts. Which provides the more convincing interpretation?

A case can be made for there being a 'real' revolution. Historian Colin Bonwick insists that 'there can be no doubt that the United States which entered the nineteenth century was very different in many, if not all, respects from the colonial America from which it emerged'. John Adams observed that the real revolution was over before a shot was fired, for its essence lay in the changes of heart and mind that turned Britons who lived overseas into Americans who lived in their own country. By 1776 Americans, who had initially resisted British impositions by citing their rights as 'Englishmen', were speaking of the natural rights of men everywhere and were emphatically denying they were Englishmen.

The revolution also – eventually – produced a federal union out of thirteen distinct colonial communities. The new nation was based on a body of ideas which differed from – indeed consciously repudiated – those of the Old World. Those ideas not only affected contemporary beliefs and attitudes but influenced succeeding generations of Americans. Many Americans, for example, were struck by the inconsistency of claiming freedom for themselves while keeping others in bondage.

Participation in the pre-war protest movement against Britain led to an increase in political consciousness among Americans who were previously marginalised within the political process. The experience of war led ordinary Americans to demand and win a greater voice in the new governments which were formed during and after the conflict. Those governments derived their authority from the people. Although total democracy was not established, the revolution had a profoundly democratising effect. The previously dominant elites were obliged to admit their social inferiors to a share of political power. Moreover, the ideals and history of the revolution gave the quest for equality of black people, women and poor whites a legitimacy it had not previously enjoyed.

Nor were the results of the revolution confined to America. As the first war for national independence in modern times to result in the rupture of an imperial connection, it was to serve as an inspiration to other colonial peoples. 'It is impossible indeed,' thought Esmond Wright, 'to find limits to the consequences for the world that have followed from the events that took place on the narrow Atlantic seaboard in the years from 1763 to 1783.'

Chapter summary

The debate as to whether the American Revolution was actually a revolution looks set to continue. Politically, the American colonies cut their ties with Britain and established republican state governments based on the idea of popular sovereignty. New men now participated in politics but the 'old' elite – or that part which had supported independence – continued to wield considerable power. Strangely, there was no element of direct popular election with regard to the national government, the Articles of Confederation. It is hard to claim that the War of Independence led to a social revolution. The structure of society remained much the same. While the war may have had an egalitarian effect, it had only a limited impact on the institution of slavery and on the status of women. The economic effects of the war were certainly not revolutionary.

Refresher questions

Use these questions to remind yourself of the key material covered in this chapter.

1 How much of a political revolution occurred in the thirteen states?

2 What were the main features of the new constitutions?

3 How strong was the Articles of Confederation?

4 What was the social impact of the war?

5 What effect did the war have on slavery?

6 Did the status of women change as a result of the war?

7 What were the main economic effects of the war?

8 How revolutionary was the American Revolution?

Question practice

ESSAY QUESTIONS

1 How important were the political changes introduced when the colonies became states?

2 Assess the social and economic consequences of the American Revolution.

3 To what extent did the Articles of Confederation provide effective national government?

4 'Loyalist emigration from 1775 caused permanent changes in America.' Assess the validity of this view.

INTERPRETATION QUESTION

1 Read the interpretation and then answer the question that follows: 'The American Revolution was marked by liberative currents, class conflicts, and egalitarian urges.' (Richard B. Morris, *The American Revolution Reconsidered*, Harper Torchbooks, 1967.) Evaluate the strengths and limitations of this interpretation, making reference to other interpretations that you have studied.

SOURCE ANALYSIS QUESTION

1 With reference to Sources 1, 2 and 3, and your understanding of the historical context, assess the value of these sources to a historian studying slavery in the decade after the Declaration of Independence.

SOURCE 1

Cato, an African American, pleads for the abolition of slavery in Pennsylvania, 1781.

I am a poor negro, who with myself and children have had the good fortune to get my freedom, by means of an act of assembly passed on the first of March 1780, and should now with my family be as happy a set of people as any on the face of the earth; but I am told the assembly are going to pass a law to send us all back to our masters ... This would be the cruellest act that ever a set of worthy good gentlemen could be guilty of. To make a law to hang us all, would be merciful, when compared with this law ... I have read the act which made me free, and I always read it with joy – and I always dwell with particular pleasure on the following words, spoken by the assembly in the top of the said law: 'We esteem it a particular blessing granted to us, that we are enabled this day to add one more step to universal civilisation, by removing as much as possible the sorrows of those, who have lived in undeserved bondage, and from which, by the assumed authority of the kings of Great Britain, no effectual legal relief could be obtained'. See it was the king of Great Britain that kept us in slavery before. – Now surely, after saying so, it cannot be possible for them to make slaves of us again – nobody, but the king of England can do it – and I sincerely pray, that he may never have it in his power.

SOURCE 2

Hector St John Crevecoeur describes slavery in the South in 1782.

The inhabitants [of Charleston] are the gayest in America; it is ... always filled with the richest planters in the province, who resort hither in quest of health and pleasure ... . An European at his first arrival must be greatly surprised when he sees the elegance of their houses, their sumptuous furniture, as well as the magnificence of their tables; can he imagine himself in a country, the establishment of which is so recent? …

While all is joy, festivity, and happiness in Charleston, would you imagine the scenes of misery overspread in the country. Their ears, by habit, are become deaf, their hearts are hardened; they neither see, hear, nor feel for, the woes of their poor slaves, from whose painful labours all their wealth proceeds. Here the horrors of slavery, the hardship of incessant toils, are unseen; and no one thinks with compassion of those showers of sweat and of tears which from the bodies of Africans daily drop, and moisten the ground they till. The cracks of the whip, urging these miserable beings to excessive labour, are too far distant from the gay capital to be heard … O Nature, where art thou? – Are not these blacks thy children as well as we?

SOURCE 3

Slaveholders in Virginia argue against the abolition of slavery in 1784–5.

When the British parliament usurped a right to dispose of our Property without our consent we dissolved the Union with our parent country and established a … government of our own. We risked our lives and waded through seas of blood … we understand a very subtle and daring attempt is made to dispossess us of a very important part of our Property … TO WREST US FROM OUR SLAVES by an act of legislature for general emancipation.

It is unsupported by Scripture. For we find in the Old Testament slavery was permitted by the Deity himself … . It is also exceedingly impolitic. For it involves in it, and is productive of want, poverty, distress and ruin to FREE citizens, neglect, famine and death to the black infant … The horrors of all rapes, murders and outrages which a vast multitude of unprincipled unpropertied, revengeful and remorseless Banditti [bandits] are capable of perpetrating … sure and final ruin to this now flourishing free and happy country.

We solemnly adjure and humbly pray that you will discountenance and utterly reject every motion and proposal for emancipating our slaves.

CHAPTER 6

The American Constitution

The central issue facing the USA after 1783 was the growth of a national union. While the War of Independence had a powerfully nationalising effect, the Articles of Confederation provided only weak national government. In 1787 a group of men (the Founding Fathers) met at Philadelphia to draw up a new Constitution: a Constitution that remains to this day. This chapter will examine the following themes:

★ The political situation 1781–7

★ Demand for stronger national government

★ The Philadelphia Convention

★ The Constitution

★ The ratification of the Constitution

The key debate on *page 158* of this chapter asks the question: Did the Founding Fathers 'ride to the rescue of the American Revolution'?

Key dates

1785	Land Ordinance	1787	May–Sept.	The Northwest Ordinance
1786	The Annapolis meeting			Meeting of the Philadelphia Convention
1786–7	Shays' Rebellion	1788		Constitution ratified

1 The political situation 1781–7

▶ *How well did the Confederation deal with the problems of the 1780s?*

The USA was governed by the terms of the Articles of Confederation from 1781 until 1789. It faced numerous problems. Its perceived failure to deal with these problems was to have major consequences.

Weak national government

During the eight years the Confederation was in operation, the USA had only the semblance of a national government and at times not even that. Charles

Thomson, secretary of Congress, complained that 'a government without a visible head must appear a strange phenomenon to European politicians and will I fear lead them to form no very favourable opinion of our stability, wisdom or Union'. Congress, in which each of the thirteen states had one vote, had some of the qualities of a national government, but it was in session only intermittently and had no fixed abode. Withdrawing from Philadelphia in 1783 to escape angry soldiers demanding back pay, it moved successively to Princeton, Annapolis and Trenton before settling in New York in 1785. Attendance at sessions was light.

Once the Articles came into full effect in 1781, three executive departments were set up: foreign affairs, finance and war. The three departments functioned with varying degrees of success. Their main problem was that the Confederation government had no coercive power over states or individuals within the states. Moreover, once independence was achieved, the states attached less importance to unity and became absorbed in their own affairs. They exercised rights they had specifically relinquished and responded belatedly or not at all to Congressional requisitions. Most ambitious politicians preferred to serve within their states rather than in Congress. Most decisions affecting the lives of Americans were made at state level, not by Congress.

The West

The Treaty of Paris (see page 101) gave America control over a huge area south of the Great Lakes and east of the Mississippi. The 1780s witnessed a flood of pioneers into the trans-Appalachian region. By 1790 the population of Kentucky had risen to 73,677 and Tennessee's reached 35,691. A coherent policy on western land distribution and territorial government was essential. American politicians, fearing that the new western territories might declare independence from the USA, realised the need for systems that would bind the western communities to the old seaboard states. As early as 1779, Congress had resolved that the West would eventually be organised into new states, to be admitted to the Union as equals.

The 1785 Land Ordinance

The 1785 Land Ordinance outlined a surveying system for the sale of northwest land. Government surveyors would first divide land into six-square-mile (15 km^2) townships. Each township was then divided into sections of one square mile (640 acres; 259 hectares). Four sections in every township were to be set aside as bounty land for ex-soldiers and one for the maintenance of schools. The rest of the land was to be sold at auction in 640-acre lots at not less than a dollar an acre. This provided a relatively quick and certain means of setting out lines, thus reducing the potential for disputes among land purchasers.

The 1787 Northwest Ordinance

The Northwest Ordinance prescribed a set of procedures for organising and admitting to statehood new territories. It provided that during the initial phase

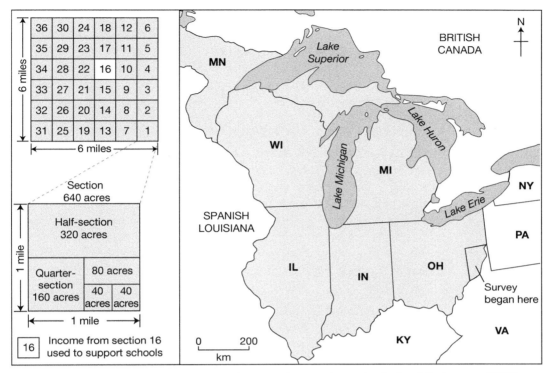

Figure 6.1 Surveying the northwest 1785–7. Sections of a township under the Land Ordinance of 1785.

of settlement a territory would not be self-governing but would have a governor and judges appointed by Congress. When the territory had 5000 adult male inhabitants, it could elect a legislature with limited powers. It could also elect non-voting representatives to Congress. Finally, when its population reached 60,000, it could form a constitutional convention and apply to Congress for admission as a state on equal terms with existing states.

Foreign policy

The weakness of the Confederation was demonstrated in foreign affairs, particularly with regard to Britain and Spain.

Relations with Britain

Despite promising in the Treaty of Paris to evacuate American soil 'with all convenient speed', Britain still clung to a number of frontier posts south of the Great Lakes in order to safeguard the fur trade and maintain contact with the northwest Native Americans. As a pretext for continuing to occupy the frontier posts, Britain cited the American failure to observe those clauses of the peace treaty concerning the repayment of pre-war debts and the restoration of loyalist property. Although Congress had urged the states to place no obstacle in the way of British merchants recovering pre-war debts, the states had ignored the advice. They had likewise turned a deaf ear when Congress 'earnestly recommended' the return of confiscated loyalist property. A government so obviously weak at home could scarcely command respect abroad. Thus, when John Adams was sent to London in 1785 with instructions to demand the evacuation of the frontier posts and seek a commercial treaty, he was rebuffed. Britain claimed there was little point negotiating with the federal government since Congress was unable to compel the states to implement its treaties.

Relations with Spain

Spain, like Britain, opposed American westward expansion. Strengthening its ties with southwest Native Americans, Spain schemed to create a Native American buffer state to protect its own possessions. Spanish control of the Mississippi River – the strategic key to the entire area south of the Great Lakes – was a huge advantage. In 1784 Spain seized Natchez on the eastern bank of the Mississippi and closed the river to American navigation, thus depriving western settlers of a vital outlet for their goods. Some American leaders feared that settlers in Tennessee and Kentucky might transfer their allegiance to Spain.

In 1786 Foreign Secretary John Jay initiated a treaty with Spain whereby in return for limited access to Spanish markets, the USA agreed to give up for 25 years the right to use the Mississippi. However, with five southern states opposed, the treaty could not be ratified by the required nine. Westerners were furious at Jay's willingness to sacrifice their interests to those of eastern

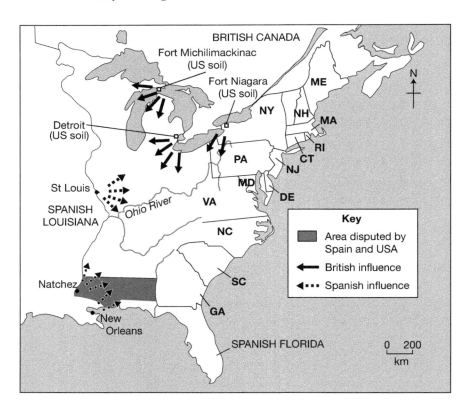

Figure 6.2 Disputed territorial claims: Spain, Britain and the USA.

merchants. Some talked of setting up an independent western republic, under Spanish protection.

Economic problems

The American economy suffered considerably from the destruction of war and the separation from Britain (see page 124). Economic difficulties were compounded by imports of large quantities of British goods after 1783. Between 1784 and 1786 the USA imported from Britain goods worth over £7.5 million, selling less than one-third of that in return. American debt and the flow of **specie** outside the country to meet the trade deficit helped to depress trade and to slow economic recovery. To many at the time, the economic situation looked bleak: prices were depressed, private and public indebtedness was heavy, and trade regulation was chaotic.

The fact that control over commercial matters was retained by individual states weakened the USA's bargaining position. When Massachusetts tried to prevent the dumping of British goods in America, New Hampshire eagerly absorbed them. After 1784 there were increasing demands that the Articles should be amended to allow Congress to regulate both international and American trade. The proposal aroused considerable intersectional rivalry since each area had different interests. The mercantile and industrial interests of New England and the middle states wanted a protective tariff against British competition. In contrast, southern states, as exporters of agricultural products, preferred free trade. However, all was not doom and gloom on the economic front:

- The US population grew from 2.75 million in 1780 to 4 million in 1790.
- The prospect of western expansion was a great bonus.
- There were new markets available in Europe and the Far East.
- Many of the British trading restrictions could be evaded, especially by Americans trading in the West Indies.
- Barriers to interstate trade were dismantled during the 1780s.

Financial problems

The Confederation inherited serious financial problems, including a nearly worthless currency (see page 124) and huge debts. In 1783 the national debt stood at a massive $41 million: the foreign debt – to the Netherlands, France and Spain – comprised nearly $8 million and domestic debt the remaining $33 million. The debt was one problem. Paying the interest on it – about $2.4 million per year – was another.

The fact that the government was unable to pay its soldiers was particularly serious. Over the winter of 1782–3 army officers met at Newburgh, New York, and pressed hard for back pay and half-pay pensions. The possibility of a coup was defused only by George Washington's use of his considerable authority. But, in June 1783, dissatisfied soldiers surrounded the Pennsylvania State House, forcing a humiliated Congress to abandon Philadelphia.

KEY TERM

Specie Gold or coined money.

Robert Morris

Bankruptcy was averted only through the dexterity and wealth of Robert Morris, appointed superintendent of finance in 1781. A Philadelphia merchant who had made huge profits during the war, Morris used some of his own money to meet expenses. Keen to develop a sound financial programme, Morris believed it was essential to create a strong national government with powers to do the following:

- set up a national bank
- secure control of the public debt (instead of parcelling it out to the individual states)
- levy import duties.

The Bank of America

Morris hoped that his privately financed Bank of North America would become a national bank (like the Bank of England), servicing the outstanding loan obligations of the government and affording it credit. His hopes soon collapsed. The government severed connection with the bank in 1784.

The public debt

Morris wanted the national government to secure control of the public debt so that it would then have to be given taxing power to raise money. He was to be disappointed. The states preferred to assume responsibility for servicing directly that part of the debt held by their own citizens instead of responding to Congressional requisitions for the same purpose. Thus, by 1786 the states had incorporated a large part of the national debt into their state debts. This was a blow to the status of Congress and meant that it had little justification for seeking enlarged financial powers.

Import duties

Morris supported efforts to amend the Articles so as to give Congress authority to levy a five per cent duty on all imports. The necessary unanimity, however, proved unattainable.

The situation by 1787

A disappointed Morris resigned in 1784. The financial situation remained serious. By 1786 Congress had levied over $15 million in requisitions from states but only $2.5 million had been paid. The states which failed to meet their obligations could not be compelled to do so. The only major source of independent income for the national government was from the sale of western lands, but this developed slowly, yielding only $760,000 before 1788. Consequently, there was still an immense overseas debt and Congress lacked sufficient revenue to pay the interest, let alone the principal.

Creditors versus debtors

The state governments faced similar financial problems. In an effort to reduce their war debts, the states imposed heavy taxes. Those in debt were particularly hard hit by the financial situation. By 1783, the paper continental currency had ceased to circulate and some states stopped issuing paper currency. Lacking the specie necessary to pay their taxes and meet their debts, debtors demanded an increase in paper money. Most creditors opposed this, contending that paper money would simply lead to inflation and economic instability.

By the late 1780s it seemed the debtors were winning political control. In 1787 seven states were issuing paper money. Rhode Island not only made paper money legal tender but compelled creditors to accept it. The value of Rhode Island paper money depreciated sharply and creditors fled the state to avoid having to accept it. For conservatives, Rhode Island was a horrifying symbol – an attack on private property. The experiment in republican government seemed to have given way to anarchy.

Social tensions

The financial problems of the 1780s resulted in social tensions and disturbances. In September 1786 the governor of New Hampshire called out 2000 militiamen to disperse several hundred farmers threatening the legislative assembly after it reneged on a promise to issue paper money. There were similar disturbances by angry farmers in Vermont, Pennsylvania, New York and Virginia.

Shays' Rebellion

The most serious trouble arose in Massachusetts. The Massachusetts state legislature, controlled by men from the commercially oriented eastern counties, rejected the demand for paper money and insisted that taxes be paid in scarce specie. Many farmers, unable to pay the taxes, lost their land; some were imprisoned. By the summer of 1786 western Massachusetts was seething with discontent. When the state legislature adjourned without heeding the farmers' demands for paper money, riotous mobs roamed from place to place, preventing the courts from hearing debt cases.

By the autumn the malcontents had found a leader in Daniel Shays, a bankrupt farmer who had been a captain in the war. In January 1787 Shays led several hundred armed men toward the federal arsenal at Springfield. The rebels were easily dispersed by 1000 militiamen led by Benjamin Lincoln and by February the insurgency had been put down. Nevertheless, Shays' Rebellion alarmed conservatives throughout the country. Again it seemed that anarchy loomed. In conjunction with the paper money issue in Rhode Island, Shays' Rebellion gave a crucial impetus to the movement to strengthen the national government's power.

Why was Washington so concerned about Shays' Rebellion?

SOURCE A

George Washington to Benjamin Lincoln, 1787, quoted in Joseph J. Ellis, *His Excellency George Washington*, Faber & Faber, 2004, p. 172.

The picture which you have drawn, & the accounts which are published, of the commotions … in the Eastern States, are equally to be lamented and deprecated. They exhibit a melancholy proof of what our trans-Atlantic foes have predicted; and of another thing perhaps, which is still more to be regretted, and is yet more unaccountable; that mankind left to themselves are unfit for their own government. I am mortified beyond expression whenever I view the clouds which have spread over the brightest morn that ever dawned upon my Country.

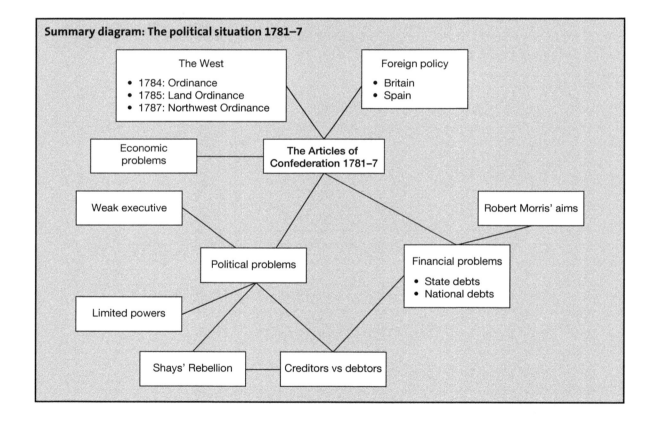

Summary diagram: The political situation 1781–7

The West
- 1784: Ordinance
- 1785: Land Ordinance
- 1787: Northwest Ordinance

Foreign policy
- Britain
- Spain

Economic problems

The Articles of Confederation 1781–7

Weak executive

Robert Morris' aims

Political problems

Financial problems
- State debts
- National debts

Limited powers

Shays' Rebellion

Creditors vs debtors

2 Demand for stronger national government

▶ *Why did many Americans wish to strengthen the national government?*

By the mid-1780s many Americans (like Washington) were dissatisfied with the Articles of Confederation:

- Many were appalled by the powerlessness of the national government in foreign affairs and commercial matters.
- Creditors wanted a national government that would put a stop to what they saw as the irresponsible legislation of states that issued paper money.
- There was a general fear that the Articles' weakness would result in disintegration and chaos.

American nationalism

While most Americans were primarily loyal to their states, there were distinct signs of growing national consciousness. The struggle for independence had increased the sense of being American. The war, besides mixing men from different states in the Continental army, had produced a crop of national heroes (for example, George Washington) and national shrines (for example, Bunker Hill). National symbols appeared in profusion:

- Congress adopted the Stars and Stripes as the national flag in 1777.
- The bald eagle took its place on the Great Seal of the USA in 1782. (Benjamin Franklin, thinking the eagle a bird of bad moral character, would have preferred the turkey as America's emblem.)

Nationalism inspired the political leaders who led the movement for constitutional reform. Men like Alexander Hamilton, James Madison and George Washington wanted a unified republic that would command the respect of the world – a truly national society in which local and state attachments were subordinate to American loyalties.

Conservative nationalism

Most of the nationalist leaders were men of substance. Some were horrified by the type of new men who now occupied so many seats in the state legislatures and even more horrified by what they considered to be the low standards of the consequent legislation. Nevertheless, the nationalists were far from crude reactionaries – as some historians have suggested. They supported much of the revolution's central ideology, including popular sovereignty. But they lacked faith in the ability of the common people to exercise careful judgement and abhorred what they saw as democratic excesses in state government. They favoured the creation of a strong national government whose power was vested in the hands of the wealthy and well educated.

Support for the Articles of Confederation

The view that the USA was falling apart was not shared by all Americans. Some believed that the Confederation was working reasonably well:

- Americans had gained independence under the Articles.
- State governments were more responsive to people's demands than ever before.
- A stronger central government might replicate the British government.
- Most Americans equated a high degree of local self-government with the preservation and enjoyment of personal liberty.
- Most state governments muddled along competently enough by eighteenth-century standards.

While many Americans accepted the need for some reform of the Articles in order to strengthen the national government, most thought that the individual states should retain considerable powers.

Interstate disharmony

Although state boundary disputes, jurisdictional rivalry and western issues were mostly resolved by 1787, sectional animosity remained a problem particularly in relation to the levying of tariff duties. From 1782 to 1785 all the states except New Jersey placed duties on imports, affecting both interstate and foreign commerce, for the purpose of raising revenue. By 1786 the New England states, New York and Pennsylvania had increased import duties to make them protective. States put their own interests first: some imposed higher tariffs than others against foreign – especially British – goods.

Virginia and Maryland agreement

The immediate origins of the Constitutional Convention lay in a dispute between Virginia and Maryland over navigation on the Potomac River. Such interstate disagreements were not uncommon during the 1780s and the national government was largely powerless to act as an arbitrator in them. In 1784 James Madison proposed that commissioners from the two states meet to negotiate a solution. Meeting at Washington's Mount Vernon estate in 1785, the delegates quickly reached agreement on the navigational issues. They then went beyond their brief and suggested that their states should co-operate on financial and customs policy, and recommended that an appeal should be made to Pennsylvania to join in future deliberations on matters of common interest. Madison, who had served in Congress and witnessed its ineffectiveness at first hand, saw an opportunity in interstate co-operation for constitutional reform. In the wake of the Mount Vernon meeting, he proposed a resolution to the Virginia assembly for a national convention to discuss commercial regulations.

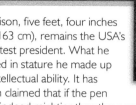

James Madison

1751	Born in Virginia
1776–9	Served on Virginia's state legislature
1780–3	Served in Congress (its youngest member)
1786–8	Served in Congress
1787	Played a crucial role in drafting the Constitution
1787–8	Contributed (with Alexander Hamilton and John Jay) to the *Federalist Papers* (see page 156)
1789–97	Served four terms in the House of Representatives
1801–9	Served as Jefferson's secretary of state
1809–17	President of the USA
1836	Died

Madison, five feet, four inches tall (163 cm), remains the USA's shortest president. What he lacked in stature he made up in intellectual ability. It has been claimed that if the pen was indeed mightier than the sword then the American capital might well have been called 'Madison, DC' rather than Washington, DC. Madison had a long political career. His role at the Philadelphia Convention in 1787 was crucially important. Many regarded Madison as the 'Father of the Constitution'. His fellow delegates rated him highly. William Pierce, a member of the Philadelphia Convention, wrote in 1787: 'every Person seems to acknowledge his greatness … he always comes forward as the best informed Man of any point in debate'. Historians have praised his work at the Convention in similar terms. Historian Clinton Rossiter (1956) regarded his performance as 'a combination of learning, experience, purpose, and imagination that not even Adams or Jefferson could have equalled'.

SOURCE B

George Washington, writing to John Jay on 1 August 1786, quoted in S.E. Morison, editor, *Sources and Documents Illustrating the American Revolution 1764–1788 and the Formation of the Federal Constitution*, Oxford University Press, 1972, p. 216.

Your sentiments, that our affairs are drawing rapidly to a crisis, accord with my own. What the event will be, is also beyond the reach of my foresight. We have errors to correct. We have probably had too good an opinion of human nature in forming our Confederation. Experience has taught us, that men will not adopt and carry into execution measures the best calculated for their own good, without the intervention of a coercive power. I do not conceive we can exist long as a nation without having lodged somewhere a power, which will pervade the whole Union in as energetic a manner as the authority of the State governments extends over the several States.

To be fearful of investing Congress, constituted as that body is, with ample authorities for national purposes, appears to me to be the very climax of popular absurdity and madness.

> What, according to Source B, did Washington want to happen?

The Annapolis meeting

Madison's resolution had effect. In September 1786 twelve men, representing five states (New York, New Jersey, Pennsylvania, Delaware and Virginia) met in Annapolis to discuss commercial problems. A meeting of such an unrepresentative body could not propose reforms, commercial or otherwise, to the nation with any credibility. But the Annapolis meeting brought together men from different states who agreed on the need for constitutional change. Most, like Madison, realised that it was impractical to hope for amendments to the Articles by Congressional action. The Articles could be amended only with the unanimous agreement of all thirteen states – an unlikely event. The meeting thus proposed that a convention of all the states should be held in Philadelphia in 1787 to redraft the Articles of Confederation.

Congress was not at first enthusiastic, but after the shock of Shays' Rebellion it called on the states in February 1787 to send delegates to a convention in Philadelphia in May 'for the sole and express purpose of revising the Articles of Confederation'.

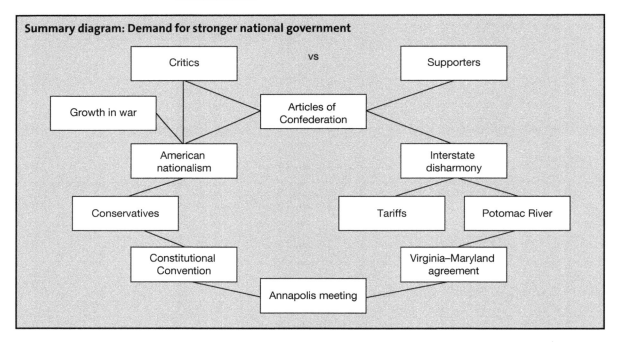

Summary diagram: Demand for stronger national government

③ The Philadelphia Convention

▶ *What were the aims of the Founding Fathers and how successful were they in realising them?*

Thomas Jefferson described the Constitutional Convention that met in Philadelphia in May 1787 as 'an assembly of demi-gods'. Many historians have agreed. The Convention delegates (the Founding Fathers) have been seen as intervening at a crucial moment to save the revolution. Their masterpiece – the Constitution – is seen as relaunching the republic and laying the foundation of all that followed. However, there are scholars who view the Convention as a meeting of self-interested elitists who sought – successfully – to undermine the revolution's democratic principles.

The influence of James Madison

The Constitutional Convention was scheduled to begin its deliberations on 17 May 1787. But when the appointed day arrived, the delegations of only Pennsylvania (the hosts) and Virginia were present. Poor weather and poorer roads delayed the arrival of the other delegates. The Virginian delegation contained two key men: George Washington and James Madison. The presence of Washington, the most famous and respected American, would lend credibility to the Convention. But Madison was to have a greater impact at the Convention than Washington. Determined to strengthen the national government, he came to Philadelphia with a clear idea of what he thought needed to be done. In a lengthy memorandum, 'The Vices of the Political System of the United States', written in April 1787, Madison outlined the need for a powerful national republic with a centralised government. He circulated the memorandum among the delegates. By the time the Convention opened, he was ready to dominate its opening stages.

The delegates

By 25 May, 29 delegates from seven states had arrived and the Convention, meeting in the Philadelphia State House, began its work. Over the next few weeks a further 26 delegates straggled in. Every state was represented except Rhode Island, which declined to participate. The 55 delegates brought a broad range of experience in public service:

- All had held public office.
- Forty-two had served in Continental or Confederation Congresses.
- Three were present and four were former governors of their states.
- Twenty had helped to draft their states' constitutions.

The Convention was a remarkably talented group – even if it lacked the abilities of Thomas Jefferson and John Adams, who were then serving as envoys to France and Britain, respectively. With an average age of 42 the delegates were relatively youthful: 30 had fought in the War of Independence; 34 had legal training; 26 were college graduates; nineteen were slave owners. The fact that there were no black people, Native Americans, women or 'poor' was hardly surprising. By law and custom, these groups were outside the recognised polity in eighteenth-century America. Small farmers, artisans and westerners, who had won an increased voice in politics since the 1760s, could not afford the time to attend.

The principles of the Founding Fathers

There was no great ideological rift between the delegates. Virtually all agreed on the necessity to strengthen the central government. But few wished to centralise power to the extent of abolishing state sovereignty altogether. There was general agreement on the need for balanced government. No one branch of government – executive, legislative or judiciary – should be allowed to monopolise power. Most delegates distrusted democracy, believing the government should be in the hands of men with experience and standing. Nevertheless, virtually all accepted that the people must have a voice in government.

Despite a large measure of agreement on principles, there was no unanimity on details:

- While the delegates accepted the need to extend the federal government's power, they disagreed as to how powerful it should be.
- They disagreed about whether the legislature should consist of one house or two.
- Representation was the most contentious issue. Should all the states be equally represented in the federal legislature, irrespective of size, as was the case under the Articles? Or should representation be based on population, an arrangement which would give Virginia, with 747,000 people (of whom 300,000 were slaves), twelve times as many representatives as Delaware, which had only 60,000?

The key men

Apart from James Madison (who spoke 161 times), other key delegates were the Pennsylvanians James Wilson (who spoke 168 times) and Gouverneur Morris (who spoke 163 times). Wilson, who had been born in Scotland, was a successful lawyer. Gouverneur Morris, with a crippled arm and only one leg, was far

SOURCE C

? How useful is this source as evidence for the historian?

A painting of the Founding Fathers at the Philadelphia Convention that is currently in the House of Representatives It was painted many years after the event.

more vocal than his namesake Robert Morris (ex-superintendent of finance), another of the Pennsylvania delegates. The presence of George Washington and Benjamin Franklin was crucial. Although they rarely spoke, the mere fact that they were present gave the Convention prestige. Washington was unanimously chosen to preside over proceedings.

Economic motivation

In the early twentieth century historian Charles Beard depicted the Founding Fathers as reactionaries whose aim was to destroy popular rule. According to Beard, they had considerable investments in **certificates of public credit**. They thus stood to gain economically if a strong central government was established. (The market value of the public credit certificates was then likely to rise.) Beard argued that the debate over the Constitution centred on rivalry between the holders of personal property (money, public securities, manufacturing, trade and shipping) and real property (land). By the mid-twentieth century Beard's thesis had been generally accepted. However, historians Robert Brown and Forrest McDonald (1965) showed that Beard's research was sloppy. In reality, the Founding Fathers' capital was largely invested in land, not public securities. Perversely, some of the largest holders of certificates of public credit voted against the proposed Constitution.

No one doubts that the Founding Fathers represented the richest groups in the USA or that they were determined to construct a system that would ensure that their wealth was protected. However, economic interest did not determine the framing of the Constitution. The Founding Fathers were men of ideas and principles. Most believed that the survival of liberty was at stake. Most were also convinced that excessive democracy was as dangerous as the monarchical tyranny from which Americans had just freed themselves.

The Virginia Plan

The Convention's first step was to consider a draft constitution, introduced on 29 May. Largely the work of Madison, the Virginia Plan provided for a national legislature of two houses, in each of which representation was to be proportionate to the population. The first house of the legislature would be directly elected by the voters. The members of the second house would be elected from among those of the first. The legislature was to have wide powers: it was to elect both the executive and the judiciary. The states would be reduced to little more than administrative units since the central government was to have the power to veto acts of state legislatures. Given that the Virginia Plan was the first proposal put before the Convention, it set the agenda. For the rest of the summer the delegates debated and amended it. Although significant changes were made to it, it remained at the centre of the Convention's deliberations.

 **KEY TERM**

Certificates of public credit Printed statements recognising that the holders were owed money by the government.

The New Jersey Plan

Although congenial to the larger states, the Virginia Plan was bitterly opposed by the smaller ones (whose representatives would easily be outvoted by those of the larger states), as well as by delegates who objected to the amount of power which would be concentrated in Congress.

In an effort to preserve the interests of the smaller states, William Patterson (from New Jersey) presented an alternative scheme (on 15 June) providing for a single legislative chamber, in which each state would have one vote. The New Jersey Plan envisaged merely the amendment of the Articles. Although Congress was to be given enlarged powers, including authority to tax and to regulate commerce, state sovereignty would be largely preserved. Although the Convention rejected the New Jersey Plan on 19 June (by seven states to three), the issue of representation in the national legislature went unresolved. For the next fortnight the issue was debated with increasing acrimony. A Grand Committee, with one delegate from each state, was finally appointed (2 July) to work out a compromise.

The Great Compromise

The Grand Committee's report is referred to as the Great Compromise. All the states, whatever their population, would have equal representation in the upper house (the Senate). However, the lower house (the House of Representatives) would have proportional representation; larger states would have more representatives. Representation and direct taxation would be distributed according to the results of regular censuses. The Great Compromise was accepted on 16 July, after a fierce debate.

North vs South

The issue of slavery representation divided northern and southern delegates. Southern states wanted slaves to be included in the population total when allotting Congressional seats, but left out in determining liability for direct taxation. Northern states, by contrast, wanted slaves excluded from representation, since they were neither citizens nor voters, but included for tax purposes since they were a form of property. The Convention eventually accepted the formula whereby a slave was counted as three-fifths of a person for the purposes of both representation and direct taxation.

Continued debate

The Convention adjourned on 26 July. A Committee of Detail was charged with producing a draft constitution, making sense of the various recommendations and amendments to the Virginia Plan made over the previous two months. The committee worked for ten days, fleshing out many of the Constitution's features.

SOURCE D

Washington's copy of the final draft of the first page of the Constitution, 17 September 1787.

Why were the first three words of the document in Source D so important?

Debate on the report of the Committee of Detail occupied five weeks from 6 August to 10 September. During this debate, slavery re-emerged as an issue. The proposed Constitution prohibited Congress from banning the slave trade. Some northern delegates wanted to end the trade. Delegates from the Carolinas and Georgia, by contrast, insisted that their states would never accept the new Constitution if the right to import slaves was impaired. However, it was not simply a case of North versus South. Some northern delegates, more concerned with securing a constitutional settlement than they were with slavery, argued against interfering with the trade. Moreover, some southern delegates wanted to abolish the slave trade, as a shortage of slaves was likely to increase the value of their – excess – slaves. In late August it was agreed that Congress would not have the authority to abolish the slave trade until 1808.

The Constitution agreed

On 8 September a Committee of Style was appointed to tidy the draft Constitution into its final form. Most of the work was done by Gouverneur Morris. On 17 September, 39 of the remaining 42 delegates approved the Constitution.

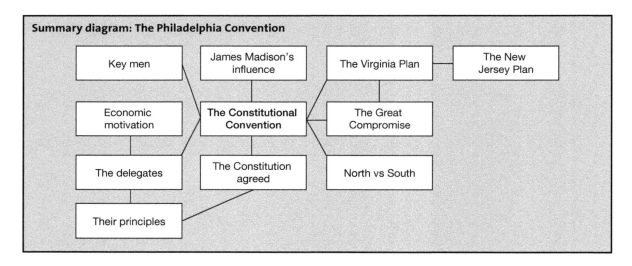

Summary diagram: The Philadelphia Convention

4 The Constitution

▶ *To what extent was the Constitution a bundle of compromises?*

The Constitution proposed a division of authority between executive, legislature and judiciary. The separation of powers (see page 112) was intended to permit the other two branches of government to check the third should it exceed its authority. Each was to be independent of the other, so that members of the executive branch were denied membership of the legislature.

The powers of the federal and state governments

Like the government of the Confederation, the federal government was authorised to maintain an army and navy, mint and borrow money, and make treaties with foreign powers. It was also given some additional powers, notably to levy taxes and to regulate commerce. Moreover, Congress was authorised to 'make all laws which shall be necessary and proper' for executing its powers. The Constitution and all laws and treaties made under it were declared to be the supreme law of the land, superior to any state law.

The states were specifically forbidden from waging war, engaging in diplomacy, coining money or laying duties on imports. Moreover, they were deprived of some powers they had hitherto exercised; in particular, they were not to issue money or make treaties. Nevertheless, the states retained considerable powers:

- The slavery issue was left to the states.
- Each state could determine its own suffrage in elections to the House of Representatives.
- The states could regulate their own intrastate or internal commerce.
- States continued to exercise jurisdiction in many important areas of civil and criminal law.

The federal executive

The federal government's executive authority would be exercised by a president:

- He was to be commander-in-chief of the army and navy.
- He could make important appointments, for example, judges and diplomats (with Senate approval).
- He could conclude treaties (in association with the Senate).
- His signature was required to make acts of Congress law.
- He could veto acts of Congress (but the veto could be overridden by a two-thirds vote of both houses).
- He could be removed from office only on **impeachment** for and conviction of 'high crimes and misdemeanours'.

Presidents were to be elected for a four-year term by an Electoral College, to which each state was to send the same number of electors as it had Congressmen.

The federal legislature

Congress was to comprise the House of Representatives and the Senate:

- The House was elected directly by voters for a two-year term.
- The Senate comprised two senators from each state and was elected by state legislatures. Senators were to serve for six years, one-third elected every two years.

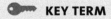 **KEY TERM**

Impeachment Charging a public official with an offence committed while in office.

- Congress had the power to raise money, make laws, declare war, ratify treaties (two-thirds of the Senate had to agree), impeach and (with a two-thirds majority) to override the president's veto.

The federal judiciary

Although much was left vague, it was agreed that there should be:

- an independent national judiciary
- a Supreme Court – appointed by the president with the approval of the Senate.

Amending the Constitution

Amendment of the Constitution required a two-thirds majority in each house of Congress and a 75 per cent majority of the states.

Criticisms of the Constitution

A common view in 1787 – and one shared by some historians since – was that the Constitution represented a conservative backlash, curbing a growing democracy:

- The Electoral College would stand between the people and the president.
- Senators would owe their office to the state governments, not direct election.
- Six-year terms would give senators considerable immunity from popular pressure.
- The House of Representatives would represent constituencies as large as 30,000 people, half the population of Delaware.
- The two-year term of its deputies was twice as long as the terms of most state assemblymen.

All these arrangements served to insulate the people's servants from the people.

Historians have attacked the Constitution for its defence of slavery (not changed until 1865). They have also criticised some of the Constitution's ineffective provisions. The Electoral College has, on occasions, prevented the candidate with the most popular votes from becoming president. The need for a two-thirds approval of the Senate for treaties has handicapped the formulation and execution of foreign policy. It is also possible to claim that the system of checks and balances ensured that nothing much would ever get done. Historian Richard Hofstadter (1948) described the Constitution as 'a harmonious system of mutual frustration'.

Much of the Constitution was couched in general terms and many issues were left open. It was unclear, for example, whether the Constitution should be strictly construed or more loosely interpreted. More importantly, the boundaries between federal and state power were far from sharply defined. Nor was it clear whether states could leave the new 'club' they had joined. These questions would provide the staple of constitutional debate for decades to come and were not to be settled until the Civil War (1861–5), a war which cost 620,000 lives.

In practice, the Constitution did not operate as envisaged. The Founding Fathers' model was parliamentary, not presidential, yet presidents – eventually – came to dominate the political scene. Although the Founding Fathers envisaged that both houses of Congress would be equal, within three generations the Senate, with its longer tenure, had become more powerful than the House. The latent power of the Supreme Court would also have surprised the Founding Fathers. Since the chief justiceship of John Marshall (1801–35), the Court has pronounced regularly on the validity of Acts of Congress. American political and social advance has thus often been determined more by the pronouncements of judges than by acts of Congress. The Constitution has 4000 words; the Supreme Court's interpretations of it number over 450 volumes.

Praise for the Constitution

George Washington gave his (considerable) seal of approval to the Constitution: 'I am fully persuaded it is the best that can be obtained at the present moment under such diversity of ideas that prevail.' Benjamin Franklin said much the same: 'I confess that there are several parts of the Constitution which I do not at present approve but I am not sure I shall never approve them … I consent, Sir, to the Constitution because I expect no better and because I am not sure that it is not the best.

Nineteenth-century British Prime Minister William Gladstone went further, describing the Constitution as 'the most wonderful work ever struck off at a given time by the brain and purpose of men'. Arguably, the Founding Fathers' work was a masterpiece of ingenuity, informed by democratic ideals, which helped to save the American Revolution. The Constitution accepted that the sole fount of legitimate political authority was the people: its preamble opened with the phrase 'We the People of the United States'. All the officers of government were to be the agents of the people. The Founding Fathers remained true to the representative principle at almost every point.

The strong national government was still made as weak and as divided as could safely be managed. Fearing tyranny in any form, the Founding Fathers were hostile to the concentration of authority in any one man or institution. They deliberately created a system of checks and balances:

- executive versus legislative versus judiciary
- House of Representatives versus Senate
- popular election versus indirect election
- federal government versus state governments.

At the same time, the Constitution reconciled the interests of:

- large and small states
- slave and free states
- federal government and state governments
- patrician leadership and popular sovereignty.

The fact that the Constitution was a sketch, not a blueprint, was a strength. Much was left for the future to clarify. The Constitution has thus been a living document, constantly reinterpreted and made responsive to new social and political needs. The Founding Fathers' good sense and political realism are evident from the fact that the Constitution has stood the test of time. With relatively few amendments (27 since 1787), a document devised 200 years ago for a small, rural republic is still the fundamental law for the world's greatest power.

SOURCE D

Gouverneur Morris writing to George Washington, 30 October 1787, quoted in S.E. Morison, editor, *Sources and Documents Illustrating the American Revolution 1764–1788 and the Formation of the Federal Constitution*, Oxford University Press, 1972, p. 305.

The States eastward of New York appear to be almost unanimous in favour of the new Constitution. … Their preachers are advocates for the adoption, and this circumstance coinciding with the steady support of the property and other abilities of the country makes the current set strongly, and I trust irresistibly that way. Jersey is so near unanimity in her favourite opinion, that we may count with certainty on something more than votes should the state of affairs hereafter require the application of pointed arguments. New York, hemmed in between the warm friends of the Constitution, could not easily (unless supported by powerful States) make any important struggle, even tho her citizens were unanimous, which is by no means the case. Parties there are nearly balanced. If the assent or dissent of the New York Legislature were to decide on the fate of America, there would still be a chance tho I believe the force of Government would preponderate and effect a rejection.

Why, according to Source D, was Gouverneur Morris optimistic about the future of the Constitution?

Summary diagram: The Constitution

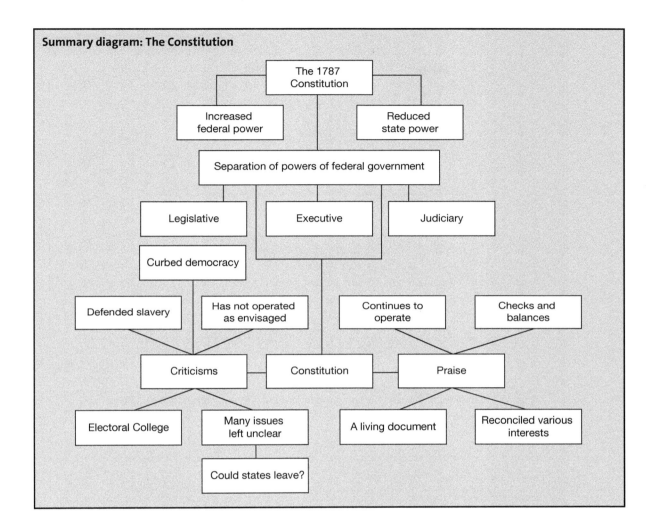

5

The ratification of the Constitution

▶ *How and why was the Constitution ratified?*

When the Convention finished its work, it transmitted a copy of the proposed Constitution to Congress. On 28 September Congress unanimously voted to submit the document to the states for ratification according to the method outlined by the Convention:

- The new document would become operative when ratified by nine – not all thirteen – states.

- The Constitution would be submitted to specially elected state conventions, not the state legislatures. Such a procedure would confer on the Constitution a status which the constitutions of all but one of the states (Massachusetts) lacked, namely that of being based directly on popular consent. It would also side-step probable opposition from the state legislatures.

Federalists vs Anti-Federalists

The process of ratification provoked fierce debate everywhere. The contest was marked by discourse of the very highest order concerning the meaning of republicanism. It was also marked by cynical political tactics.

The supporters of the Constitution won an important first point when they appropriated the word 'Federalist' to describe themselves. (Given that their intentions were for increased central and less state power, the word was probably a more apt title for their opponents.) The fact that the Federalist opponents were dubbed 'Anti-Federalists' immediately cast them in a negative role. In the struggle over ratification, the Federalists were most strongly supported by men of property and position: planters, merchants and lawyers. Many of their Anti-Federalist opponents were small farmers, especially from the more isolated regions. But opinion did not divide neatly along lines of class or economic interest. Some rich men were Anti-Federalist. Many poor men, like the labourers and artisans of the cities, were Federalist. Every major town had a Federalist majority. According to historian Jackson Turner Main, the crucial socio-economic factor in distinguishing Federalists from Anti-Federalists was their level of engagement in commercial trading (see page 113).

Anti-Federalists were aware of the problems of the 1780s but believed that the proposed cure was far worse than the disease. Anti-Federalist leaders made a number of criticisms of the Constitution:

- They claimed that the Convention had exceeded its mandate in proposing a whole new framework of government to replace the Articles.
- They feared that a powerful national government would destroy the sovereignty of the states.
- They argued that state legislatures were more representative of the people than the new Congress was likely to be.
- Many deplored the absence of a Bill of Rights – a list of legally protected liberties such as were appended to many of the state constitutions.

Anti-Federalists also raised a host of specific objections, all reflecting a suspicion of centralised power. Federalists addressed the criticisms in hundreds of pamphlets and newspaper articles. Their greatest fear was that rejection of the Constitution would lead to collapse of the Union, anarchy, interstate warfare and ultimately the loss of American independence.

Federalist advantages

It seems likely that at the outset a majority of American voters were opposed to the Constitution. Nevertheless, the Federalists had several advantages:

- They offered a specific set of solutions to the pressing problems that faced the nation. While most Anti-Federalists conceded that some political reform was necessary, they had no alternative to offer the public.
- Federalist support was strong in the towns. Local people thus often gave delegates to state ratifying conventions (which met in towns) the impression that most people favoured the Constitution.
- The support of the two most famous men in America – Washington and Franklin – added lustre to the Federalist cause.
- Anti-Federalist support, scattered across isolated small farms, was difficult to organise.
- The vast majority of newspapers were Federalist owned and inclined. Only five major newspapers, out of approximately 100, consistently opposed the Constitution.

Where their support was strong the Federalists moved rapidly to secure approval, and where it was weak they delayed, allowing themselves time to campaign effectively. The crucial states were the largest ones: Pennsylvania, Massachusetts, Virginia and New York.

Delaware, New Jersey, Georgia, Pennsylvania and Connecticut

In some states, ratification was easily achieved. Of the first five states to ratify, Delaware (7 December 1787), New Jersey (18 December 1787) and Georgia (2 January 1788) did so unanimously. Pennsylvania (12 December 1787) approved by a comfortable majority (46–23) and Connecticut (9 January 1788) by an overwhelming one (128–40). Thus, the Federalist cause built up an early momentum.

Massachusetts

In Massachusetts there was a long and spirited contest. The stance of revolutionary stalwarts Samuel Adams and John Hancock was vital. Both had Anti-Federalist leanings. Federalist pressure was put on both men when the Massachusetts Convention met in January 1788. Pro-Constitution demonstrations by Boston artisans persuaded Adams to support the Constitution. Hancock changed sides when Federalists suggested that he might become vice president if the Constitution were ratified. Eventually, moderate Anti-Federalists were won over by a Federalist pledge to consider appending a Bill of Rights to the Constitution. Thus, in February 1788 the Federalists triumphed by 187 votes to 168.

Maryland, South Carolina and New Hampshire

Maryland (63–11) voted in favour of the Constitution in April 1778 and South Carolina (149–73) fell into line in May. In June New Hampshire (57–47) became the ninth state to ratify. Remote and non-commercial, the state had been initially strongly Anti-Federalist. When its people elected their convention, they instructed it not to ratify. When it met over the winter, it followed instructions. But rather than reject the Constitution, it adjourned until June without taking a final decision. That gave the Federalists an opportunity. Raising the issue in town meetings, they put pressure on delegates to change their minds. The New Hampshire Convention finally ratified on an afternoon when Federalists had got a number of their opponents drunk enough at lunch to miss the session. Technically, the Constitution could now go into force. However, without Virginia and New York it could hardly succeed.

Virginia

In Virginia, the opposing forces were evenly balanced. Patrick Henry's eloquent attacks on the Constitution, ably seconded by Richard Henry Lee's *Letters from a Federal Farmer*, had a profound effect. However, Washington's support for the Constitution and Madison's reasoned advocacy, along with his promise to work for a Bill of Rights, was crucial. On 26 June 1788 the Virginia Convention ratified by 89 votes to 79. In essence, in Virginia, the division was between the commercial Tidewater counties (Federalist) and the less well-developed regions (Anti-Federalist).

New York

When the New York Convention met, Alexander Hamilton thought that four-sevenths of the people of the state were against the Constitution. He, Madison and Jay, using the joint pseudonym Publius, wrote a series of 85 articles for the New York press, urging the adoption of the Constitution. These essays, subsequently published as *The Federalist Papers*, came to be regarded as a classic of American political thought. However, it appears that they did not have a significant influence on contemporary opinion. More important in softening the intransigence of the New York Anti-Federalists was Virginia's decision to ratify and the fear, cultivated by Hamilton, that New York city would secede if the state

SOURCE F

Look at Source F. What point was the paper trying to make?

The *Massachusetts Centinel* 1788.

Table 6.1 Ratification of the Constitution

	State	Date	Vote in Convention	Rank in population	1790 population
1	Delaware	7 Dec 1787	Unanimous	13	59,096
2	Pennsylvania	12 Dec 1787	46–23	3	433,611
3	New Jersey	18 Dec 1787	Unanimous	9	184,139
4	Georgia	2 Jan 1788	Unanimous	11	82,548
5	Connecticut	9 Jan 1788	128–40	8	237,655
6	Massachusetts (incl. Maine)	7 Feb 1788	187–168	2	475,199
7	Maryland	28 Apr 1788	63–11	6	319,728
8	South Carolina	23 May 1788	149–73	7	249,073
9	New Hampshire	21 June 1788	57–47	10	141,899
10	Virginia	26 June 1788	89–79	1	747,610
11	New York	26 July 1788	30–27	5	340,241
12	North Carolina	21 Nov 1789	195–77	4	395,005
13	Rhode Island	29 May 1790	34–32	12	69,112

rejected the Constitution. On 26 July 1788 New York's Convention approved ratification by 30 votes to 27.

Conclusion

Although North Carolina and Rhode Island still stood aloof, the new Constitution could now begin to function. As its last act, the Confederation Congress ordered national elections for January 1789.

Only about a quarter of adult white males voted for the state ratifying conventions. The rest were either disfranchised or uninterested. Those most likely to stay away were farmers in isolated communities. Federalist success was the result of several factors: better organisation, big names, newspapers and Anti-Federalist divisions. The Bill of Rights concession was vital (see page 156).

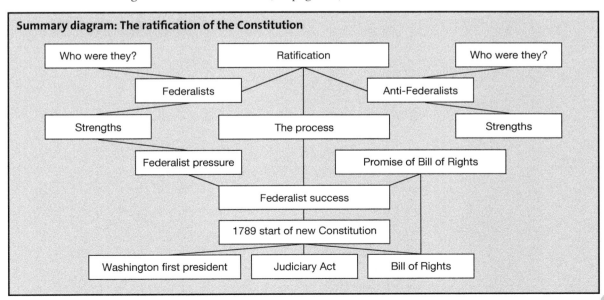

Summary diagram: The ratification of the Constitution

Key debate

▶ *Did the Founding Fathers 'ride to the rescue of the American Revolution'?*

In the late nineteenth century, historian John Fiske called the years from 1781 to 1787 the 'Critical Period'. He depicted the Articles of Confederation as a weak government, unable to deal with a host of political, social and economic problems. Fiske claimed that the USA was close to disintegration until the Founding Fathers rode to the rescue, drafting a more effective Constitution. For much of the nineteenth century, the Constitution was seen as the fitting end of the revolution. Most nineteenth-century historians believed that the revolution had been a struggle to secure American liberty: the Constitution was seen as liberty's greatest protection. However, twentieth-century historians like Charles Beard, Merrill Jensen and Jackson Turner Main had a different view.

EXTRACT 1

Charles Beard (1935), quoted in E. Latham, editor, *The Declaration of Independence and the Constitution*, D.C. Heath, 1962, p. 71.

A survey of the economic interests of the members of the Convention presents certain conclusions. A majority of the members were lawyers by profession.

Most of the members came from towns, on or near the coast … Not one member represented in his immediate personal economic interests the small farming or mechanic classes. The overwhelming majority of members, at least five-sixths, were immediately, directly, and personally interested in the outcome of their labours at Philadelphia, and were to a greater or less extent economic beneficiaries from the adoption of the Constitution.

EXTRACT 2

Merrill Jensen (1950), quoted in R.D. Brown, editor, *Major Problems in the Era of the American Revolution 1760–1791*, D.C. Heath, 1992, p. 406.

The [Confederation] government was 'weak', of that there is no question. It had been created that way deliberately because its founders had feared, and during the 1780s they continued to fear, a strong central government as they had feared and fought against the British government before 1776.

Yet one cannot understand the history of the Confederation government if one talks of it only in terms of efforts to remedy its obvious weaknesses. To do so is to miss much of the point of the political history of the American Revolution. One misses also the fact that the central government struggled mightily with problems left by the war and with still others arising from the birth of a new nation. Furthermore, one loses sight of the fact that the government of the Confederation achieved a measure of success, at least according to the likes of those who believed in the kind of central government provided by the Articles of Confederation.

Beard, Jensen and Main saw the years from 1781 to 1787 as years of achievement, not failure. Rather than defenders of the revolution, they claimed that the Founding Fathers were upper-class conservatives, conspiring to protect their own economic interests. Thus, by the mid-twentieth century the Constitution was depicted as a reactionary document: the product not so much of democracy but of devious men who feared it.

It is now generally accepted that the 1780s was not a period of unrelieved gloom. Nor is it fair to blame all the troubles of the period on the weakness of the Articles of Confederation. In some respects the Confederation acquitted itself well (for example, successfully regulating western settlement). The Articles aimed to prevent the central government from infringing the rights of states. Arguably, there was nothing wrong in the USA remaining a loose collection of independent states. Nevertheless, the authority of Congress steadily diminished after 1783. With peace, the states no longer felt the necessity of co-operating with each other or with Congress. Thus, the once-respected institution became increasingly weak. By 1785 American finances were in disarray and the USA was treated with contempt by Britain and Spain.

EXTRACT 3

Hugh Brogan, *Longman's History of the United States of America*, Longman, 1985, pp. 221–2.

The Constitution as it emerged between 1789 and 1791 crowned the American Revolution and provided a safe compass for the future. In theory, it settled all those problems – whether of taxation; of foreign relations; of collective duties and individual rights; of political and legal organisation – which had proved so intractable that they had brought about the downfall of the old British Empire … The political thought on which it was based was realistic, accepting that men were not angels, but that their aspirations were mostly legitimate, and it was the business of the political framework to give them scope. Liberty and law were its two inescapable guiding lights; as understood by the Founding Fathers they have served America pretty well … it seems best to end this section by pointing once more to the astonishing fact that so wise and effective a settlement emerged from thirty years of revolution; and to the equal marvel of its adaptability … No other revolution, worthy of the name, has ended so happily.

Which of the three extracts provides the most convincing interpretation?

American nationalists wanted a stronger central government. The result – the Constitution – has survived the test of time. As have the Founding Fathers. Over the past 60 years historians have put the Founding Fathers back on their pedestal. Stanley Elkins and Eric McKitrick consider them to be the 'Young Men of the Revolution', driven not by self-interest but by youthful energy and the frustrations they had known as Congressmen, diplomats and army officers. John Roche sees them as modern politicians who understood the need for reform and who carefully calculated the best strategy for achieving it. Esmond Wright stresses that the Founding Fathers were patriots, 'men with principles as well as pocketbooks'. If they represented property, they spoke for many constituents for most Americans were property owners. They sought to create a strong government not only, and perhaps not mainly, to curb democracy, but also to preserve the Union and the gains of the revolution.

While the Critical Period may have been less critical than its critics implied, the Articles of Confederation certainly deserves some criticism. The Founding Fathers may not have been 'demi-gods', but they did produce an extraordinary document which ensured that the 'great experiment' in republicanism would endure at a national as well as at state level. In that sense, they came to the rescue of the revolution.

Chapter summary

By the mid-1780s many influential Americans were concerned at the weakness of the Articles of Confederation. Angry at its perceived failings, especially in foreign and financial matters, and fearful of anarchy and disunity, nationalists demanded stronger central government. Congress, concerned by Shays' Rebellion, agreed to set up a Constitutional Convention, the purpose of which was to revise the Articles of Confederation. The Convention delegates, who met at Philadelphia in May 1787, devised a new Constitution. Despite considerable opposition from Anti-Federalists, the Constitution was ratified by eleven states, ensuring that it came into effect in 1789. Historians continue to debate whether the Founding Fathers were devious reactionaries or saviours of the American Revolution.

Refresher questions

Use these questions to remind yourself of the key material covered in this chapter.

1 How well did the Confederation deal with the problems of the 1780s?

2 Why did many Americans wish to strengthen the national government?

3 What were the aims of the Founding Fathers?

4 Why was Madison's role at Philadelphia so crucial?

5 Were the Founding Fathers motivated by economic self-interest?

6 To what extent was the Constitution a bundle of compromises?

7 Why has the Constitution been criticised?

8 Why has the Constitution been praised?

9 How was the Constitution ratified?

10 Did the Founding Fathers ride to the rescue of the American Revolution?

Question practice

ESSAY QUESTIONS

1 'The Articles of Confederation of 1781 were doomed from the start.' Assess the validity of this view.

2 Assess the reasons why some Americans demanded stronger national government in 1786–7.

3 How far did the Founding Fathers achieve their aims?

4 To what extent was the 1787 Constitution a 'bundle of compromises'?

INTERPRETATION QUESTION

1 Read the interpretation and then answer the question that follows: 'The direct, impelling motive [of the Founding Fathers] was the economic advantages which the beneficiaries expected would accrue to themselves from their action.' (Sidney Fine and Gerald S. Brown, editors, *The American Past: Conflicting Interpretations of the Great Issues*, Macmillan, 1963.) Evaluate the strengths and limitations of this interpretation, making reference to other interpretations that you have studied.

SOURCE ANALYSIS QUESTION

1 With reference to Sources 1, 2 and 3, and your understanding of the historical context, assess the value of these sources to a historian studying the ratification of the 1787 Constitution.

SOURCE I

Gouverneur Morris, writing to George Washington in 30 October 1787.

I have observed that your name to the new Constitution has been of infinite service. Indeed I am convinced that if you had not attended the Convention, and the same paper had been handed out to the world, it would have met with a colder reception, with fewer and weaker advocates, and with more and more strenuous opponents. As it is, should the idea prevail that you would not accept of the Presidency, it would prove fatal in many parts. Truth is, that your great and decided superiority leads men willingly to put you in a place which will not add to your personal dignity, nor raise you higher than you already stand; but they would not willingly put any other person in the same situation, because they feel the elevation of others as operating (by comparison) the degradation of themselves. ...

Thus much for the public opinion on these subjects, which must not be neglected in a country where opinion is everything. I will add my conviction that of all men you are the best fitted to fill that office.

SOURCE 2

Patrick Henry of Virginia, speaking to the Virginia Ratifying Convention in 1788.

Have they said, We, the states? Have they made a proposal of a compact between states? If they had, this would be a confederation. It is otherwise most clearly a consolidated government. The question turns, sir, on that poor little thing – the expression. We, the people, instead of the states, of America. I need not take much pains to show that the principles of this system are extremely pernicious, impolitic and dangerous … Here is a resolution as radical as that which separated us from Great Britain. It is radical in this transition; our rights and privileges are endangered, and the sovereignty of the states will be relinquished … The rights of conscience, trial by jury, liberty of the press, all your immunities and franchises, all pretensions to human rights and privileges, are rendered insecure, if not lost, by this change … It is said that eight states have adopted this plan. I declare that if twelve states and a half had adopted it, I would, with manly firmness, and in spite of an erring world, reject it. You are not to inquire how your trade may be increased, nor how you are to become a great and powerful people, but how your liberties can be secured; for liberty ought to be the direct end of your government.

SOURCE 3

James Madison, author of No. 39 of *The Federalist Papers* in 1788.

The first question that offers itself is whether the general form and aspect of the government be strictly republican. It is evident that no other form would be reconcilable with the genius of the people of America; with the fundamental principles of the Revolution; or with that honourable determination which animates every votary of freedom, to rest all our political experiments on the capacity of mankind for self-government. If the plan of the convention, therefore, be found to depart from the republican character, its advocates must abandon it as no longer defensible.

What then, are the distinctive characters of the republican form? … We may define a republic to be … a government which derives all its power directly or indirectly from the great body of the people, and is administered by persons holding their offices during pleasure, for a limited period, or during good behaviour …

On comparing the Constitution planned by the convention with the standard here fixed, we perceive at once that it is, in the most rigid sense, conformable to it. The House of Representatives, like that of one branch at least of all the State legislatures, is elected immediately by the great body of the people. The Senate, like the present Congress, and the Senate of Maryland, derives its appointment indirectly from the people. The President is indirectly derived from the choice of the people according to the example in most of the States.

CHAPTER 7

George Washington and John Adams

The period from 1789 to 1801 was a particularly formative one for the USA. A new federal government, based on the 1787 Constitution, had to be developed. The USA's first president, George Washington, would be crucial in this process. So would his chief men, especially Alexander Hamilton and Thomas Jefferson. Within a short time Hamilton and Jefferson were at odds on a host of issues. Their disagreements and rivalry encouraged the growth of political parties, a situation not envisaged by the Founding Fathers. In 1796, when Washington stood down, John Adams was elected president. This chapter will assess the success of the USA's first two presidents by focusing on:

★ Organising the federal government

★ Hamilton's financial programme

★ Foreign and western affairs

★ The 1796 presidential election

★ The Adams administration 1797–1800

★ The 1800 presidential election

The key debate on *page 191* of this chapter asks the question: How successful was George Washington as president?

Key dates

1789	April	Washington elected president	1794	Nov.	Jay's Treaty with Britain
	Sept.	Judiciary Act	1795		Treaty of San Lorenzo
1791	Feb.	Bank of the United States chartered	1796		John Adams elected president
	Dec.	Bill of Rights added to the Constitution	1797		XYZ affair
1792		Washington re-elected president	1798		Alien and Sedition Acts
1794	June	Whiskey Insurrection	1801		Thomas Jefferson elected president

Organising the federal government

▶ *Why were the actions of Congress and president so important in 1789?*

There was no guarantee that the new Constitution would work successfully. There was not even any certainty about how it would work or indeed exactly how it was meant to work.

The new government

The election of 1789, the first under the new Constitution, gave the Federalists control of the new government. There were large Federalist majorities in both the Senate and the House of Representatives. As the most famous and popular man in the country, George Washington was chosen as president by Electoral College representatives; no one stood against him. John Adams, with 34 votes, the second highest number, became vice president.

The new Congress met on 4 March 1789 in New York city, the temporary seat of the federal government. It could muster only eight senators and thirteen members of the House. A month passed before both chambers gathered a quorum. Meanwhile, Washington left his home at Mount Vernon to be inaugurated president on 30 April. His journey to New York turned into a triumphal procession, confirming the universal confidence he commanded and the hopeful expectancy with which the new constitutional experiment was awaited. Washington was less optimistic. Burdened with dread that so much was expected of him, he declared that he felt like a condemned man going to the place of execution.

Problems facing the new government

Washington's apprehensions were understandable:

- The USA was far from united.
- Rhode Island and North Carolina were still not in the Union.
- The nation had an untried Constitution.
- The new government, burdened with a colossal debt, had almost no revenue or machinery for collecting money.
- No judiciary department existed.
- The USA had no navy and its army consisted of 672 officers and men.
- The USA's western borders were open to Native American attack.
- British and Spanish troops still occupied parts of the national territory.

Nevertheless, the new government entered office with two advantages:

- The worst of the post-war depression was over and the economy was expanding.
- There was widespread support for both the new government and the Constitution. Despite the passion that had characterised the ratification debates, Anti-Federalists accepted the popular verdict and agreed to participate in the new political system in good faith.

The first Congress

Congress set about the work of building on the Constitution's general framework. In assuming this task, it set a number of precedents which permanently influenced American constitutional development. James Madison, working closely with Washington in 1789–90, played a key role in the House of Representatives.

The Judiciary Act

The Constitution had created a federal judiciary but left the detail as to how it should be structured and what its precise responsibilities and relationship with the state courts should be for settlement at another time. The 1789 Judiciary Act established a hierarchical system of federal courts. At the top was the Supreme Court. This was to consist of a chief justice and five associate justices. Beneath it there were to be district courts in each state and three circuit courts of appeal. By creating an entire apparatus, the Judiciary Act ensured that federal laws and rights would be adjudicated uniformly throughout the nation. The act also provided that the Supreme Court should rule on the constitutionality of state court decisions and nullify state laws which violated the federal Constitution.

Washington selected the six members of the Supreme Court (three from the South and three from the North) and named **John Jay** as the first chief justice.

The Bill of Rights

During the ratification debates, there had been much criticism of the lack of specific guarantees of popular rights. In some states, the Federalists had promised to remedy this omission in order to secure ratification. James Madison made the adoption of a Bill of Rights one of the first items of business. The House of Representatives adopted seventeen amendments; the Senate adopted twelve, the states ratified ten.

These ten constitutional amendments, known collectively as the Bill of Rights, went far towards reconciling Anti-Federalists to the Constitution. Nine of the amendments were concerned with the rights of the individual. They guaranteed freedom of religion, of speech, of assembly and of the press, the right to petition and to bear arms, and immunity against arbitrary search and arrest. They also prohibited excessive bail, cruel and unusual punishments and the quartering of

 **KEY FIGURE**

John Jay (1745–1829)
Helped to negotiate peace with Britain in 1782–3, served Congress as secretary for foreign affairs for six years, helped Hamilton and Madison to write the *Federalist Papers*, became the first chief justice of the US Supreme Court and was responsible for a controversial treaty with Britain in 1794.

troops in private houses. The tenth amendment reserved to the states all powers except those specifically delegated to the federal government.

The amendments took effect in December 1791 when Virginia became the final state to ratify them. The adoption of the amendments helped to convince North Carolina (1789) and Rhode Island (1790) to enter the Union.

Raising revenue

Aware that revenue was the government's most critical need, Congress passed two measures:

- There was to be a trade duty of five per cent on most items, 7.5 per cent on certain listed items, and duties as high as 50 per cent on 30 specific items, including steel, nails, hemp, molasses, ships, tobacco, salt, indigo and cloth, to protect American manufacturers from foreign competition.
- The Tonnage Act (1789) stated that American ships should pay a duty of six cents per ton, American-built but foreign-owned ships 30 cents/ton and foreign-built and -owned ships 50 cents/ton.

The importance of Washington

If Congress had an important role in building the new framework of government, so too did George Washington. Washington had earned the right to be trusted with power. In 1783 he had shown no desire to become the military dictator that many had feared. Realising that his actions would set important precedents, he was determined to create a vigorous and effective executive.

Presidential dignity

Washington, aware of the symbolic significance of forms and ceremonies, set out to invest the office of president with an aura of dignity (without appearing to be a monarch):

- Every week Washington held an open-house reception which struck a middle note between courtly formality and republican simplicity.
- Visiting Boston, Washington declined to visit Governor John Hancock until Hancock paid a call on him, thus making the point that a president took precedence over a mere governor.
- The first Congress spent a month discussing a proper title for the president. Vice President John Adams favoured some high-sounding designation like 'His Elective Majesty', 'His Highness the President' or 'His Mightiness'. But Congress settled for the simplicity of 'President of the United States.' In short, he was simply Mr President.

The relationship between president and Congress

Among the questions the Constitution had not answered in detail was that of the relationship between the executive and the legislature. The Constitutional Convention had evidently intended that the Senate should function as the president's advisory council. Thus, the Constitution had provided that the president was to appoint high officials and make treaties 'by and with the advice and consent of the Senate'. But when Washington appeared before the Senate in August 1789 to seek advice about a number of draft Native American treaties, some senators refused to discuss the matter in his presence and the debate became a shouting match over questions of procedure. Washington eventually stormed off in a huff. Since the Senate insisted on its independence, it was clear to him that he would have to look elsewhere for advice.

The federal 'civil service'

Washington inherited only a shadow of a bureaucracy from the Confederation: a foreign office with John Jay and two clerks; a Treasury Board with little or no treasury; a secretary of war with a very small army and no navy. While the Constitution said nothing about government departments, it was clear that new bodies were needed. The state, treasury and war departments were established in the autumn of 1789 along with the offices of attorney general and postmaster general. Washington was determined that the heads of the executive departments should be responsible to him alone. In the end, Congress reluctantly conceded that the president should have the right to appoint and dismiss them without consulting Congress.

Washington's cabinet

Washington selected his department heads on the basis of three criteria: merit, service and geography – aiming to preserve a balance between North and South:

- As secretary to the treasury, Washington chose his wartime aide-de-camp Alexander Hamilton, who in helping to organise the Bank of New York had acquired a knowledge of public finance.
- Thomas Jefferson, minister to France since 1784, became secretary of state.
- General Henry Knox, the secretary of war, continued in the office he had held under the Confederation.
- Edmund Randolph, former governor of Virginia, became attorney general, the government's legal adviser.

At first, it was Washington's practice to consult his officials individually on matters of policy. But very soon he routinely called these men to sit as a group for discussion and advice on matters of policy. The department heads thus evolved into the president's cabinet, an advisory body for which the constitution made no formal provision.

SOURCE A

Why was Washington, in Source A, so pleased by events?

George Washington, writing to Catherine Macaulay Graham on 9 January 1790, quoted in S. Elkins and E. McKitrick, *The Age of Federalism: The Early American Republic 1788–1800*, Oxford University Press, 1993, p. 75.

That the government, though not absolutely perfect, is one of the best in the world, I have little doubt … It was indeed next to a miracle that there should have been so much unanimity in points of such importance, among such a number of citizens so widely scattered, and so different in their habits in many respects as the Americans were. Nor are the growing unanimity and increasing goodwill of the citizens to the government less remarkable than favorable circumstances. So far as we have gone with the new government (and it is completely organized and in operation) we have had greater reason than the most sanguine could expect to be satisfied with its success.

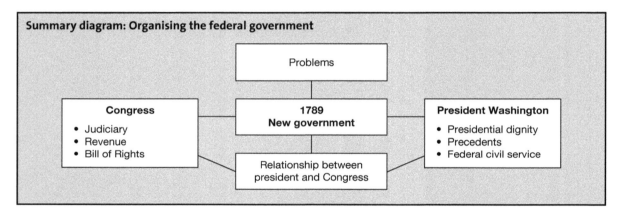

Summary diagram: Organising the federal government

Hamilton's financial programme

▶ *Why did Hamilton's financial measures generate so much hostility?*

Alexander Hamilton soon became the main driving force of the administration for several reasons:

- He was talented and ambitious.
- He was a favourite of Washington.
- Finance was crucially important to the fledgling government.
- Washington believed it was not his function to initiate legislation.
- The secretary of the treasury occupied a special place among the executive heads in that he was required to report (in writing) directly to Congress.

Hamilton's main ideas

Hamilton was essentially a nationalist. He wanted the new nation to be united and strong. He hoped that the states' power would eventually wither away,

Alexander Hamilton

1755	Born in the British West Indies, the illegitimate son of a Scottish father and a French mother
1772	Sent to North America to improve his education
1777	Became one of Washington's aides-de-camp
1780	Married Elizabeth Schuyler, daughter of General Philip Schuyler, a wealthy and prominent New Yorker
1781	Played a major role in the siege of Yorktown
1782–3	Served in Congress
1787	Represented New York in the Philadelphia Convention
1787–8	Published the *Federalist Papers* (see page 156)
1789	Appointed secretary of the treasury
1790–1	Published a series of important financial reports
1795	Resigned as treasury secretary
1804	Died in a duel with his political enemy **Aaron Burr**

Hamilton was a many-sided personality. Charming, articulate, immensely talented and honest (though he had a number of unethical friends), he could also be petty, manipulative, headstrong and combative. Thomas Jefferson was convinced that Hamilton was power hungry (correctly) and corrupt (wrongly). In political and financial matters, Hamilton consistently took the side of greater federal power at the expense of the states. Although not all his plans came to fruition, he played a monumental role in establishing the new republic, including his service as Washington's main adviser and confidant and his shaping of the national financial system. His political thought, which contrasted sharply with that of Jefferson, continued to influence American political discourse for the next two centuries. Some scholars see Hamilton as a forerunner of modern liberal capitalist economics, opposed to the agrarianism advocated by slaveholders like Jefferson and Madison. (Hamilton abhorred slavery.) Hamilton favoured the creation of an essentially British system, with a republican 'monarch' (the president), limited democracy (with government by 'rich and the well-born') and strong institutions (such as the Bank of the United States).

ensuring the federal government's supremacy. Admiring the British system of government, he saw Washington as a sort of constitutional monarch and himself as prime minister. He believed that the federal government must dominate financial policy. Determined to restore national credit, he believed it was essential to bind the moneyed classes to the new government.

In a series of reports, submitted to Congress from January 1790 to December 1791, Hamilton outlined his programme for government finances.

Hamilton's report on public credit

Hamilton's first and most important report was on the issue of public credit (January 1790). Hamilton recommended:

- the funding at face value of the entire domestic and foreign debt incurred by the government of the Confederation and amounting to about $56 million
- federal assumption of the war debts of the states, totalling some $21 million.

Hamilton believed a national debt would be a powerful cement of the Union, enabling it to establish sound finances and ensuring its credit for the future. It would also follow that Congress would have to assert a national taxing power, which would instil respect for the federal government's authority.

 KEY FIGURE

Aaron Burr (1756–1836)

Having served with distinction in the Continental army, Burr became a lawyer and politician in New York, where he was a rival of Hamilton. Burr became vice president in 1801. He is best remembered for his duel with Hamilton (1804) and for his failed attempt to create a separate empire in the western USA in 1805-6.

Opposition to Hamilton

There was virtually no opposition to the repayment of the foreign debt at face value rather than at the depreciated market rate. Such a step was obviously essential to the new government's financial standing. The proposal to do the same for the domestic debt, however, was bitterly attacked, especially by southerners. Nearly all the debt was held by (mostly northern) speculators who had bought bonds cheaply when hard times had forced original creditors to sell. Protesting that the measure would enrich a tiny minority at the public expense, Madison suggested an alternative plan which discriminated between the original holders and subsequent purchasers. Hamilton answered Madison's argument by claiming that it would be impossible to judge who might have benefited from selling bonds and investing the proceeds in more productive ways. Moreover, speculators were entitled to consideration for the risk they had taken and the faith they had shown in the government. Congress accepted Hamilton's proposal.

There was greater opposition, much of it sectional, to Hamilton's state debt assumption scheme. Southern states, except for South Carolina, had provided for the repayment of their debts and objected to paying a share of the large debts owed by northern states, which thus stood to gain most from the assumption plan. Southerners also feared that the assumption would expand federal power at the expense of the states.

Hamilton had hoped that Madison would guide his measure through Congress. However, it would have been political suicide for Madison (a Virginian) to support Hamilton's proposals. Instead, he became Hamilton's leading opponent, persuading Congress in April 1790 to reject the state debt proposal.

Compromise

A series of political bargains with Madison and Jefferson enabled Hamilton to reverse the verdict. In exchange for southern votes for assumption, Madison agreed:

- to make generous allowances to states that had already settled most of their debts
- that the permanent national capital would be in the South, at a site on the Potomac River to be chosen by President Washington.

Congress finally passed the legislation for Hamilton's plan in August 1790.

The second report on public credit

Hamilton's programme resulted in the USA's national debt soaring to over $80 million. No less than 80 per cent of the federal government's annual expenditure was needed to service the debt. More revenue had to be found if the government was to remain solvent.

In December 1790 Hamilton issued a second report on public credit which included a proposal for a tax on distilled spirits to aid in raising revenue to cover the nation's debts. This measure, which established the precedent of a federal **excise tax**, was passed by Congress in March 1791.

KEY TERM

Excise tax A tax on certain home commodities.

Success?

Most historians agree that Hamilton's credit measures were financially successful:

- The value of new government bonds rose sharply.
- The federal government was able to borrow money both at home and abroad.

However, Hamilton's measures had political repercussions. Madison, echoing the views of many Virginian planters, opposed Hamilton's funding schemes, which he saw as threatening the Constitution, especially state powers. In December 1790 the Virginia Assembly protested that it could 'find no clause in the Constitution authorizing Congress to assume the debts of the States!' To Hamilton this was 'the first symptom of a spirit which must either be killed, or will kill the Constitution of the United States'.

SOURCE B

The Virginian governor, writing to George Washington in 1790, quoted in Joseph J. Ellis, *His Excellency George Washington*, Faber & Faber, 2004, p. 205.

In an Agricultural Country like this, to erect and concentrate and perpetuate a large insured interest … must in the course of human events, produce one or other of two evils – the Prostration of Agriculture at the feet of Commerce, or a change in the present form of Federal Government, fatal to the existence of American liberty.

Why, according to Source B, did the governor of Virginia so oppose Hamilton's financial measures?

Report on the national bank

Hamilton now proposed to create a national bank, a revival of Robert Morris's idea (see page 136). Modelled on the Bank of England, the proposed Bank of the United States would have a capital of $10 million, one-fifth to be subscribed by the government, four-fifths by private investors. It would:

- act as a depository for government funds
- facilitate the collection of taxes
- provide a source of capital for loans to stimulate the development of business and commerce
- issue paper money and curb excessive note issue by state banks
- ensure that the bank's stockholders had a vested interest in supporting the federal government.

Opposition

When the bill to charter the bank came before Congress, Madison insisted that the Constitution had not specifically conferred on Congress the power to charter companies; therefore no such power existed. Congress passed the bill despite Madison's opposition. But Washington, disturbed by Madison's arguments, consulted his cabinet on the constitutional question. Jefferson (and Randolph) supported Madison, arguing for a strict interpretation of the Constitution and contending that Congress should be allowed no powers not expressly delegated to it.

In reply, Hamilton advanced the doctrine of 'implied powers'. Although a central bank had not been authorised in so many words, it was the 'necessary and proper' means of exercising such explicitly granted Constitutional powers as the levying of taxes and the regulation of currency and trade.

Washington, although not wholly persuaded by Hamilton's argument, signed the bill into law. He was influenced by the fact that the matter came within the jurisdiction of the treasury secretary. Moreover, by and large he supported Hamilton's measures: the president, while not committing himself in the year-long debates over financial issues, was just as much an economic nationalist as Hamilton.

Success?

The Bank of the United States, with a charter for twenty years, opened for business in Philadelphia in December 1791. Over the next three decades it contributed to the USA's economic development. Its banknotes maintained their value. It also exercised some control over the state banks that mushroomed in the 1790s. However, the Bank, loathed in the South and West, did little for Hamilton's popularity.

The report on manufactures

The last of Hamilton's state papers, the report on manufactures (December 1791), was his most visionary. Determined to encourage manufacturing, the report laid down a comprehensive plan for industrialisation through a system of protective tariffs and government subsidies for new industries and new inventions. Congress was not ready for such bold economic planning. The report was shelved and although Congress passed a new tariff act in 1792, this was for revenue rather than for protection.

The results of Hamilton's financial programme

Hamilton's financial programme was substantially the one that Robert Morris had urged on the Confederation a decade before (see page 136) and one that Hamilton had strongly endorsed at the time. His measures were undoubtedly successful financially. They restored public credit, ensuring that foreign capital flowed into the USA. Productivity increased and prosperity returned.

But far from cementing the Union, as Hamilton had hoped, his measures served to sharpen divisions and to give them political form. Many southerners feared that Hamilton's programme resulted in a threatening aggregation of political power by the federal government at the expense of the states. They also saw his measures as a hostile takeover of the revolution by northern bankers and speculators. Hamilton succeeded in tying more closely to the government those who were already on its side. Unfortunately, he antagonised those who had their doubts.

The Republican alternative

The Founding Fathers regarded political parties as corrupt and disruptive and hoped that the USA would be spared them. That national parties soon arose was in part due to the disputes resulting from Hamilton's measures. His appeal to northern commercial elements aroused sectional jealousies in the South and West and alienated debtors everywhere. His efforts to centralise power in the federal government provoked fears of tyranny. His admiration of the British form of government fed suspicions that he planned to reintroduce monarchy.

Hamilton vs Jefferson

Opposition to Hamilton had initially centred around Madison. But once Secretary of State Thomas Jefferson had become convinced, as he had by 1791, that Hamilton's principles were 'adverse to liberty', it was he that anti-Hamiltonians looked to mainly for leadership. A great letter writer, Jefferson worked mostly behind the scenes. Madison continued to direct the opposition in Congress.

Ideologically, Hamilton and Jefferson were perhaps not as far apart as they have sometimes been depicted: they were both republican, patriotic, democratic and in favour of property rights. But they also had sharply different visions of the USA's future:

- Hamilton foresaw a diversified economy, agriculture balanced by commerce and industry. Jefferson, suspicious of money interests, wanted a republic of sturdy, independent yeoman farmers, whom he regarded as the backbone of American society.
- Hamilton, pessimistic about the people, feared anarchy and loved order. Jefferson, optimistic about the people, feared tyranny and loved liberty.
- Hamilton wanted a stronger federal government. Jefferson supported the rights of states.

To counter the influence of John Fenno, editor of the Hamiltonian *United States Gazette*, Jefferson brought the poet and journalist Philip Freneau to Philadelphia in 1791 to edit a rival newspaper, the *National Gazette*. The disagreements between Hamilton and Jefferson soon became widely visible in a journalistic war of words between the two editors.

In the course of a 'botanizing expedition' up the Hudson in the summer of 1791, Jefferson and Madison came to an understanding with some of Hamilton's political rivals in New York, including Governor George Clinton and Aaron Burr. While the significance of this trip has sometimes been exaggerated, it did lead to the forging of an informal alliance between the South and New York.

By 1792 Hamilton had become the embodiment of a party known as the Federalists, while Jefferson and Madison had become the leaders of those who took the name Republican (thereby implying that the Federalists aimed at a monarchy). While neither the Federalists nor the Republicans (or Democratic-Republicans as they sometimes called themselves) had yet formed fully fledged national parties, they were in the throes of development. Historian J.C. Miller claimed (1960) that the ideological differences between Federalists and Republicans were 'greater than those which have generally existed between major American political parties'.

The 1792 presidential election

Washington was still a revered figure: a man above party, the concept of which he loathed. In his first term he had performed his main mission flawlessly, providing invaluable legitimacy to the 'more perfect union' that was still a work in progress. He had avoided the major political battles, not committing himself to either side. While he longed to return to Mount Vernon, he was urged by both Hamilton and Jefferson to continue in public life: 'North and South will hang together', Jefferson warned, but only 'if they have you to hang on'. Washington agreed to stand again in 1792 and was again unopposed. But the Republicans were sufficiently well-organised to nominate Clinton as their vice presidential candidate. He received 50 electoral votes to Adams's 75.

The Federalists had a clear majority in the Senate but Federalists and Republicans were roughly equal in the House, where many men remained unattached to either of the two factions.

Jefferson's resignation

Hamilton and Jefferson remained in Washington's cabinet. However, the differences between the two men became increasingly bitter and personal. Each sought to undermine the other and organise a following in Congress and in the country. Jefferson's actions nearly led Washington to dismiss him. In December 1793 Jefferson left the cabinet voluntarily. Washington, regarding him as disloyal, never spoke to him again.

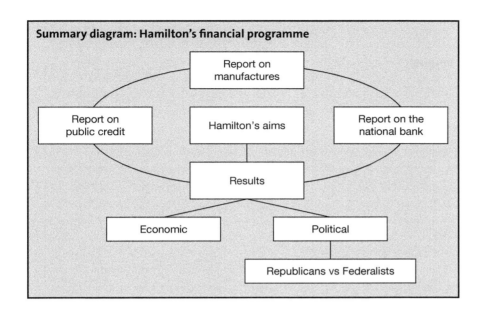

Summary diagram: Hamilton's financial programme

 ## Foreign and western affairs

▶ *What were the USA's main problems in foreign and western policy between 1793 and 1796?*

During Washington's second term, problems arising from the French Revolution and the outbreak of war in Europe sharpened party differences. So too did western developments.

The impact of the French Revolution

The outbreak of revolution in 1789 in France had met with general approval by most Americans, who believed the French were following their example. But by 1793, with the execution of King Louis XVI and the **Jacobin** reign of terror, opinion in America diverged sharply. Federalists interpreted events in France as confirming their fears that popular government could easily generate into mob rule. Republicans, by contrast, continued to sympathise with the revolutionaries. Jefferson declared that 'the tree of liberty must be refreshed from time to time with the blood of patriots and tyrants'. If Hamilton's fiscal programme had first divided Federalists and Republicans, the French Revolution had become the touchstone for determining political allegiance in American politics by the early 1790s.

France's declaration of war on Britain in 1793 exacerbated the conflict of opinion. The European war raised the question of American obligations to France. By the treaty of 1778 (see page 92) the USA remained an ally of France, obligated

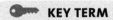

KEY TERM

Jacobins An extremist group in the French Revolution. In power in France in 1793–4, they became associated with the guillotine and the Reign of Terror.

to defend French possessions in the West Indies. Hamilton argued that the 1778 alliance should be declared invalid on the grounds that it was made with a government that no longer existed. As well as holding strong pro-British sentiments, he was aware that British imports were the chief source of the tariff revenues on which his financial programme depended. Seventy-five per cent of American trade was with Britain and 90 per cent of its imports came from Britain.

Jefferson supported France but he did not want war. He believed that the USA should proclaim neutrality but should delay abandoning the 1778 treaty, using it as a bargaining tool with Britain. Washington, who regarded foreign affairs as a presidential concern, was essentially a realist. He believed in interests, not ideals. He did not share Jefferson's views that American ideals were necessary American interests. Aware of the USA's military and economic weakness, he believed that its main interest was to avoid another war with Britain at almost any cost. In April 1793 he issued a proclamation of neutrality. It simply declared the USA to be 'friendly and impartial toward the belligerent powers'.

Citizen Genêt

Washington accepted Jefferson's argument that the USA should recognise the new French Jacobin government (becoming the first country to do so) and received its new ambassador, Citizen Edmond-Charles Genêt. Landing in Charleston in 1793, Genêt immediately organised a Jacobin Club. The enthusiasm with which he was received as he headed north and his talks with Jefferson in New York confirmed his belief that the bonds uniting Americans with the French Revolution were more powerful than any presidential proclamation of neutrality. Intriguing with frontiersmen and land speculators with an eye to attacking Spanish Florida and Louisiana (issuing French military commissions in the process), Genêt quickly became an embarrassment, even to his Republican friends. Jefferson decided that the French minister had overreached himself when he violated a promise not to outfit a captured British ship as a French privateer. When Genêt threatened to appeal his cause directly to the American people over the head of their president, Washington (in August 1793) demanded his recall. Meanwhile the French government had sent over a new minister with a warrant for Genêt's arrest. Instead of returning to France to risk the guillotine, Genêt sought asylum in the USA.

Despite Genêt's foolishness and the growing excesses of the Jacobins, the French revolutionary cause remained popular with many Republicans through 1793–4. Mass demonstrations took place in many towns as Americans demanded war with Britain. Federalists, abhorring the prospect of mob rule, feared that French practices might spread across the Atlantic, with guillotines set up on Broadway.

Problems with Britain

British actions did not make it easy for the Federalists to rally to their side:

- Americans were incensed that Britain had not relinquished its military posts south of the Great Lakes as it had agreed to do in 1783. To make matters worse, British troops were suspected of encouraging Native Americans to attack American settlers.
- Just as galling was Britain's disregard of the maritime rights of neutral America. US commerce had derived a great boost from the wartime needs of the belligerents, especially from France's decision to allow neutrals to trade with its West Indian colonies. Britain, unwilling to accept such an obvious attempt to evade its blockade, declared its intent in November 1793 to maintain the blockade. This resulted in the seizure of some 250 American ships carrying goods from the French West Indies to France and the imprisonment of their crews.

By the spring of 1794 it seemed that the USA and Britain were close to war. In April 1794 a bill supporting the boycott of trade with Britain passed the House of Representatives. It was defeated in the Senate only by the casting vote of Vice President Adams.

Jay's Treaty

Washington, aware that the USA was totally unprepared for war and fearful of war's potentially divisive consequences, sent Chief Justice Jay to London to try to negotiate a settlement. The British government was in an uncompromising mood, partly because it had been secretly informed by Hamilton that the USA would not join a projected League of Armed Neutrality to uphold neutral rights on the seas. Jay's Treaty, signed in November 1794, thus fell far short of what he had been instructed to demand. Its main provisions were as follows:

- Britain promised to evacuate the northwest forts by 1796.
- Britain agreed to submit American claims for compensation for ship seizure to arbitration.
- Britain granted American commerce (very) limited access to the British West Indies.

In return:

- Jay agreed to refer the pre-revolutionary debts and northeast boundary questions to mixed commissions.
- Britain gained the most favoured nation treatment in American commerce.
- Jay promised that French privateers would not be outfitted in American ports.

Jay failed to secure either a hoped-for commercial treaty or compensation for the slaves carried off by Britain in 1783. He was also forced tacitly to accept the British position on neutral rights at sea. Prime Minister William Pitt said that the treaty had been 'dictated on both sides by a spirit of fairness and mutual accommodation'. This was not the way Republicans saw it. Jefferson declared that Jay's Treaty was 'really nothing more than a treaty of alliance between England and the Anglomen of this country against the legislature and people of the United States'.

Jay's Treaty resulted in uproar in the USA. Republicans denounced the agreement as a base surrender and a pact with the British devil. Jay was burned in effigy and there were demands for his impeachment. Only after long debate did the Senate ratify the document with the necessary two-thirds majority (twenty votes to ten). Edmund Randolph, who had succeeded Jefferson as secretary of state, opposed the treaty. Washington hesitated for two months before signing it in August 1795. He signed it because he thought the treaty was a sensible compromise and better than the only alternative – war with Britain.

Jay's Treaty was largely successful. Britain surrendered its forts. An economic boom followed the treaty as American trade with Britain and its empire increased threefold.

Relations with Spain

Spain had encouraged secessionist plots among western settlers and also incited southern Native Americans to attack American settlements. By creating the impression that Britain and the USA were drawing closer together and might be contemplating joint action against Louisiana, Jay's Treaty induced Spain to soften its attitude towards the USA. Thomas Pinckney, sent to Madrid as a special envoy, was thus able to conclude the Treaty of San Lorenzo (October 1795) by which Spain:

- granted the USA free use of the Mississippi and the right to deposit goods in New Orleans
- accepted the American claim to the thirty-first parallel as the Florida boundary
- promised to restrain Native Americans from attacking frontier settlements.

Pinckney's Treaty ended a decade of Spanish intrigue. A separate western Confederacy lost its point once the Mississippi had been opened to American trade.

Western developments

Washington was more concerned with western developments than with European foreign policy. His main wish was to consolidate US control of the continent between the Appalachians and the Mississippi. Americans continued to edge westwards throughout the 1790s. New western states joined the Union: Kentucky (in 1792) and Tennessee (in 1796).

Native American policy 1789–93

Washington declared in 1789 that a just Native American policy was one of his highest priorities. Working closely with Knox (Native American affairs came under the authority of the secretary of war), Washington supported a policy designed to create several sovereign Native American 'homelands'. He envisaged that the Native American occupants of these areas would gradually become assimilated as fully fledged American citizens.

Attempting to make this policy a reality occupied more of Washington's time and energy than any foreign or domestic issue during his first term. In 1790 he negotiated the Treaty of New York with a Creek leader, Alexander McGillivray, a mixed-race chieftain. This restored to the Creeks some of the lands ceded in treaties with Georgia and provided generous payments for the rest of the land. In the same year, Washington issued a proclamation forbidding private or state encroachments on all Native American lands guaranteed by treaty with the USA.

Washington soon found that it was one thing to proclaim and quite another to sustain:

- In the South, the Georgia state legislature defied the proclamation by selling more than 15 million acres (6 million hectares) on its western border to speculators calling themselves the Yazoo Companies.
- In the North, white settlers simply moved on to Native American lands, breaking formal treaties.

With some misgivings, Washington approved a series of military expeditions into the Ohio Valley to put down uprisings by Native American tribes. In the autumn of 1791 an expedition commanded by Arthur St Clair was annihilated, provoking congressional cries for reprisals in what became an escalating cycle of violence that defied Washington's efforts at conciliation. Eventually, he acknowledged that his vision of secure Native American sanctuaries could not be enforced. He realised that there was no holding back the tide of white settlers.

SOURCE C

The Pittsburgh Gazette, April 1796, quoted in S. Elkins and E. McKitrick, *The Age of Federalism: The Early American Republic 1788–1800*, Oxford University Press, 1993, p. 447.

But in which treaty has the western country the most interest? I think in the British; at least the most immediate interest. I would rather have the posts [forts] and command of the Indians and peace, until we get our country settled, than have the privilege of selling flour without duty, for a while. If we cannot get the command of the Indians, and keep them in peace, the descent of the river will be disturbed, and though the Spaniards make it open, the Indians will make it shut; and come upon our settlements and hinder our making flour, so that we shall not have much to take to market.

Why did the writer of Source C prefer Jay's to Pinckney's treaty?

The Treaty of Greenville

In 1794, the northwestern Native Americans suffered a crushing defeat at the hands of 5000 troops led by General Wayne at the battle of Fallen Timbers. Native American tribes eventually agreed to the Treaty of Greenville (August 1795). The USA acquired the right to the lands which are now Ohio and Indiana.

Western land policy

Once Jay and Pinckney had settled matters with Britain and Spain, the West was open for a renewed surge of settlers. It was soon apparent that Federalists and Republicans disagreed on land policy. Influential Federalists, like Hamilton and Jay, favoured:

- high land prices, which would enrich the treasury
- the sale of large parcels of land to speculators, which was easier and more profitable than the sale of small amounts to actual settlers.

Jefferson and Madison reluctantly accepted the need for revenue in order to reduce the national debt. But Jefferson hoped that lands could be sold cheaply in small chunks, benefiting ordinary settlers.

Federalist policy prevailed. In the Land Acts of 1796, Congress extended the rectangular surveys ordained in 1785 (see page 132). But it doubled the price of land to $2 per acre with only a year in which to complete payment. Half the townships would go in 640-acre sections, making the minimum cost $1280 – well beyond the means of most settlers and even too pricey for most speculators. By 1800 government land offices had sold fewer than 50,000 acres under the act.

The Whiskey Insurrection

The 1791 tax on liquor (see page 171) bore heavily on frontier farmers. Lacking adequate transport facilities, they found it difficult to dispose of their surplus corn and rye unless its bulk was reduced by distillation into whiskey. In western Pennsylvania the discontent with the excise boiled over in 1794 into armed resistance. Mobs terrorised federal agents and prevented courts from functioning. In August 1794 some 6000 men gathered near Pittsburgh, setting up mock guillotines to register their solidarity with revolutionary France. Federalists saw this as American Jacobinism in action.

At Hamilton's urging, Washington raised a militia force of 13,000 men to deal with the trouble. He marched part of the way before leaving Hamilton in charge. Hamilton led the army to Pittsburgh, rapidly suppressing the 'Whiskey Boys' and granting an amnesty to all the rebels who signed an oath to obey the federal government's laws.

While the government had shown its strength, it had alienated frontiersmen. Hamilton's role in the Whiskey Insurrection conjured up among Republicans fears of a standing army and military dictatorship. Hamilton, however, disillusioned by politics and anxious to earn money to maintain his large family, retired from office in January 1795. Nevertheless, he remained a power behind the scenes, exerting huge influence on both the cabinet and Washington.

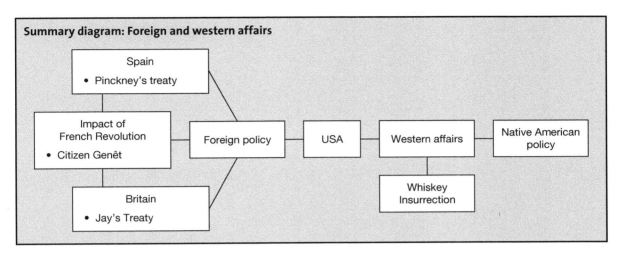

Summary diagram: Foreign and western affairs

 # The 1796 presidential election

▶ *Why did the Federalists win the 1796 election?*

Although political parties were far from fully developed, it was clear that the 1796 presidential election was likely to be bitterly fought.

Washington stands down

Regarding himself as the national leader, Washington had no wish to evolve into a party chieftain. But he could do little about it. By the mid-1790s, he believed that the leading Federalists (like Hamilton) were men of sense and patriotism. He considered many Republicans (especially Jefferson) to be fools and troublemakers.

During his second term, the Republican press depicted Washington as either a Federalist or a senile dupe of Federalist leaders. By claiming the president was under the evil influence of Hamilton, Jefferson and Madison, the press was able to criticise Washington's administration without overtly criticising Washington himself. Nevertheless, Washington was subjected to sustained criticism of both his character and his policies. Worn out by the burdens of the presidency and hurt by the partisan abuse heaped on him, Washington declined to stand for re-election in 1796. His decision established a two-term presidential tradition that all his successors (except Franklin D. Roosevelt) were to follow.

Before leaving public life, Washington issued a Farewell Address (17 September 1796). It was not delivered as a speech. Instead, it was first published in the Philadelphia *Daily American Advertiser*. Hamilton was the draftsman, writing most of the words; Washington was the author whose ideas prevailed throughout. Washington advised Americans to 'steer clear of permanent alliances with any portion of the foreign world'. He also warned Americans against 'the baneful effects of the spirit of party'. According to historian Joseph Ellis (2004), Washington left the presidency as he came in: 'dignified, defiant and decisive; clear about what was primary, what peripheral'.

SOURCE D

Part of Washington's Farewell Address, quoted in R.D. Brown, editor, *Major Problems in the Era of the American Revolution 1760–1791*, D.C. Heath, 1992, pp. 580–1.

Towards the preservation of your Government and the permanency of your present happy state, it is requisite, not only that you steadily discountenance irregular opposition to its acknowledged authority, but also that you resist with care the spirit of innovation upon its principles however specious the pretexts …

I have already intimated to you the danger of parties in the State, with particular reference to the founding of them on geographical discriminations. Let me now take a more comprehensive view and warn you in the most solemn manner against the baneful effects of the Spirit of Party, generally. This spirit … exists under different shapes in all Governments … but in those of the popular form it is seen in its greatest rankness and is truly their worst enemy.

? Examine Source D. Why do you think Washington was so critical of the 'baneful effects of the Spirit of Party'?

The candidates

The party strife that Washington deprecated was made more intense by his retirement. In 1796 the presidency became for the first time a party question. The Republicans chose Jefferson as their candidate, adding geographical balance to the ticket with Aaron Burr of New York. The logical choice of the Federalists was Washington's protégé Hamilton. But accused (wrongly) of mishandling public money, he was not in a position to stand. Torn by factional rivalries, the Federalists settled on John Adams.

Hamilton, who disliked Adams's moderation as well as his independence, hoped to manipulate the electoral machinery so that the Federalist vice presidential candidate, Thomas Pinckney of South Carolina, became president. The Constitution did not then require separate balloting for president and vice president. Electors simply cast two votes without specifying which candidate they favoured for president. The candidate with the highest number of electoral votes became president, the runner-up vice president. Hamilton hoped that southern Republicans, whose first votes would go to Jefferson, might be persuaded to make another southerner, Pinckney, their second choice.

The result

Some of Adams's supporters, aware of Hamilton's scheme, withheld their second ballots from Pinckney. Thus, Adams with 71 electoral votes became president. Astonishingly, the vice presidency went to Jefferson, whose 68 electoral votes exceeded those of Pinckney (with 59) and Burr (with 30). Accordingly, candidates of different parties were elected president and vice president.

In the Senate the Federalists won a majority. The House was more equally divided. Half its members still prided themselves upon being free of party ties.

Party divisions

Besides demonstrating the deficiencies in the electoral system, the 1796 result also showed how well founded were Washington's fears of geographical divisions. Adams's electoral votes came almost entirely from the northern states; Jefferson carried nearly all the South plus the new western states, Kentucky and Tennessee. It was somewhat ironic that New England, once the most democratic part of America, should have become the chief stronghold of Federalism, whereas Virginia, where society had been – and still was – more stratified, became the most Republican.

The two parties were not completely sectional. If the Federalists drew their main support from New England and to a lesser extent from the middle states, they had some support in the South, especially in South Carolina. Conversely, the Republicans, while distinctly southern and western, had sizeable support in the North, especially in New York.

Nor did the parties divide along strict socio-economic lines. By and large, merchants, bankers, ship owners and manufacturers were Federalists while farmers and planters were Republican. But with farmers making up about 90 per cent of the population, it is evident that many farmers supported the Federalists. It has been suggested that small-scale farmers tended to support the Republicans while commercial farmers whose crops were produced for the market were generally Federalist.

Most contemporaries believed that people of the 'better sort' (the richer) were Federalist, those of the 'meaner sort' (the poorer) Republican. Voting returns lend support to this view. But there was wealth on both sides. Certainly the Federalist Party was not wholly a 'gentlemen's' party. Many urban artisans voted Federalist. So did northern free black men, not surprisingly given the slaveholding leadership of the Republican Party.

A variety of factors influenced partisan allegiance. Some voted Federalist out of veneration for George Washington. Others followed the lead of a local magnate. Religion also played an important role. Congregationalists, Episcopalians and Quakers were overwhelmingly Federalists. Baptists, Methodists and Presbyterians tended towards Republicanism.

Most Americans who were entitled to vote did not do so, possibly because of the inconvenience of travelling many miles to the ballot.

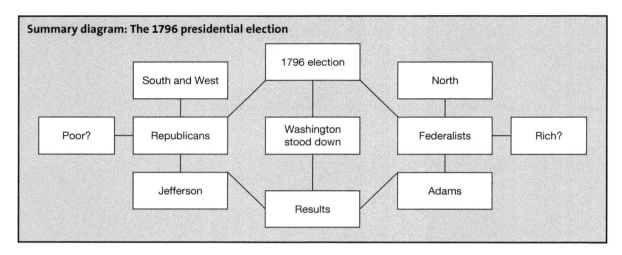

Summary diagram: The 1796 presidential election

5 The Adams administration 1797–1800

▶ *How effective was Adams as president?*

Able, courageous and honest, Adams was determined to continue Washington's policies. He thus made the mistake of retaining Washington's cabinet, most of whose members acknowledged Hamilton as their leader and continued to look to him for advice. Hamilton, therefore, stayed as the real power behind Adams's administration. While Adams tried to remain his own man, disagreeing with the **High Federalists** almost as much as with the Republicans, he was slow to exert his authority.

KEY TERM

High Federalists
Supporters of Alexander Hamilton.

The problem of France

The most urgent problem facing the Adams administration was the deterioration of relations with France.

The XYZ affair

The French believed that by accepting Jay's Treaty, the USA had virtually become Britain's ally. The new French government, the Directory, retaliated by:

- refusing to receive the newly appointed American minister, Charles Pinckney
- ordering the seizure of American ships carrying British cargoes: by June 1797 over 300 merchantmen had been captured.

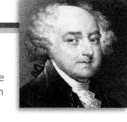

John Adams

1735	Born into a modest family in Massachusetts
1755	Graduated from Harvard College; became a lawyer in Boston
1764	Married Abigail Smith. They had five children including a future US president (John Quincy Adams)
1774	Published *Novanglus*, an influential pamphlet critical of British imperial actions
1774–7	Sat in the first and second Continental Congress
1782–3	Helped to secure the Treaty of Paris
1785–8	Served as first American minister to Britain
1796	Elected president
1800	Defeated by Jefferson in the presidential election
1826	Died on the same day as Jefferson (ironically 4 July)

Adams's political philosophy was somewhere between Jefferson's and Hamilton's. He shared neither Jefferson's faith in the common people nor Hamilton's fondness for an aristocracy of wealth. He favoured the classic mixture of aristocratic, democratic and monarchical elements, although his use of 'monarchical' interchangeably with 'executive' exposed him to the attacks of Republicans who tended to see a monarchist in every Federalist.

While Adams is not considered one of the USA's greatest presidents, his influence on the American Revolution was considerable. He played an active role in Massachusetts against British policy pre-1775. Dedicated to the principles of republicanism, he was a 'thinker', not a rabble-rouser (like his cousin, Samuel Adams). A major figure in the second Continental Congress, he chaired scores of important committees and went on to negotiate the Treaty of Paris. He largely wrote the Massachusetts Constitution in 1779 – the model for other state constitutions and for the 1787 Constitution.

In an attempt to avert war, Adams sent a special mission, led by Charles Pinckney, to France. When it reached Paris it was greeted not by Charles Maurice de Talleyrand, the French foreign minister, but by three of his subordinates (later identified in the envoys' dispatches as X, Y and Z) with the news that before negotiations could begin the USA must pay a bribe of $250,000 and agree to lend France $12 million. Outraged by this insult, the American commissioners returned home. Adams was similarly outraged, as was the nation when the president submitted the matter to Congress in March 1798.

The Quasi-War

With war fever mounting, Congress abrogated the 1778 treaty of alliance with France, created a navy department, authorised the capture of armed French ships, suspended trade with France, and voted for funds for the expansion of the army and navy. Washington was appointed commanding general of a 10,000-strong army, accepting only on condition that Hamilton was made second in command.

Adams, however, resisted a formal declaration of war. Between 1798 and 1800 the USA and France fought a limited and undeclared naval war. The infant US navy more than held its own in a series of engagements, capturing more than 80 French privateers.

The Alien and Sedition Acts

War hysteria gave the Federalists an opportunity to strike at both their domestic opponents and foreign influence. Republican leaders opposed the Quasi-War; Jefferson saw the creation of a standing army as a threat to liberty and still regarded Britain as the USA's natural enemy. Federalists were also incensed by the fact that many recent European political refugees, mainly from France and Ireland, supported France.

In the summer of 1798 the Federalists enacted a series of measures known collectively as the Alien and Sedition Acts. Proposed by High Federalists in Congress, the measures did not originate with Adams but had his blessing:

- The Naturalization Act, designed to deprive the Republicans of immigrant votes, increased the residential requirement for citizenship from five years to fourteen.
- Two Alien Acts gave the president power to deport any alien whom he deemed 'dangerous to the peace and safety of the United States'.
- The Sedition Act prescribed heavy fines and imprisonment for persons convicted of publishing 'any false, scandalous or malicious writing' bringing into disrepute the government, Congress or the president of the USA.

The Sedition Act was the most controversial. Transparently partisan, it was designed to punish Republicans whom Federalists could scarcely distinguish from traitors. To his credit, Adams did not enforce the Alien Acts. But under the Sedition Act some 25 people were arrested, including some prominent Republican editors. Ten were convicted and imprisoned.

The Virginia and Kentucky resolutions

Republicans denounced the Alien and Sedition Acts as arbitrary extensions of federal power and violations of the Bill of Rights. The few convictions under the acts served to create martyrs to the cause of freedom of speech and the press. In 1798–9 the legislatures of Virginia and Kentucky adopted protest resolutions, drafted respectively – and anonymously (at the time) – by Madison and Jefferson. Maintaining that the Alien and Sedition Acts were unconstitutional, the Virginia and Kentucky resolutions declared that the federal government had no right to exercise powers not specifically delegated to it by the states. They went on to assert the right of a state to judge when infractions of the Constitution had occurred, and to nullify those acts it deemed unconstitutional. Jefferson even suggested that Kentucky might secede from the Union, in effect calling for rebellion against the government of which he was vice president. Had this been revealed at the time, he might well have been impeached for treason. In 1798–9, however, both Virginia and Kentucky affirmed their attachment to the Union and took no steps to obstruct the execution of the offending acts.

Arguably, Jefferson's radical doctrine of states' rights was far more dangerous than the threat to freedom posed by the Alien and Sedition laws. Washington declared that if the resolutions were 'systematically and pertinaciously pursued', they would lead to the Union's dissolution.

The end of hostilities

Northern states supported the Alien and Sedition Acts. High Federalists were eager for an outright declaration of war on France. Such a step, they believed, would unite the country behind Federalist leadership. It might also open the way to foreign adventure. Hamilton dreamed of leading an expedition to seize Louisiana and the Floridas from Spain, France's ally, and then, with British help, going on to liberate South America. But Adams still hoped for a peaceful solution. He disliked the militarism that had infected his party and feared Hamilton's martial ambitions. Early in 1799, in response to overtures from Talleyrand, he decided to reopen negotiations with France. When the American commissioners arrived in France, they found Napoleon Bonaparte now First Consul. He was in a conciliatory mood. The resulting treaty, signed in 1800, settled the outstanding differences between the USA and France and formally released the USA from the 1778 defensive alliance with France.

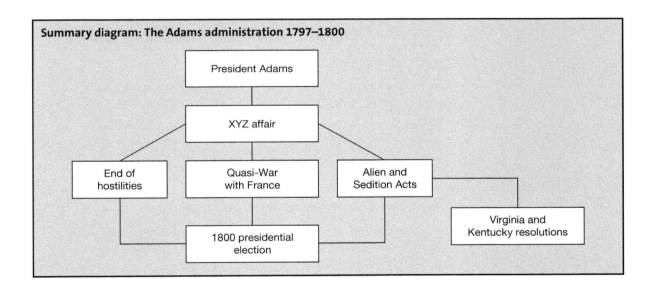

Summary diagram: The Adams administration 1797–1800

6 The 1800 presidential election

▶ *Why did Adams lose the 1800 election?*

Adams's insistence on peace created a rift within his party. He also faced other problems as the 1800 election approached.

SOURCE E

John Marshal, a Federalist supporter, writing to his brother in December 1799, quoted in S. Elkins and E. McKitric, *The Age of Federalism: The Early American Republic 1788–1800*, Oxford University Press, 1993, p. 728.

The eastern people are very much dissatisfied with the President [Adams] on account of the late missions to France. They are strongly disposed to desert him and to push some other candidate … King or Ellsworth with one of the Pinckneys … .

If they are deterred from doing this by the fear that the attempt might elect Jefferson I think it not improbable that they will vote generally for Adams and Pinckney so far as to give the latter gentleman the best chance if he gets the southern vote to be President. Perhaps this ill humour may evaporate before the election comes on – but at present it wears a very serious aspect.

> ? Why, according to Source E, was the situation likely to be serious for Adams in the 1800 presidential election?

Federalist problems

In 1798 Congress imposed a direct tax on houses, land and slaves to pay for the USA's military growth. This tax, which reached every property holder in the nation, was more unpopular than the Alien and Sedition Acts, which touched comparatively few individuals. In 1799 a group of Pennsylvania farmers, led by Captain John Fries, rioted in protest against the federal property tax. Adams used troops to restore order. But High Federalists thought he displayed weakness in pardoning Fries on his conviction for treason, along with a general pardon to all participants in the affair.

As the 1800 presidential election approached, grievances were mounting against Federalist policies: taxation to support an army that did little except chase Pennsylvanian farmers (see page 180); the Alien and Sedition Acts which threatened liberty. Washington's death in December 1799 deprived the Federalist Party of its most effective symbol. When Adams decided to make peace with France he probably doomed his one chance for re-election: a wave of patriotic war fever with a united party behind him.

In early 1800 the schism within the Federalist Party could no longer be concealed. Soon after being renominated by his party, Adams dismissed Secretary of State Timothy Pickering and Secretary of War James McHenry – two leading Hamiltonians – from his cabinet. As Adams ran for re-election few Federalist leaders stood by him. Hamilton wrote a pamphlet declaring Adams unfit to be president and, adopting the same tactic as in 1796, hoped to defeat him by throwing support to the Federalist vice presidential candidate Charles Pinckney.

The 1800 campaign

In 1800 the Republicans again nominated Jefferson and Aaron Burr. A bitter campaign now ensued. Republicans condemned the Alien and Sedition Acts and the heavy taxes, and accused Adams of having monarchical tendencies. Jefferson directed the Republican campaign by mail from his home at Monticello. He was depicted as the farmers' friend, the champion of states' rights, frugal government, liberty and peace. The Federalists, for their part, depicted Jefferson as a Jacobin and an atheist.

The result

The Republicans won a narrow victory. Jefferson and Burr each had 73 electoral college votes, Adams 65 and Pinckney 64. The Federalists won the New England states, New Jersey and Delaware. The Republicans won New York, the South and West, while Pennsylvania and Maryland split their votes. The decisive states were New York and South Carolina, either of which might have given the victory to Adams. In New York Burr's organisation had – just – won control of the legislature which cast the electoral college votes.

Adams's defeat originated in his refusal to subordinate national interests to party ends. Withstanding the belligerent clamour of important elements in his own party, he made peace with France because he thought it was the right thing to do. This action divided his party.

Next to the split in the Federalist ranks, the key factor was superior Republican organisation and electioneering. While their opponents still equated party with faction and made little attempt to woo popular support, the Republicans had been building an efficient, tightly disciplined national machine, holding popular meetings and founding party newspapers. In New York, especially, they worked tirelessly to get every voter to the polls, and New York's votes proved crucial. As well as winning the presidential election, the Republicans won control of both the House and Senate.

The House of Representatives decides

Although Adams had been clearly defeated, the identity of the next president remained in doubt. While Jefferson was the Republican choice for president, both he and Burr had received the same number of electoral votes. The Constitution provided that, in the event of a tie, the choice devolved on the House of Representatives, with each state delegation casting a single vote. Since the Federalists were still in a majority in the House (it would be many months before the new Republican-dominated House assembled), the decision would be up to them.

Ballot after ballot was taken in the winter of 1800–1 without result. Some diehard Federalists, who detested Jefferson, were prepared to make Burr president. But Hamilton thought Burr, his long-standing rival in New York, unprincipled and dangerous. Much as he distrusted Jefferson, Hamilton feared Burr more. His views influenced enough Congressmen for Jefferson to be elected on the thirty-sixth ballot. To avoid another such crisis in future the twelfth amendment to the Constitution, adopted in 1804, required separate ballots for president and vice president.

How united was the USA in 1801?

Americans in the eighteenth century had been far from united. Prior to 1775 the loyalty of most people had been first to their colony and then to Britain. In 1775 little had united the thirteen colonies except hostility to Britain. Whatever unity had been established in the war years was seen in danger of falling apart after 1783 under the weak Articles of Confederation. That was why men like Madison, Hamilton and Washington had supported the creation of a new form of government. The 1787 Constitution was designed to pull the various states together. To what extent had the Federalists succeeded in creating a united nation?

Disunity

It is possible to claim that American unity was still superficial in 1801:

- There were strong differences between northern and southern states (for example, over slavery) and between eastern and western states.
- There were deep economic and social divisions within and between the various states.
- These divisions were reflected in the rise of political parties and the bitter political debates of the 1790s, culminating in the 1800 presidential election.

Growing unity

The Federalists had spent twelve years in power. In many ways those years had been remarkably successful. They had:

- launched the new Constitution
- established a national government with demonstrated power
- built a fiscal structure which safeguarded the nation's credit
- recovered territory from Britain and Spain
- created a stable northwest frontier
- avoided wars which could have caused the country to fall apart.

The Federalists' main failure was political. Their policies, designed to build a strong, united nation, resulted in the rise of the Republicans who, in 1800, won the support of most Americans. Most contemporaries regarded the development of political parties in the 1790s as a major failure. This was undoubtedly so for the Federalists: they never again won a national election. In 1800 Americans were bitterly divided politically. In retrospect, however, the development of the two-party system was one of the most significant and enduring legacies of the Federalist era. By forcing the wide spectrum of political opinion into two camps, it institutionalised political debate into an organised format that helped to tame dissension, enabling Americans to settle differences relatively peacefully.

Thus, by 1801 the new Constitution had ensured a strong national government which, in turn, helped to establish a greater sense of unity among Americans. The Federalists deserve great credit for this development.

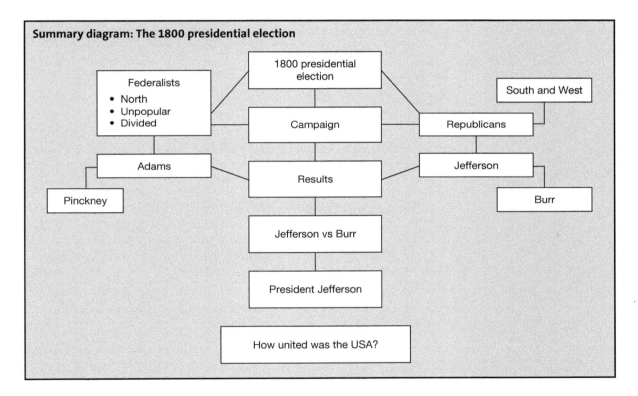

Summary diagram: The 1800 presidential election

7 Key debate

▶ *How successful was George Washington as president?*

Washington's (perceived) military accomplishments were the reason why he was unanimously elected as the USA's first president in 1789. Some have claimed that his presidential achievements were greater than his military achievements. But many Americans in 1796 would not have agreed with this view. Nor, for that matter, have all historians.

Criticism of Washington

EXTRACT 1

An extract from a review by Larzer Ziff in *The New York Times*, 13 September 1987, of a book by Barry Schwartz, *George Washington: The Making of an American Symbol*, Free Press, 1987.

Perhaps the most extraordinary of the many remarkable circumstances that surrounded the transformation of a Virginian planter into an object of permanent national veneration is that it took place during his lifetime, when he was still present for comparison with his image … Free of a desire to debunk, I would point out that many of Washington's contemporaries were acutely aware of a sizeable discrepancy between man and symbol. John Adams, for instance, pondered the matter at some length, as if the phenomenon were one of the greatest curiosities of his age.

Critics at the time, like Jefferson and Madison, depicted Washington as past his sell-by date, a quasi-senile frontman for a Federalist conspiracy, inadvertently lending his enormous credibility to treacherous plans to undermine American liberties. Had he stood again for the presidency in 1796, he would almost certainly have been re-elected but he would not have been chosen unanimously (as in 1789 and 1792).

Recent historical opinion has also been critical of Washington's presidential leadership. While he found time to write meticulous instructions to his managers about estate matters at Mount Vernon, he wrote and said very little about crucial political events. This raises the question as to whether Washington took the helm or merely occupied the bridge of the American ship of state. Given that he regarded his role as primarily ceremonial and symbolic, it is possible to argue that whatever success his administration achieved was due more to his subordinates than to himself.

Washington has also become an inviting target for (what have been perceived to be) the glaring failures of the revolutionary generation: failure to tackle the issue of slavery and harshness to Native Americans. When the slavery issue came before Congress in February 1790, Washington washed his hands of the matter, declaring that it was Congress's concern, not the president's. Although Washington was eager to treat Native Americans fairly, in the event he did little to assist their cause.

Washington's achievements

EXTRACT 2

From Joseph Ellis, *His Excellency George Washington*, Faber & Faber, 2004, p. xiv.

It seemed to me [on beginning my research] that Benjamin Franklin was wiser than Washington; Alexander Hamilton was more brilliant; John Adams was better read; Thomas Jefferson was more intellectually sophisticated; James

Extracts 1 and 2 differ in emphasis. Which provides the more convincing explanation?

*Madison was more politically astute. Yet each and all of these prominent figures acknowledged that Washington was their unquestioned superior. Within the gallery of greats so often mythologized and capitalized as Founding Fathers, Washington was recognized as **primus inter pares**, the Foundingest Father of them all.*

> **KEY TERM**
>
> ***Primus inter pares***
> First among equals.

Washington's accomplishments as president far outweigh his failures. One of the revolutionary legacies was a suspicion of political power being in the hands of one man. As head of the new federal government, Washington walked a fine line and walked it skilfully. Aware that everything he did set a precedent, he attended carefully to the pomp and ceremony of office, making sure that the trappings were suitably republican. Turning his natural aloofness into an advantage, he preferred to avoid political in-fighting, removing the presidency from partisan battles.

Exercising executive authority called for a different set of leadership skills from symbolising it. His administrative style had evolved through decades of experience as master of Mount Vernon and commander of the Continental army. According to Jefferson, Washington made himself the 'hub of the wheel', with routine business delegated to the departmental heads at the rim. It was a system that maximised executive control while also creating distance from details. Its successful operation depended on Washington:

- identifying and recruiting talented young men
- trusting his appointments with considerable responsibility
- knowing when to keep his distance and when to interfere.

Recruiting perhaps the most intellectually sophisticated collection of statesmen in US presidential history, he had no need to interfere too much; he simply let his heads of department get on with it. And they did so, for the most part effectively. Under his leadership, Hamilton's policies brought financial stability to the new nation.

But Washington by no means washed his hands of matters of state. Asserting the power of the new federal government, he mobilised and led militia forces against tax-resisting frontiersmen in 1794. In foreign affairs his administration succeeded in maintaining US neutrality between France and Britain. Washington's support ensured that Jay's Treaty secured ratification in the Senate.

Although he was a slave owner, Washington came to believe that slavery was a moral and political anachronism. In 1785 he wrote, 'There is not a man living who wishes more sincerely that I do, to see a plan adopted for the abolition of slavery.' As president, it is true he did nothing to tackle the problem of slavery. But in his defence, his chief political priority was the creation of a unified American nation. He was fully aware that any attempt on his part to do anything to challenge the institution of slavery would divide that nation.

Far from being a failure of moral leadership, he saw his action as a prudent exercise in political judgement. In his will, he freed his own slaves. According to historian Gordon Wood, 'he did this in the teeth of opposition from his relatives, his neighbours, and perhaps even Martha [his wife]. It was a courageous act, and one of his greatest legacies.'

Washington's action with regard to Native Americans can also be praised. He wished to create sovereign Indian enclaves within the USA, trusting that Native Americans would eventually assimilate with white Americans. His great hope was the Cherokee tribe. No tribe had done as much to adapt its own customs to permit peaceful co-existence with white settlers. In an open letter in 1796, Washington promised the Cherokee that if they continued to do their part, then the federal government would enforce its treaties honourably so as to assure Cherokee survival as a people and a nation. Unfortunately, his successors did not honour his commitment.

As the USA's first president, he oversaw the creation of a strong, well-financed national government. He sought to use federal government to improve infrastructure, open western lands, promote commerce and build a spirit of American nationalism. As he had done as commander-in-chief, he embodied national authority, providing something of an illusion of cohesion to what was still a mix of regional and state allegiances.

It is much to his credit that he surrendered political power in 1796 as he had surrendered military power in 1783. Without him at the centre of affairs, the political experiment in republicanism might well have failed. 'With him, and in great part because of him, it succeeded', says Joseph Ellis.

Chapter summary

The years 1789–1801 saw the new Constitution brought into effect. Important precedents were established by Congress and by President Washington. The Constitution was made to work. Secretary of the Treasury Andrew Hamilton played a key role on the financial front. However, his policies generated opposition, especially in the South and West. Jefferson and Madison led the Republican opposition to the Federalists – the supporters of Washington's administration. When Washington stepped down in 1796, John Adams, the Federalist candidate, won the presidential election. In office, Adams avoided open war with France but faced opposition from within his own party and from Republicans who particularly opposed the Alien and Sedition Acts. In the 1800 election Adams was defeated by Jefferson. While the Federalists were never again to hold national office, they had done much to ensure that the new nation was established on firm foundations.

Refresher questions

Use these questions to remind yourself of the key material covered in this chapter.

1 Why were the actions of Congress and president so important in 1789?

2 How did Washington set about creating an effective presidency?

3 How successful were Hamilton's financial measures?

4 Why did political parties develop?

5 What were the USA's main problems in foreign policy between 1793 and 1796?

6 Why did foreign policy divide Federalists and Republicans?

7 Why did western developments divide Federalists and Republicans?

8 Why did the Federalists win the 1796 election?

9 Why were France and America virtually at war in 1798–9?

10 Why did the Alien and Sedition Acts arouse so much passion?

11 Why did Adams lose the 1800 election?

12 How great a president was Washington?

 # Question practice

ESSAY QUESTIONS

1 Assess the reasons for the growth of parties in the 1790s.

2 How successful was Alexander Hamilton's financial programme?

3 How far did the French Revolution affect political developments in the USA in the 1790s?

4 How successful were the Federalists between 1789 and 1801?

INTERPRETATION QUESTION

1 Read the interpretation and then answer the question that follows: 'Only George Washington himself excelled Alexander Hamilton in the durability of his achievements as the early builder of the Republic.' (Sidney Fine and Gerald S. Brown, editors, *The American Past: Conflicting Interpretations of the Great Issues*, Macmillan, 1963.) Evaluate the strengths and limitations of this interpretation, making reference to other interpretations that you have studied.

SOURCE ANALYSIS QUESTION

1 With reference to Sources 1, 2 and 3, and your understanding of the historical context, assess the value of these sources to a historian studying the rise of political parties in the USA in the 1790s.

SOURCE 1

The National Gazette, 15 March 1792, a newspaper supported by Thomas Jefferson.

It is a deplorable truth that a system of finance has issued from the Treasury of the United States and has given rise to scenes of speculation calculated to aggrandise the few and the wealthy, by oppressing the great body of the people, to transfer the best resources of the country forever into the hands of the speculators, and to fix a burden on the people of the United States and their posterity, which time, instead of diminishing will serve to strengthen and increase … with unlimited import and excise laws pledged for its support and copied from British statute books.

SOURCE 2

The Gazette of the United States, a newspaper which supported Alexander Hamilton. This paragraph was placed in the newspaper in 1792 by Hamilton, who signed it T.L.

The Editor of the 'National Gazette' receives a salary from government.

Quere [query] – Whether this salary is paid him for translations; *or for* publications, *the design of which is to vilify those to whom the voice of the people has committed the administration of our public affairs – to oppose the measures of government, and by false insinuations, to disturb the public peace?*

In common life it is thought ungrateful for a man to bite the hand that puts bread in his mouth; but if the man is hired to do it, the case is altered.

SOURCE 3

Alexander Hamilton writing to Washington on 9 September 1792.

I know that I have been an object of uniform opposition of Mr. Jefferson, from the first moment of his coming to the City of New York to enter upon his present office. I know, from the most authentic sources, that I have been the frequent subject of the most unkind whispers and insinuating from the same quarter. I have long seen a formed party in the Legislature under his auspices, bent upon my subversion. I cannot doubt from the evidence I possess that the National Gazette *was instituted by him for political purposes and that one of the leading objects of it has been to render me and all the measures connected with my department as odious as possible …*

Nevertheless, I pledge my honour to you, Sir, that if you shall hereafter form a plan to rewrite the members of your administration upon some steady principle of cooperation, I will faithfully concur in executing it during my continuance in office.

OCR A level History

Essay guidance

The assessment of OCR Units Y212 and Y242: The American Revolution 1740–1796 depends on whether you are studying it for AS or A level:

- for the AS exam, you will answer one essay question from a choice of two, and one interpretation question, for which there is no choice
- for the A level exam, you will answer one essay question from a choice of two, and one shorter essay question also from a choice of two.

The guidance below is for answering both AS and A level essay questions. Guidance for the shorter essay question is at the end of this section. Guidance on answering interpretation questions is on page 202.

For both OCR AS and A level History, the types of essay questions set and the skills required to achieve a high grade for Unit Group 2 are the same. The skills are made very clear by both mark schemes, which emphasise that the answer must:

- focus on the demands of the question
- be supported by accurate and relevant factual knowledge
- be analytical and logical
- reach a supported judgement about the issue in the question.

There are a number of skills that you need to develop to reach the higher levels in the marking bands:

- understand the wording of the question
- plan an answer to the question set
- write a focused opening paragraph
- avoid irrelevance and description
- write analytically
- write a conclusion which reaches a supported judgement based on the argument in the main body of the essay.

These skills will be developed in the section below, but are further developed in the 'Period Study' chapters of the *OCR A level History* series (British Period Studies and Enquiries).

Understanding the wording of the question

To stay focused on the question set, it is important to read the question carefully and focus on the key words and phrases. Unless you directly address the demands of the question you will not score highly. Remember that in questions where there is a named factor you must write a good analytical paragraph about the given factor, even if you argue that it was not the most important.

Types of AS and A level questions you might find in the exams	The factors and issues you would need to consider in answering them
1 Assess the reasons for the outbreak of the American Revolution.	Weigh up the relative importance of a range of factors as to why the American Revolution broke out.
2 To what extent were economic factors the most important cause of the American Revolution?	Weigh up the relative importance of a range of factors, including comparing the importance of economic factors with other factors.
3 'Political factors were the most important cause of the American Revolution.' How far do you agree?	Weigh up the relative importance of a range of factors, including comparing the importance of political factors with other issues to reach a balanced judgement.
4 How successful were British policies in America in the period from 1763 to 1775?	This question requires you to make a judgement about the success of British policies. Instead of thinking about factors, you would need to think about issues such as: • The aims of British policy. • The response of the colonies to the policy.

Planning an answer

Many plans simply list dates and events – this should be avoided as it encourages a descriptive or narrative, rather than an analytical, answer. The plan should be an outline of your argument; this means you need to think carefully about the issues you intend to discuss and their relative importance before you start writing your answer. It should therefore be a list of the factors or issues you are going to discuss and a comment on their relative importance.

For question 1 in the table, your plan might look something like this:

- Economic factors, but trade kept Britain and colonies together.
- Unpopular taxes/duties, but these were low and colonists could afford them.
- Political principles/ideology: colonists often stressed they were entitled to same rights as Englishmen.
- Importance of town and country meetings, local churches and newspapers; link to attack on liberty.
- The role of the mob: force Britain to act, but most colonists were not urban.
- British government policy; links to economic factors and taxes.

The opening paragraph

Many students spend time 'setting the scene'; the opening paragraph becomes little more than an introduction to the topic – this should be avoided. Instead, make it clear what your argument is going to be. Offer your view about the issue in the question – what was the most important reason for the outbreak of the American Revolution – and then introduce the other issues you intend to discuss. In the plan it is suggested that ideology was the most important factor. This should be made clear in the opening paragraph, with a brief comment as to why – perhaps that this was often emphasised by colonists, but could be linked to economic factors and taxes as they were the issues that caused the ideology to develop. This will give the examiner a clear overview of your essay, rather than it being a 'mystery tour' where the

argument becomes clear only at the end. You should also refer to any important issues that the question raises. For example:

There are a number of reasons why the American Revolution broke out, including economic factors, such as taxes and duties, British government policy and a developing ideology among the colonists[1]. However, it was the developing ideology which was the most important factor as the colonists often stressed they were entitled to the same rights as Englishmen[2], whereas taxes and duties were low and the colonists could afford to pay them[3].

1 The student is aware that there were a number of important reasons.
2 The student offers a clear view as to what it considers to be the most important reason – a thesis is offered.
3 There is a brief justification to support the thesis.

Avoid irrelevance and description

Hopefully the plan will stop you from simply writing all you know about why the revolution broke out and force you to weigh up the role of a range of factors. Similarly, it should also help prevent you from simply writing about the military events of the revolution. You will not lose marks if you do that, but neither will you gain any credit, and you will waste valuable time.

Write analytically

This is perhaps the hardest, but most important skill you need to develop. An analytical approach can be helped by ensuring that the opening sentence of each paragraph introduces an idea, which directly answers the question and is not just a piece of factual information. In a very strong answer it should be possible to simply read the opening sentences of all the paragraphs and know what argument is being put forward.

If we look at the second question on the importance of economic factors (see page 197), the following are possible sentences with which to start paragraphs:

- The Trade and Navigation laws were irksome to many colonists.
- Custom duties were a drain on colonial finances and caused many to oppose British rule.
- Trade grievances were not important as the colonists benefited from the mercantilist policies.
- Principle, rather than economic factors, was the main cause of the revolution.
- American leaders developed an ideology that provided a philosophical basis for their actions.
- There was a view among many colonists that a small clique of British ministers wanted to destroy American liberties.

You would then go on to discuss both sides of the argument raised by the opening sentence, using relevant knowledge about the issue to support each side of the argument. The final sentence of the paragraph would reach a judgement on the role played by the factor you are discussing in the outbreak of the American Revolution. This approach would ensure that the final sentence of each paragraph links back to the actual question you are answering. If you can do this for each paragraph you will have a series of mini essays which discuss a factor and reach a conclusion or judgement about the importance of that factor or issue. For example:

Although the colonists disliked the British government's economic policies, such as the Townshend duties on colonial imports of glass, wine, china and tea, these were not major grievances for the colonists[1]. The Americans were aware that they gained a great deal from the mercantilist policies pursued by the British and moreover, if economic concerns were a major factor in the outbreak of the revolution it would be expected that complaints about economic policies would feature heavily in the Declaration of Independence, but they are mentioned only once[2].

1   The sentence puts forward a clear view that economic policies were not a major grievance, and provides an example of what economic grievances there might be – this could be added to in a full essay.

2   The response develops the idea outlined in the opening sentence and explains why economic grievances were not a major issue and provides evidence to support the claim, both through reference to mercantilism and the Declaration of Independence, thus fully supporting the argument made in the opening sentence.

The conclusion

The conclusion provides the opportunity to bring together all the interim judgements to reach an overall judgement about the question. Using the interim judgements will ensure that your conclusion is based on the argument in the main body of the essay and does not offer a different view. For the essay answering question 1 (see page 197), you can decide what was the most important factor in the outbreak of the American Revolution, but for questions 2 and 3 you will need to comment on the importance of the named factor – economic issues or political factors – as well as explain why you think a different factor is more important, if that has been your line of argument. Or, if you think the named factor is the most important, you would need to explain why that was more important than the other factors or issues you have discussed.

Consider the following conclusion to question 2: to what extent were economic factors the most important cause of the American Revolution?

The benefits the American colonists made from their trade with Britain were a factor that would keep Britain and America together, rather than divide them. Trade grievances were scarcely mentioned by the colonists. Taxation and duties were also not a major issue for the colonists as the British proposals were low and could easily be paid by the Americans. However, they did provide the principle around which opposition developed and grew, culminating in the revolution[1]. It was the absence of colonial consent to the taxes which sparked colonial anger. Taxation provided the opportunity for the colonists to argue that if they were Englishmen they were entitle to the same rights as people in England and therefore they should have to give their consent. It was ideology and principle which were the most important causes of the revolution[2], but economic factors, particularly taxes, provided the incidents around which the argument was based[3].

1 The opening of the conclusion considers the relative importance of the named factor and offers a very clear judgement.
2 This provides a balance and shows how economic factors were linked to principle and ideology, which is put forward as the most important reason for the revolution.
3 The last sentence offers a very clear overall judgement, as to the most important factor, but also the relative importance of the named factor. Throughout the conclusion judgement as to the relative importance of factors is made.

How to write a good essay for the A level short answer questions

This question will require you to weigh up the importance of two factors or issues in relation to an event of development. For example:

Which of the following was more responsible for the failure of the Articles of Confederation?

(i) Economic problems

(ii) Civil disobedience

Explain your answer with reference to both (i) and (ii).

As with the long essays, the skills required are made very clear by the mark scheme, which emphasises that the answer must:

- analyse the two issues
- evaluate the two issues
- support your analysis and evaluation with detailed and accurate knowledge
- reach a supported judgement as to which factor was more important in relation to the issue in the question.

The skills required are very similar to those for the longer essays. However, there is no need for an introduction, nor are you required to compare the

two factors or issues in the main body of the essay, although either approach can still score full marks. For example, you could begin with:

The Failure of the Articles of Confederation was due to a number of issues and economic problems were certainly important. The Articles did not refer to the provision for a national tax, as central government power was kept quite limited. Congress was not given the power to tax and could only request money from the states, which meant that it and the army were often short of money[1]. Moreover, Congress had also been denied the power to regulate international and inter-state trade and as a result each state retained control over its own trade policies[2]. These issues created serious problems for the new Confederacy and this was made worse because of the economic legacy of the War of Independence. Congress printed more money, but this caused inflation, and these problems were added to by the loss of preferential trade with Britain following the war.

1 The answer explains one of the economic problems and the problems it created.
2 The answer explains a second economic problem.

The answer would need to go on to explain how these economic problems resulted in the failure of the Articles.

Most importantly, the conclusion must reach a supported judgement as to the relative importance of the factors in relation to the issue in the question. For example:

Both of the factors played a role in the failure of the Articles. However, although the economic problems were serious, they could have been managed if the states had been willing to respond to the requests made to them and the problem of state war debts became a major issue as some paid the off and others did not[1]. However, civil disobedience was a more serious concern as Shays' Rebellion showed how vulnerable the Confederacy was to mob rule, while civil unrest in areas such as Massachusetts was symptomatic of discontent across all former thirteen colonies**[2]**. Unrest was a direct challenge to the new Confederation and could require armed force to control, but which the Confederation might lack the funds to suppress.

1 The response explains the relative importance of the first factor and suggests that its importance was limited.
2 The response explains the importance of the second factor and why it was more important than the first factor.

Interpretations guidance

The guidance below is for answering the AS interpretation question for OCR Unit Y242: The American Revolution 1740–1796. Guidance on answering essay questions is on page 197.

The OCR specification outlines the two key topics from which the interpretation question will be drawn. For this book these are:

- The causes of the American Revolution.
- The early republic 1783–96.

The specification also lists the main debates to consider.

It is also worth remembering that this is an AS unit and not an A level historiography paper. The aim of this element of the unit is to develop an awareness that the past can be interpreted in different ways.

The question will require you to assess the strengths and limitations of a historian's interpretation of an issue related to one of the specified key topics.

You should be able to place the interpretation within the context of the wider historical debate on the key topic. However, you will *not* be required to know the names of individual historians associated with the debate or to have studied the specific books of any historians. It may even be counterproductive to be aware of particular historians' views, as this may lead you to simply describe their view, rather than analyse the given interpretation.

There are a number of skills you need to develop to reach the higher levels in the mark bands:

- To be able to understand the wording of the question.
- To be able to explain the interpretation and how it fits into the debate about the issue or topic.
- To be able to consider both the strengths and weaknesses of the interpretation by using your own knowledge of the topic.

Here is an example of a question you will face in the exam:

Read the interpretation and then answer the question that follows:

'America was close to disintegration until the Founding Fathers rode to the rescue and drafted a more effective Constitution.'

Adapted from: John Fiske, *The War of Independence*, 1894.

Evaluate the strengths and limitations of this interpretation, making reference to other interpretations that you have studied.

Approaching the question

There are several steps to take to answer this question:

1 Explain the Interpretation and put it into context

In the first paragraph you should explain the interpretation and the view it is putting forward. This paragraph places the interpretation in the context of the historical debate and explains any key words or phrases relating to the given interpretation. A suggested opening might be as follows:

The interpretation puts forward the view that the Articles of Confederation had left America with a weak government and that the new country was close to disintegration because of the social, political and economic problems and challenges it faced[1]. He goes on to suggest that the country was saved by the actions of the Founding Fathers, who in his opinion, played a crucial role and rescued the nation through drawing up a more effective Constitution, which secured liberty for the people[2].

1 The opening sentence is clearly focused on the given Interpretation, it clearly explains the first part and briefly suggests why it might be considered close to disintegration – but there is no detailed own knowledge added at this point.
2 The second sentence deals with the second half of the Interpretation and puts forward the argument that the crucial role was played by the Founding Fathers. The first two sentences have therefore clearly explained the view in the interpretation.

In order to place Fiske's view in the context of the debate about the role of the Founding Fathers you could go on to suggest that this view was consistent with those in the nineteenth century who thought that the aim of the revolution had been to secure liberty and that was only achieved by the Constitution. You might also want to point out that this view has been challenged and many historians now argue that the period between 1781 and 1787 was a period of achievement, not failure.

2 Consider the strengths of the interpretation

In the second paragraph consider the strengths of the interpretation by bringing in your own knowledge that supports the given view. A suggested response might start as follows when considering the strengths of the view:

There is some merit to Fiske's view as the authority of Congress gradually diminished after 1783 and once peace had been made after the War of Independence the states no longer felt that it was essential to co-operate with each other or with Congress[1]. As a result, there was little holding the former colonies together and disintegration was a real prospect, particularly as Congress was weak and increasingly losing respect[2].

1 The answer clearly focuses on the strength of the given interpretation.
2 The response provides some support for the view in the interpretation from the candidate's own knowledge, this is not particularly detailed or precise, but this could be developed in the remainder of the paragraph as suggested.

Answers might go on to develop this and could make reference to the fact that American finances were weak and Britain and Spain treated America with contempt. In support of the second part of the interpretation, answers might argue that the importance of the Founding Fathers has been upheld by other historians and that they were reformers with principles who worked to create a strong government to preserve the Union and the gains of the revolution.

It can be argued that Fiske is right to stress the importance of the Constitution.

3 Consider the weaknesses of the interpretation

In the third paragraph consider the weaknesses of the given interpretation by bringing in knowledge that can challenge the given interpretation and explains what is missing from the interpretation.

A suggested response might start as follows when considering the weaknesses of the view:

However, there are a number of weaknesses in Fiske's interpretation[1]. Most importantly, it ignores the achievements of the period, particularly as the Confederation had ensured that independence was won and the settlement of the west was regulated[2]. Moreover, the Articles prevented American central government from infringing the rights of the states. All of these were important achievements which the interpretation ignores[3].

1 The opening makes it very clear that this paragraph will deal with the weaknesses of the interpretation.
2 It explains clearly the first weakness and provides evidence to support the claim, the evidence is not detailed and could be developed, but the answer focuses on explaining the weakness, rather than providing lost of detail.
3 A second weakness is explained, again the infringement of state rights could be expanded.

Answers might go on to argue that the Founding Fathers did not ride to the rescue, but instead were more concerned with protecting their own economic interests, as they were upper-class conservatives. Instead, therefore, of seeing the Constitution as the saviour, answers could suggest that it was a reactionary document that prevented, or at least curbed, democracy. It might therefore be argued that the period does not deserve to be described as 'The critical period', even if the Articles did have some weaknesses.

There is no requirement for you to reach a judgement as to which view you find more convincing or valid.

Assessing the interpretation

In assessing the interpretation you should consider the following:

- Identify and explain the issue being discussed in the interpretation: the importance of the Founding Fathers to the creation of the Republic.
- Explain the view being put forward in the interpretation: the Founding Fathers were crucial in saving America after the failings of the Articles of Confederation.
- Explain how the interpretation fits into the wider debate about the issue: whether the period from 1781 to 1787 should be seen as one of failure or success.

In other interpretations you might need to:

- Consider whether there is any particular emphasis within the interpretation that needs explaining or commenting on, for example, if the interpretation says something is 'the only reason' or 'the single most important reason'.

- Comment on any concepts that the interpretation raises, such as 'total war', 'authoritarian system', 'liberalisation'.
- Consider the focus of the interpretation, for example, if an interpretation focuses on an urban viewpoint, what was the rural viewpoint? Is the viewpoint given in the interpretation the same all areas of society?

In summary: this is what is important for answering interpretation questions:

- Explaining the interpretation.
- Placing the interpretation in the context of the wider historical debate about the issue it considers.
- Explaining the strengths *and* weaknesses of the view in the extract.

AQA A level History

Essay guidance

At both AS and A level for AQA Component 2: Depth Study: The American Revolution: 1740–96, you will need to answer an essay question in the exam. Each essay question is marked out of 25:

- for the AS exam, Section B: answer **one** essay question from a choice of two
- for the A level exam, Section B: answer **two** essay questions from a choice of three.

There are several question stems which all have the same basic requirement: to analyse and reach a conclusion based on the evidence you provide.

The AS questions often give a quotation and then ask whether you agree or disagree with this view. Almost inevitably your answer will be a mixture of both. It is the same task as for A level – just phrased differently in the question. Detailed essays are more likely to do well than vague or generalised essays, especially in the Depth Studies of Paper 2.

The AQA mark scheme is essentially the same for AS and the full A level (see the AQA website, www.aqa.org.uk). Both emphasise the need to analyse and evaluate the key features related to the periods studied. The key feature of the highest level is sustained analysis: analysis that unites the whole of the essay.

Writing an essay: general skills

- *Focus and structure.* Be sure what the question is asking and plan what the paragraphs should be about.
- *Focused introduction to the essay.* Be sure that the introductory sentence relates directly to the focus of the question and that each paragraph highlights the structure of the answer.
- *Use detail.* Make sure that you show detailed knowledge, but only as part of an explanation

being made in relation to the question. No knowledge should be standalone; it should be used in context.

- *Explanatory analysis and evaluation.* Consider what words and phrases to use in an answer to strengthen the explanation.
- *Argument and counter-argument.* Think of how arguments can be balanced so as to give contrasting views.
- *Resolution.* Think how best to 'resolve' contradictory arguments.
- *Relative significance and evaluation.* Think how best to reach a judgement when trying to assess the relative importance of various factors, and their possible interrelationship.

Planning an essay

Practice question 1

To what extent was the American Constitution (1787) designed to meet the problems faced by the USA after 1783?

This question requires you to analyse the aims of the Founding Fathers in 1787. You must discuss the following:

- The main problems faced by the USA after 1783 and the perceived failure of the Articles of Confederation to deal with those problems (your primary focus).
- Other influences on the framing of the US Constitution, such as disagreements among the Founding Fathers (your secondary focus).

A clear structure makes for a much more effective essay and is crucial for achieving the highest marks. You need three or four paragraphs to structure this question effectively. In each paragraph you will deal with one factor. One of these *must* be the factor in the question.

A very basic plan for this question might look like this:

- Paragraph 1: the problems faced by the USA in 1783 and the effects of the weakness of the Articles of Confederation.
- Paragraph 2: another influence on the framing of the US Constitution, such as disagreements among the Founding Fathers.
- Paragraph 3: the nature of the compromise – leading to the conclusion of the essay (answering the question).

It is a good idea to cover the factor named in the question first, so that you don't run out of time and forget to do it. Then cover the others in what you think is their order of importance, or in the order that appears logical in terms of the sequence of paragraphs.

The introduction

Maintaining focus is vital. One way to do this from the beginning of your essay is to use the words in the question to help write your argument. The first sentence of question 1, for example, could look like this:

In 1787 the Founding Fathers met at Philadelphia to draw up a new Constitution which they hoped would enable the USA to meet the problems faced by the new nation after 1783 and do so more successfully than the flawed Articles of Confederation – itself one of the major problems.

This opening sentence provides a clear focus on the demands of the question, though it could, of course, be written in a more exciting style.

Focus throughout the essay

Structuring your essay well will help with keeping the focus of your essay on the question. To maintain a focus on the wording in question 1, you could begin your first main paragraph with 'problems'.

Perhaps the main problem facing the USA after 1783 was the weakness of the Articles of Confederation.

- This sentence begins with a clear point that refers to the primary focus of the question (the problems facing the USA) while linking it to a factor (the weakness of the Articles of Confederation).
- You could then have a paragraph for each of your other factors.
- It will be important to make sure that each paragraph focuses on analysis and includes relevant details that are used as part of the argument.
- You may wish to number your factors. This helps to make your structure clear and helps you to maintain focus.

Deploying detail

As well as focus and structure, your essay will be judged on the extent to which it includes accurate detail. There are several different kinds of evidence you could use that might be described as detailed. This includes correct dates, names of relevant people, statistics and events. For example, for sample question 1 you could use terms such as the Virginia Plan and Separation of Powers. You can also make your essays more detailed by using the correct technical vocabulary.

Analysis and explanation

'Analysis' covers a variety of high-level skills including explanation and evaluation; in essence, it means breaking down something complex into smaller parts. A clear structure which breaks down a complex question into a series of paragraphs is the first step towards writing an analytical essay. The purpose of explanation is to provide evidence for why something happened, or why something is true or false. An explanatory statement requires two parts: a *claim* and a *justification*.

For example, for question 1, you might want to argue that one important reason was the failure of the Articles of Confederation to deal with the financial situation. Once you have made your point, and supported it with relevant detail, you can then explain how this answers the question. For example, you could conclude your paragraph like this:

So the Article of Confederation's failure to resolve the USA's financial problems and the growing tensions between creditors and debtors**[1]**, as shown by Shays' Rebellion, led to many Americans demanding stronger national government**[2]** because they feared the alternative was disintegration and chaos**[3]**.

1 The first part of this sentence is the claim while the second part justifies the claim.
2 The relationship between the claim and the justification.
3 The justification.

Evaluation

Evaluation means considering the importance of two or more different factors, weighing them against each other, and reaching a judgement. This is a good skill to use at the end of an essay because the conclusion should reach a judgement which answers the question. Your conclusion to question 1 might read as follows:

Clearly, the problems facing the Articles of Confederation had led a number of powerful Americans (like George Washington) to demand stronger national government. However, the Founding Fathers did not see eye to eye on what that government should be like. Therefore, they had to compromise. The 1787 Constitution, albeit a bundle of compromises, was better designed to meet the problems of the future than the Articles of Confederation – the main problem of the period 1783-7.

Words like 'however' and 'therefore' are helpful to contrast the importance of the different factors.

Complex essay writing: argument and counter-argument

Essays that develop a good argument are more likely to reach the highest levels. This is because argumentative essays are much more likely to develop sustained analysis. As you know, your essays are judged on the extent to which they analyse.

After setting up an argument in your introduction, you should develop it throughout the essay. One way of doing this is to adopt an argument–counter-argument structure. A counter-argument is one that disagrees with the main argument of the essay. This is a good way of evaluating the importance of the different factors that you discuss. Essays of this type will develop an argument in one paragraph and then set out an opposing argument in another paragraph. Sometimes this will include juxtaposing the differing views of historians on a topic.

Good essays will analyse the key issues. They will probably have a clear piece of analysis at the end of each paragraph. While this analysis might be good, it will generally relate only to the issue discussed in that paragraph.

Excellent essays will be analytical throughout. As well as the analysis of each factor discussed above, there will be an overall analysis. This will run throughout the essay and can be achieved through developing a clear, relevant and coherent argument.

A good way of achieving sustained analysis is to consider which factor is most important.

Here is an example of an introduction that sets out an argument for question 1:

In 1787 the Founding Fathers met at Philadelphia to draw up a new Constitution which they hoped would enable the USA to meet the problems faced by the new nation after 1783 and do so more successfully than the flawed Articles of Confederation – itself one of the major problems**[1]**. The problems besetting the USA's powerlessness in foreign and commercial affairs, financial problems caused by the irresponsible actions of individual states, and the threat of chaos and disintegration of the USA in the face of this**[2]**. Given that the Articles of Confederation was unable to resolve the problems – not surprisingly because in many respects it was the problem – there was need for a stronger national government. The Founding Fathers, while accepting the need for stronger national government, disagreed about the precise nature of the new government[3]. After weeks of deliberation, and willingness to compromise, they finally agreed a Constitution – a Constitution which, with relatively few amendments, is still the fundamental law for the world's greatest power.

1 The introduction begins with a claim.
2 The introduction continues with another reason.
3 Concludes with outline of argument of the most important reason.

- This introduction focuses on the question and sets out the key factors that the essay will develop.
- It introduces an argument about which factor was most significant.
- However, it also sets out an argument that can then be developed throughout each paragraph, and is rounded off with an overall judgement in the conclusion.

Complex essay writing: resolution and relative significance

Having written an essay that explains argument and counter-argument, you should then resolve the tension between the argument and the counter-argument in your conclusion. It is important that the writing is precise and summarises the arguments made in the main body of the essay. You need to reach a supported overall judgement. One very appropriate way to do this is by evaluating the relative significance of different factors, in the light of valid criteria. Relative significance means how important one factor is compared to another.

The best essays will always make a judgement about which was most important based on valid criteria. These can be very simple, and will depend on the topic and the exact question.

The following criteria are often useful:

- Duration: which factor was important for the longest amount of time?
- Scope: which factor affected the most people?
- Effectiveness: which factor achieved most?
- Impact: which factor led to the most fundamental change?

As an example, you could compare the factors in terms of their duration and their impact. A conclusion that follows this advice should be capable of reaching a high level (if written, in full, with appropriate details) because it reaches an overall judgement that is supported through evaluating the relative significance of different factors in the light of valid criteria.

Having written an introduction and the main body of an essay for question 1, a concluding paragraph that aims to meet the exacting criteria for reaching a complex judgement could look like this:

By 1787 a number of influential and powerful Americans – men like George Washington, Robert Morris, Alexander Hamilton and James Madison – were convinced that the Articles of Confederation was failing the USA. Appalled by the powerlessness of the national government in foreign affairs and commercial matters, angered by (what they saw as) the irresponsible legislation of states that issued paper money, and fearful that the weakness of the Articles threatened impending disintegration and chaos, they demanded stronger national government. The shock of Shays' failed Rebellion in 1787 resulted in Congress calling on the states to send delegates to a convention in Philadelphia in May 1787 'for the sole and express purpose of revising the Articles of Confederation'. This is what the Founding Fathers proceeded to do. Not seeing eye to eye on precisely what the new government should be like, they had to compromise. There is no doubt, however, that the resultant 1787 Constitution, albeit a bundle of compromises, was better designed to meet the problems of the future than the Articles of Confederation – the main problem of the period 1783-7.

Sources guidance

Whether you are taking the AS exam or the full A level exam for AQA Component 2: Depth Study: The American Revolution: 1740–96, Section A presents you with sources and a question which involves evaluation of their utility or value.

AS exam	A level exam
Section A: answer question 1 based on two primary sources. (25 marks)	Section A: answer question 1, based on three primary sources. (30 marks)
Question focus: with reference to these sources and your understanding of the historical context, which of these two sources is more valuable in explaining … ?	Question focus: with reference to these sources and your understanding of the historical context, assess the value of these three sources to an historian studying …

Sources and sample questions

Study the sources. They are all concerned with the American colonies' relationship with Britain in the early 1760s.

SOURCE I

From a book by the Reverend Andrew Burnaby, an Anglican minister, writing about his visit to America in 1760.

My first attachment, as it is natural, is to my native country [England]. My next is to America and such is my affection for both that I hope nothing will ever happen to dissolve that union, which is necessary to their common happiness …

The province of Massachusetts Bay has been for some years past, I believe, rather on the decline, Its inhabitants have lost several branches of trade

which they are not likely to recover again … Their ship trade is considerably decreased, owing to their not having been so careful in the construction of vessels as formerly. Their fisheries too have not been equally successful … However, notwithstanding what has been said, Massachusetts Bay is a rich, populous and well-cultivated province.

SOURCE 2

Thomas Hutchinson, a Bostonian and the last royal governor of Massachusetts, writing in 1784 about the situation in Massachusetts in 1763.

Advantages in any respect enjoyed by the subjects in England, which were not enjoyed by the subjects in the colonies began to be considered in an invidious light and men were led to inquire, with greater attention than formerly, into the relation in which the colonies stood to the state from which they sprang … It is well known in America that the people of England, as well as administration, were divided upon the expediency of retaining

Canada rather than the islands [Guadeloupe and other French Caribbean islands] and it was also known the objection to Canada proceeded from an opinion that the cession of it by France would cause in time a separation of the British colonies from the mother country. This jealousy [suspicion] in England being known, it was of itself sufficient to set enterprising men upon considering how far such a separation was expedient and practicable.

SOURCE 3

James Otis (who later became a major opponent of Britain) speaking in the town meeting of Boston in 1763.

We in America have certainly abundant reasons to rejoice. The heathen are not only driven out, but the Canadians, much more formidable enemies are conquered and become fellow subjects. The British dominions and power may now be said, literally to extend from sea to sea ... And we may safely conclude from his majesty's wise administration hitherto that liberty and knowledge, civil and religious, will be co-extended, improved and preserved to the latest posterity. No other constitution of civil government has yet appeared in the world so admirably adapted to these great purposes as that of Great Britain.

AS style question

With reference to Sources 1 and 2, and your understanding of the historical context, which of these two sources is more valuable in explaining the strength of the relationship between Britain and the American colonies in the early 1760s?

A level style question

With reference to Sources 1, 2 and 3, and your understanding of the historical context, assess the value of these sources to a historian studying the strength of the relationship between Britain and the American colonies in the early 1760s.

The mark schemes

AS mark scheme

See the AQA website (www.aqa.org.uk) for the full mark schemes. This summary of the AS mark scheme shows how it rewards analysis and evaluation of the source material within the historical context.

Level 1	Describing the source content or offering generic phrases.
Level 2	Some relevant but limited comments on the value of one source or some limited comment on both.
Level 3	Some relevant comments on the value of the sources and some explicit reference to the issue identified in the question.
Level 4	Relevant well-supported comments on the value and a supported conclusion, but with limited judgement.
Level 5	Very good understanding of the value in relation to the issue identified. Sources evaluated thoroughly and with a well-substantiated conclusion related to which is more valuable.

A level mark scheme

This summary of the A level mark scheme shows how it is similar to the AS one, but covers three sources. Also the wording of the question means that there is no explicit requirement to decide which of the three sources is the most valuable. Concentrate instead on a very thorough analysis of the content and evaluation of the provenance of each source, using contextual knowledge.

Level 1	Some limited comment on value of at least one source.
Level 2	Some limited comments on the value of the sources or on content or provenance or comments on all three sources but no reference to the value of the sources.
Level 3	Some understanding of all three sources in relation to both content and provenance, with some historical context; but analysis limited.
Level 4	Good understanding of all three sources in relation to content, provenance and historical context to give a balanced argument on their value for the purpose specified in the question.
Level 5	As Level 4, but with a substantiated judgement.

Working towards an answer

It is important that knowledge is used to show an understanding of the relationship between the sources and the issue raised in the question. Answers should be concerned with the following:

- provenance
- arguments used (and you can agree/disagree)
- tone and emphasis of the sources.

You will need to assess the *value of the content* by using your own knowledge. Is the information accurate? Is it giving only part of the evidence and ignoring other aspects? Is the tone of the writing significant?

You will need to evaluate the *provenance* of the source by considering who wrote it, and when, where and why. What was its purpose? Was it produced to express an opinion; to record facts: to influence the opinion of others? Even if it was intended to be accurate, the writer may have been biased – either deliberately or unconsciously. The writer, for example, might have only known part of the situation and reached a judgement solely based on that.

Here is a guide to analysing the provenance, content and tone for Sources 1, 2 and 3.

Analysing the sources

To answer the question effectively, you need to read the sources carefully and pull out the relevant points as well as add your own knowledge. You must remember to keep the focus on the question at all times.

Analysing the sources

To answer the question effectively, you need to read the sources carefully and pull out the relevant points as well as add your own knowledge. You must remember to keep the focus on the question at all times.

Source 1 (page 209)

Provenance:

- The source is from a book by an Englishman, the Reverend Andrew Burnaby, visiting the 'province of Massachusetts Bay' in 1760.
- Reverend Andrew Burnaby is not a politician. He writes of his experiences and gives his opinion of what he has seen.

Content and argument:

- The source believes that the union of England and America is beneficial to both.
- Massachusetts is suffering economically, particularly its shipbuilding and fishing industries.
- Nevertheless, Massachusetts is prosperous, well populated and well cultivated.

Tone and emphasis:

- The tone is positive. Burnaby asserts that the English–American connection is beneficial to both. The fact that he 'hopes nothing will ever happen to dissolve that union' perhaps suggests he has some fears on that score.

Own knowledge:

- Your knowledge to agree/disagree with the source, for example: details about whether the American colonies did benefit economically from mercantilism.

Source 2 (page 209)

Provenance:

- The source is from Thomas Hutchinson, an ex-royal governor of Massachusetts.
- Hutchinson is clearly writing with hindsight – after the split between the colonies and Britain.

Content and argument:

- The source claims that some Americans in 1763 were beginning to question their relationship with Britain, asserting their rights and suspicious of British government actions.
- The source suggests that the British government considered not taking Canada from the French on

the grounds that this might cause a split between the colonies and Britain. It also suggests that some colonists knew – and resented – this.

Tone and emphasis:

- Hutchinson gives the impression that some Americans were seeking to pick a quarrel with Britain. (Remember, he is writing with hindsight!)

Own knowledge:

- Your knowledge to agree/disagree with the source, for example: evidence about the way that most Americans viewed their relationship with Britain in 1763: were Americans as suspicious of Britain as Hutchinson implies?

Source 3 (page 210)

Provenance:

- The source is from James Otis, speaking at a political meeting in Boston in 1763.
- Otis was speaking in 1763, the year when the Seven Years' War came to a successful conclusion and France lost its North American colonies to Britain.

Content and argument:

- The source is positive about America's relationship with Britain which has resulted in the defeat of both the 'heathen' (Native Americans) and the French Canadians.
- Otis praises King George's government, particularly the way it protects people's liberties.

Tone and emphasis:

- Otis seems optimistic about the future relationship between the American colonies and Britain.

Own knowledge:

- Your knowledge to agree/disagree with the source, for example: detailed knowledge about the situation in 1763 and about the irony of the fact that Otis, who praised the British government in 1763 was soon (within a year) to be one of one of its leading critics.

Answering AS questions

You have 45 minutes to answer the question. It is important that you spend at least one-quarter of the time reading and planning your answer. Generally when writing an answer, you need to check that you are remaining focused on the issue identified in the question and are relating this to the sources and your knowledge.

- You might decide to write a paragraph on each 'strand' (that is provenance, content and tone), comparing the two sources, and then write a short concluding paragraph with an explained judgement on which source is more valuable.
- For writing about content, you may find it helpful to adopt a comparative approach, for example when the evidence in one source is contradicted or questioned by the evidence in another source.

At AS level you are asked to provide a judgement on which is more valuable. Make sure that this is based on clear arguments with strong evidence, and not on general assertions.

Planning and writing your answer

- Think how you can best plan an answer.
- Plan in terms of the headings above, perhaps combining 'provenance' with 'tone and emphasis', and compare the two sources.

As an example, here is a comparison of Sources 1 and 2 in terms of provenance, and tone and emphasis:

The two sources have different viewpoints. In terms of their provenance, Source 1 is writing without the benefit of hindsight and is simply an account of impressions of a visit to Massachusetts. There is no obvious political content except the hope that the English–American link will continue. Source 2 gives us the views of Thomas Hutchinson, a leading American politician. Written with the benefit of hindsight, the source is far more political. It suggests that a number of Americans, resenting British rule, were seeking to break the links with the mother country in 1763.

Then compare the *content and argument* of each source, by using your knowledge. For example:

Source 1 wants the English and American link to continue, claiming that both the colonies and the mother country benefit from the connection. Although the source claims that Massachusetts has some economic problems, it goes on to assert that the province is generally prosperous and thriving.

Source 2 focuses on the increasing tensions between Britain and its American colonies. It claims that a number of American colonists were concerned about their rights and the nature of their relationship with Britain. It suggests that Britain considered taking Guadeloupe and other French Caribbean islands from France rather than Canada, fearful that the acquisition of Canada might lead to a split between the American colonies and the mother country. Some Americans began to consider whether such a split might be beneficial.

Which is *more valuable*? This can be judged in terms of which is likely to be more valuable in terms of where the source came from; or in terms of the accuracy of its content. However, remember the focus of the question – in this case, the relationship between Britain and its American colonies in 1763.

With these sources, you could argue that Source 1 is the more valuable because it was written at the time whereas Source 2 is written with the benefit of hindsight. However, you could argue that Source 2 is the more valuable on account of the fact that it was written by an important politician whose opinion of events are worth knowing.

Then check the following:

- Have you covered the 'provenance' and 'content' strands?
- Have you included sufficient knowledge to show understanding of the historical context?

Answering A level questions

The same general points for answering AS questions (see 'Answering AS questions') apply to A level questions, although of course here there are three sources and you need to assess the value of each of the three, rather than choose which is most valuable. Make sure that you remain focused on the question and that when you use your knowledge it is used to substantiate (add to) an argument relating to the content or provenance of the source.

If you are answering the A level question with Sources 1, 2 and 3 above:

- Keep the different 'strands' explained above in your mind when working out how best to plan an answer.
- Follow the guidance about 'provenance' and 'content' (see the AS guidance).
- Here you are *not* asked to explain which is the most valuable of the three sources. You can deal with each of the three sources in turn if you wish.
- However, you can build in comparisons if it is helpful, but it is not essential. It will depend to some extent on the three sources.
- You need to include sufficient knowledge to show understanding of the historical context. This might encourage cross-referencing of the content of the three sources, mixed with your own knowledge.
- Each paragraph needs to show clarity of argument in terms of the issue identified by the question.

Glossary of terms

Absolutist system of government   Government by a ruler with unrestricted power and usually with no democratic mandate.

Arbitrary power   Power that is not bound by rules, allowing a monarch to do as he or she wishes.

Artisans   Skilled manual workers.

Autonomy   Independence or self-government.

Backcountry   The western areas furthest from the coast.

Boston town meeting   The town council of Boston.

Certificates of public credit   Printed statements recognising that the holders were owed money by the government.

Charters   Formal documents, granting or confirming titles, rights or privileges.

Circular letter   A letter of which copies are sent to several people.

Colony   Territory, usually overseas, occupied by settlers from a 'mother country' that continues to have political power over the settlers.

Corporate colonies   Connecticut and Rhode Island possessed charters granted by the king, which gave them extensive autonomy.

Court martial   A court held by officers of the army or navy for the trial of offences against service laws.

Deflation   The situation resulting from a decreasing amount of money in circulation. People have insufficient money to buy goods or to invest.

Divine right of kings   The view that kings ruled by the authority of God rather than by the consent of the people.

East India Company   A powerful company that controlled much of Britain's trade with India.

Economic self-sufficiency   The situation when a country or a community produces all it needs and is not dependent on others.

English/British   England and Scotland signed the Act of Union in 1707. Thus, it is correct to term the policy British (rather than English) after 1707.

Enlightenment   The name given to a school of European thought of the eighteenth century. Those influenced by the Enlightenment believed in reason and human progress.

Enumerated commodities   Listed items which were affected by the Trade and Navigation Acts.

Excise tax   A tax on certain home commodities.

Executive   The power or authority in government that carries the law into effect; a person (or persons) who administer(s) the government.

Freeholders   People who own, rather than rent, their land.

Frontiersmen   People who lived close to the colonial borders or in Native American territory and who were able to survive in what was often a hostile environment.

The Glorious Revolution   In 1688 King James II fled from Britain. William III and Mary became joint monarchs. Parliament assumed greater control.

Guerrilla war   Warfare by which small units harass conventional forces.

Hanoverian succession   In 1714 Queen Anne, the last Stuart monarch, died childless. George, Elector of Hanover, a small state in Germany, became King George I of Britain.

Hessians   German auxiliaries who fought for Britain.

High Federalists   Supporters of Alexander Hamilton.

Impeachment   Charging a public official with an offence committed while in office.

Industrial Revolution   The economic and social changes arising out of the change from industries carried on in the home to industries in factories with power-driven machinery.

Jacobins   An extremist group in the French Revolution. In power in France in 1793–4, they became associated with the guillotine and the Reign of Terror.

Liberty Tree   An actual (but also symbolic) tree in Boston, representing freedom from tyranny.

Liquid assets   Wealth that may be easily converted into cash.

Loyalists   Those Americans who supported Britain.

Manumission laws   Laws that allowed owners to free their slaves.

Mayflower   The name of the ship on which the Pilgrim Fathers, a small group of English Puritans, sailed to America in 1620.

Mercantilism   The belief that colonies existed essentially to serve the economic interests of the mother country.

Militia   A force, made up of all military-aged civilians, called out in times of emergency.

Minutemen   Men who were pledged to rush to America's defence at a minute's notice.

National debt   The money borrowed by a government and not yet paid back.

Native Americans   The people, often known as Indians, who first lived in North America.

Oligarchy   Government by a small (usually wealthy) exclusive class.

Patriots   Americans who supported independence.

Patronage   The right of bestowing jobs or offices – offices usually given to supporters, family or friends.

Planters   Southern landowners who owned more than twenty slaves.

Popular sovereignty   The idea that political power should be held by the people.

Primus inter pares   First among equals.

Privateers   Privately owned vessels granted permission by a government to capture enemy ships.

Privy Council   The private council of the British king, advising on the administration of government.

Proprietary colonies   Colonies in which the Crown had vested political authority in the hands of certain families: the Calverts (in Maryland) and the Penns (in Pennsylvania and Delaware).

Quorum   A minimum number of members necessary for transaction of business.

Ratification   Official approval and sanction.

Separation of powers   A system of government in which power is shared between the legislative, the executive and the judiciary, ensuring that no branch can become dominant.

Ships of the line   The great wooden battleships employed from the seventeenth to the mid-nineteenth centuries.

Sinecure   An office without much, if any, work; in other words, a cushy job.

Sovereignty   Ultimate power.

Specie   Gold or coined money.

Stamp duty   A tax on legal documents, its payment being confirmed by the affixation of a stamp.

Tarred and feathered   Victims were stripped naked, covered with hot tar and then rolled in goose feathers.

Tea agents   Men responsible for collecting tea duties.

Tidewater   The eastern areas nearest the coast.

Tories   Members of the Tory Party – a party which usually opposed radical change.

Trans-Appalachian region   The land west of the Appalachian mountains.

Whigs   Members of the Whig Party – a party which had once upheld popular rights and opposed royal power.

Further reading

The causes and course of the American War of Independence

B. Bailyn, *The Ideological Origins of the American Revolution* (Belknap Press, 1992)

A crucial text on the importance of ideas underpinning the American Revolution

S. Conway, *The War of American Independence 1775–1783* (Edward Arnold, 1995)

This provides an excellent coverage of the War of Independence – and not just from an American perspective

S. Conway, *A Short History of the American Revolutionary War* (I.B. Tauris, 2013)

The best short history of the war

E. Countryman, *The American Revolution* (Hill & Wang, 2003)

A readable and accessible account of the struggle for independence

J.E. Ferling, *Almost a Miracle: The American Victory in the War of Independence* (Oxford University Press, 2009)

A gripping account of the War of Independence

S.B. Griffiths, *The War for American Independence: From 1760 to the Surrender at Yorktown* (University of Illinois, 2002)

Another well-written and comprehensive text

R. Middlekauff, *The Glorious Cause: The American Revolution, 1763–1789* (Oxford University Press, 2005)

A wonderful book: engaging and masterful

H.M. Ward, *The American Revolution: Nationhood Achieved 1763–1788* (St Martin's Press, 1995)

An excellent work, covering the entire Revolutionary War period

E. Wright, *The Search for Liberty: From Origins to Independence* (Wiley-Blackwell, 1995)

A splendid overview of early American history

The American Revolution

C. Bonwick, *The American Revolution* (Macmillan 2005)

A succinct account of the revolution in all its aspects

F.D. Cogliano, *Revolutionary America 1763–1815: A Sourcebook* (Routledge, 2010)

An excellent introduction to the American Revolution

J.P. Greene and J.R. Pole, editors, *The Blackwell Encyclopedia of the American Revolution* (Wiley-Blackwell, 1994)

An invaluable reference book covering all aspects of the period

H.M. Ward, *The War for Independence and the Transformation of American Society* (Routledge, 1999)

Very good on the social history of the war

G.S. Wood, *The Creation of the American Republic* (University of North Carolina Press, 1998)

A classic work examining the evolution of political thought from the Declaration of Independence to the Constitution

Biographies

R.B. Bernstein, *Thomas Jefferson* (Oxford University Press, 2005)

The definitive short biography of Jefferson

R. Chernow, *Alexander Hamilton* (Penguin, 2005)

Easily the best book on Hamilton

R. Chernow, *Washington: A Life* (Penguin Press, 2010)

An award-winning biography which presents Washington warts and all

F.D. Cogliano, *Thomas Jefferson: Reputation and Legacy* (Edinburgh University Press, 2006)

A probing study of this revered American

J.J. Ellis, *His Excellency: George Washington* (Vintage, 2005)

An excellent book on His Excellency!

J.E. Ferling, *Setting the World Ablaze: Washington, Adams, Jefferson and the American Revolution* (Oxford University Press, 2000)

Three for one! Not to be missed

J.E. Ferling, *First of Men: A Life of George Washington* (Oxford University Press, 2010)

Another wonderful, well-written and compelling book on Washington

J.E. Ferling, *John Adams* (Oxford University Press, 2010)

This remains a sterling study of Adam's work and character

R.L. Ketcham, *James Madison: A Biography* (University of Virginia Press, 1990)

A well-researched biography of an important politician

E.G. Lengel, *General George Washington: A Military Life* (Random House, 2005)

This book deals specifically with Washington's military career

D.S. McCullough, *John Adams* (Simon & Schuster, 2002)

A best-selling popular biography and deserved winner of the 2002 Pulitzer Prize

The Constitution and the Federalist Age

R. Beeman, *Plain Honest Men: The Making of the American Constitution* (Random House, 2010)

An interesting book showing why the Constitution emerged as it did

S. Elkins and E. McKitrick, *The Age of Federalism: The Early American Republic 1788–1800* (Oxford University Press, 1995)

Probably too wordy for most students but still worth dipping into for extra detail

J.J. Ellis, *Founding Brothers: The Revolutionary Generation* (Ballantine Books, 2002)

A great read! It focuses on six vital moments in the life of the new nation

J. Ferling, *Adams v Jefferson: The Tumultuous Election of 1800* (Oxford University Press, 2005)

The best book on this important election

P. Maier, *Ratification: The People Debate the Constitution* (Simon & Schuster, 2010)

Examines (in depth) the issues dividing Americans in 1787–8

J.C. Miller, *The Federalist Era 1789–1801* (Waveland Press, 1998)

The fact that it is still in print (it was first published in 1960) speaks volumes

E. Wright, *An Empire for Liberty: From Washington to Lincoln* (Wiley-Blackwell, 1995)

The second volume in Wright's excellent trilogy on American history

Index